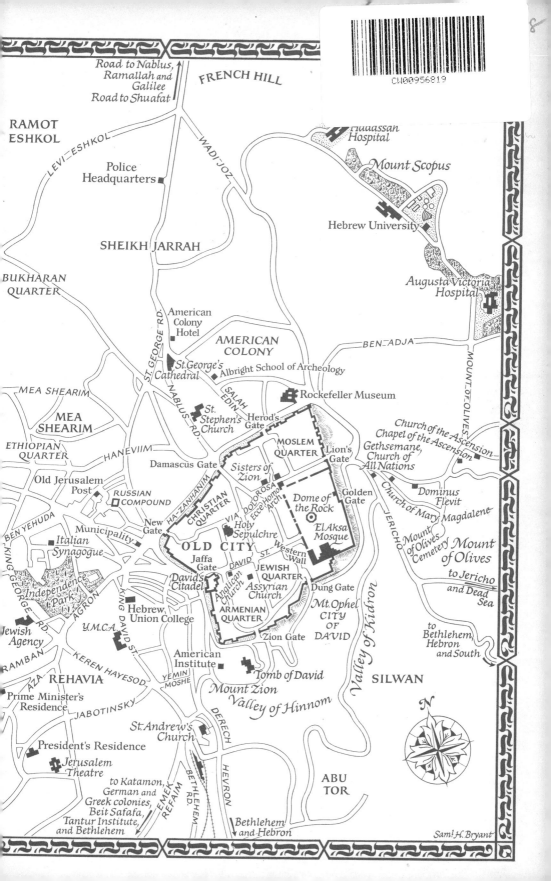

Road to Nablus,
Ramallah and
Galilee
Road to Shuafat

FRENCH HILL

RAMOT
ESHKOL

Hadassah
Hospital

Mount Scopus

Police
Headquarters

WADI JOZ

LEVI ESHKOL

SHEIKH JARRAH

Hebrew University

BUKHARAN
QUARTER

Augusta Victoria
Hospital

American
Colony
Hotel

AMERICAN
COLONY

BEN ADJA

ST. GEORGE RD.

St.George's
Cathedral

Albright School of Archeology

MEA SHEARIM

MEA
SHEARIM

NABLUS RD.

SALAH EDIN

Rockefeller Museum

Church of the Ascension
Chapel of the Ascension
Gethsemane,
Church of
All Nations

ETHIOPIAN
QUARTER

HANEVIIM

St.
Stephen's
Church

Herod's
Gate

MOUNT OF OLIVES

Old Jerusalem
Post

Damascus Gate

Sisters of
Zion

MOSLEM
QUARTER

Lion's
Gate

Dominus
Flevit

RUSSIAN
COMPOUND

BEN YEHUDA

HA-ZANHANIM

CHRISTIAN
QUARTER

New
Gate

Municipality

VIA DOLOROSA

Ecce Homo
Arch

Dome of
the Rock

Golden
Gate

Church of Mary Magdalene

JERICHO

Italian
Synagogue

Holy
Sepulchre

El Aksa
Mosque

Mount
of Olives
Cemetery

Mount
of Olives

KING GEORGE

OLD CITY

Jaffa
Gate

ST. DAVID

Western
Wall

to Jerico
and Dead
Sea

Independence
Park

AGRON

David's
Citadel

JEWISH
QUARTER

Assyrian
Church

Anglican
Church

Dung Gate

Mt.Ophel
CITY
OF
DAVID

Valley of Kidron

Jewish
Agency

Hebrew
Union College

KING DAVID ST.

ARMENIAN
QUARTER

Zion Gate

to
Bethlehem
Hebron
and South

RAMBAN

Y.M.C.A.

KEREN HAYESOD

American
Institute

SILWAN

AZA

REHAVIA

YEMIN
MOSHE

Tomb of David

N

Prime Minister's
Residence

JABOTINSKY

Mount Zion
Valley of Hinnom

President's Residence

St.Andrew's
Church

DERECH

ABU
TOR

Jerusalem
Theatre

to Katamon,
German and
Greek colonies,
Beit Safafa,
Tantur Institute,
and Bethlehem

EMEK REFAIM

BETHLEHEM RD.

HEVRON

Bethlehem
and Hebron

Sam! H. Bryant

The Flavor
of Jerusalem

The Flavor of Jerusalem

Joan Nathan and Judy Stacey Goldman

LITTLE, BROWN AND COMPANY

BOSTON / TORONTO

FIRST EDITION

T 03/75

The authors are grateful to *Israel* magazine for permission to reprint the following recipes:

"Teddy's Favorites" from vol. 5, no. 1; "Yankee Treats" from vol. 4, no. 2; "Armenian Kebabs" from vol. 5, no. 3–4; "Hadassah Herring" from vol. 5, no. 5; "Golda's Chicken Soup" from vol. 5, no. 6; "Yakne the Greek" from vol. 5, no. 7; as well as recipes from "Sabbath Breakfast," vol. 5, no. 11–12. Copyright © 1973 by *Israel* magazine.

Drawings on pages 70, 93, 162, and 199 by Mary Purcell.

LIBRARY OF CONGRESS CATALOGING IN PUBLICATION DATA

Nathan, Joan.
  The flavor of Jerusalem.

  Includes index.
  1. Cookery, International. I. Goldman, Judith
Stacey, joint author. II. Title.
TX725.A1N28   641.5'9   74-23574
ISBN 0-316-59843-7

Designed by Barbara Bell Pitnof.

Published simultaneously in Canada by Little, Brown & Company (Canada) Limited

PRINTED IN THE UNITED STATES OF AMERICA

To Jerusalem, with love

Come thou over with me, and I will sustain
thee with me in Jerusalem.

— II SAMUEL 19:32

Contents

Foreword

Over the centuries, Jerusalem has been the inspiration for thousands of books: religious, historical, archaeological and political. But few people know of the city's rich culinary treasures.

One of the delights of living in Jerusalem is the daily contact with the rich mosaic of different traditions that are contained within its small population. The people of Jerusalem come from all over the world — each bringing not only his own speech, dress and prayer but also his own traditional style of cooking. In Jerusalem the three great religions of the world live side by side in more ways than one. The neighborhoods of their many sects and communities merge into one another, the only warning being the distinct aroma of their nationalities. This book gives a veritable "Cook's tour" of Jerusalem and the diversity of our city comes through in the wide range of recipes given and stories told.

We had thought that during the many years we have lived in Jerusalem we had tasted every cuisine available here. *The Flavor of Jerusalem* only shows how wrong we were.

TAMAR AND TEDDY KOLLEK

Acknowledgments

Our first thanks to Mayor Teddy Kollek and the members of the Municipal Council — Meron Benvenisti, David Bergman, Rabbi Sharyashuv Cohen and Menashe Nehemia — who introduced us to the people of the various districts of Jerusalem they represent.

Our thanks also to veteran Jerusalemites Armenian Archbishop Shahe Ajamian, Rhoda Cohen, Genia Gilat, Sarah Gilat, Asher Harris, Salah Jarallah, Jean Jasper, Ganit Katznelson, Tamar Kollek, Marlin Levin, Esther Reifenberg, Salim Sayage, Raanan Sivan, Greek Orthodox Archbishop Vasilios, Horatio and Valentine Vester and all the many people who advised us on "who's who" in Jerusalem cooking.

We are very grateful to Cornell Capa and the International Fund for Concerned Photography, who generously gave of their time and talent to provide us with the photographs.

Our very sincere thanks also to our friends in Israel, Canada and the United States who helped us test the recipes: Betty Gerson, Anne Goldman, Kathy Stacey Mason, John Phillips, Julie Radovan, Pat Rainey, Jane Rogul, June Rogul, Jean Scheckman, Florence Stacey, Ceci Tripp, Ginny and Pearl Nathan and their many helpful friends in Providence, Rhode Island.

Warm thanks to Marsh Clark, Judy Doneson, Shula Eisner, Allan Gerson, Janet Kaplan, Irene Nobel, Mary Purcell and Raymond Westbrook, who truly gave of themselves and without whose advice, encouragement and assistance our book could never have been completed.

Special thanks to all the Jerusalemites we had the pleasure to meet during our culinary trip and to our families and friends, who had the patient palates to taste our recipes.

Introduction

Most tourists to Israel, when asked to name a local dish, can remember only the kibbutz breakfast, that healthy and very substantial start to the day, which has become standard fare in Israel's hotels. In fact, there is no single Israeli cuisine in the sense that there is a French or Italian cuisine. Except for the kibbutz breakfast, native Israeli cooking depends on which native is doing the cooking: that is, what his or her land of origin is. This is especially true in Jerusalem, whose natives include not only Jews from various lands but a great many non-Jews as well — Copts from Egypt, Greek Orthodox from Greece, Armenian exiles and Moslems from the entire eastern Mediterranean world. Each has preserved his own community's style of cooking along with its cultural and religious heritage. Jerusalemites have come to know and appreciate each other's specialties and to embrace the culinary influence of the neighboring Arab countries. But a Jerusalem cookery — like the people of Jerusalem themselves — remains a rich mixture of tastes rather than a single flavor of a melting pot.

A typical gastronomic tour of the city might begin with Turkish coffee in a café, followed by ten o'clock caviar and vodka at one of the two Russian churches or perhaps at a new immigrant's home, lunch at a Hungarian Jewish or a Moslem restaurant, tea and crumpets at the Anglican archbishop's and dinner at an Oriental bar mitzvah or a wedding in Mea Shearim, the very Orthodox section, where females must dress modestly, with long sleeves and skirts that cover their knees.

At any reception at the Jerusalem City Hall (called the Municipality) one can see cloaked Christian clergymen, Moslem notables in traditional headdress, and Chassidic Jews in sidelocks mingling with elegant foreign diplomats and casually dressed Israelis. A Moslem *mukhtar* (chief) from Chad rubs shoulders with a Jew from the Soviet Union, while a black-robed Ethiopian priest descended from the Queen of Sheba listens to an Evangelical Christian from the United States describe an archaeological excavation which he is directing. All in one room, people speak-

*Christian leaders toast each others' health at a reception
in the home of Israel's President*

ing a variety of languages, with little in common but a love for
Jerusalem, enjoy fresh fruit and Middle Eastern hors d'oeuvres which
have been carefully prepared so that guests from all the city's ethnic
groups can partake of them. On this occasion and similar ones the true
meaning of Jerusalem's "large mosaic," as Mayor Teddy Kollek is fond
of saying, makes itself apparent.

The city's population of 230,000 Jews, 11,500 Christians and 64,000
Moslems can be divided and subdivided into over a hundred Jewish and
Moslem groupings and some thirty-two Christian denominations. In the
seventh century the Khalif Omar ibn Kattab brought the first Moslems
to Jerusalem. Today the Moslems, representing one-fifth of the population, are divided not so much by religion as by place of birth, which
might be Jerusalem, a small village nearby, Hebron or some other part
of the Middle East.

All the Christian communities fall into four main groups: Eastern
Orthodox, Roman Catholic, Monophysite, and Protestant. Besides the
local Arab-Christian members of almost all the thirty denominations,
there are the church dignitaries. Most are the heads of Christian communities in all parts of the Holy Land and the rest of the Middle East.
The most important are the three patriarchs: the Greek Orthodox, the

Armenian Orthodox and the Latin (Roman Catholic). In addition to them there are also several archbishops and bishops, whose dioceses have Jerusalem as their centers; among these are the Anglican (Protestant), the Greek Catholic, the Coptic, the Syrian and the Ethiopian. Besides the spiritual leaders of these churches thousands of monks, priests, and nuns also live in the city, and they are the custodians of the holy sites, the teachers in church-affiliated schools, and nurses and doctors.

The rest of the population — three-fourths of the total — is composed of Jews emanating from seventy different countries. There has been a continual stream of Jews into Jerusalem since the time of David, a thousand years before Jesus. Despite centuries of diffusion in the Diaspora there has always been one common bond between all Jews, "the yearning for Jerusalem," in a sense their unifying element. (While Moslems turn toward Mecca in prayer and Christians to Rome, Jews have always turned eastward toward Jerusalem.) Until the nineteenth century Sephardic Jews comprised the majority, many having come at the time of the Spanish Inquisition. In the nineteenth century Ashkenazic Jews from eastern Europe settled in the Holy Land; the Holocaust brought many more. But the largest number (over 60 percent of the population of Jerusalem today) came after the creation of the State of Israel in 1948, Jews who were expelled from Arab lands. Although the latest wave of immigration is from the Soviet Union, other Jews, attracted by Jerusalem, have come here from throughout the world.

The attraction of Jerusalem for the faithful of so many religions has brought with it a curious side effect on the city's cuisine. Dietary laws of varying strictness govern the selection, preparation and consumption of food, and a brief survey of these rules is necessary to understand the recipes.

According to *kashrut*, ancient dietary laws, religious Jews are permitted to eat meat only from an animal which has cloven hooves and chews its cud. "Whatsoever parteth the hoof and is wholly cloven-footed and cheweth the cud, that may you eat" (Leviticus 11:3). The Biblical permission includes cows, sheep and goats and excludes rabbits, horses, dogs, cats and, of course, pigs. Eatable fowl include turkeys, chicken, and doves but not birds of prey. In addition, *kashrut*-observing Jews may eat only fish having both fins and scales, thus excluding all shellfish.

Flesh may not be torn from a living animal and all animals and birds require a *shochet*, a rabbi specially instructed in the ritual of slaughter so that the animal is killed instantly with no suffering. The knife that the *shochet* uses must be sharp and smooth without the slightest perceptible notch so that he will strike cleanly. The law states: "The knife must be tested as to its three sides upon the flesh of the finger and upon

"If I forget thee, O Jerusalem." Psalms 137:5.
A Hassidic Jew prays at the Western Wall

the nail." (The reason this requirement does not apply to fish is that they have no "physical feelings.") After the animal is killed, the meat is put through a process called *melihah*, which consists of first soaking it in water for one half hour and then covering it with salt for one hour, before it may be prepared for food.

Milchig (dairy) dishes must be cooked and eaten separately from *fleishig* (meat) dishes, because three times in Exodus and Deuteronomy the Old Testament states that a kid cannot be cooked in its mother's milk. Neutral or *pareveh* food such as fish and eggs may be eaten with either meat or milk. Two sets of dishes, for milk and meat meals, are used, stored and cleaned separately. In fact, some sects of Jews are accustomed to waiting for as long as six hours after a meat meal before having milk products. The normal wait is about three hours.

No cooking is permitted on the Sabbath, the day of rest, except that food prepared in advance can simmer for a long time under a low flame, like the traditional Cholent, a robust stew, or Kugels, vegetable and noodle puddings which cook in a low oven throughout the night.

According to the Koran, Moslems, too, are prohibited from eating pork products; they are prohibited as well from drinking alcohol. Their form of ritual butchering is similar to that of the Jews described above and they salt their meat in the same manner; in fact, in the reunited city Jews and Moslems use the same municipal slaughtering house. Moslems do mix meat and milk, however, and many feel that *leben*, a light form of yoghurt, helps to wash down a heavy meal of meat and rice. Every day during the month of Ramadan, religiously strict Moslems fast throughout the day from sunrise to sunset and then eat a rather sumptuous dinner in the evening. This Ramadan fast is central to their religious belief.

The Christian communities in Jerusalem have no dietary restrictions throughout the year except during Lent, when each sect has its own way of abstaining from certain foods for forty days prior to Easter. Members of the Greek Orthodox Church, for example, do not eat meat, fish, eggs, butter, milk and cheese throughout the Lenten period. Some of the sects, like the Ethiopians, have as many as 270 fast days throughout the year.

Despite all the prohibitions and traditions, we noticed that many Jews, Moslems and Christians in Jerusalem nowadays do not adhere strictly to religious dietary laws. Consequently, while many of the recipes are from the kitchens of religious Jerusalemites, we have also included favorites that do not conform to some of the religious prohibitions.

Before becoming familiar with the people and their communities, it might be helpful for the uninitiated to be able to visualize the city of

Bargaining for grapes in the Old City

Jerusalem physically. Ever since King David proclaimed Jerusalem his capital over three thousand years ago, the city has grown northward and upward from the valleys of Kidron and Hinnon near Mount Zion to its present area, covering all the surrounding hilltops. Always the center of the Jewish religion, Jerusalem was naturally selected as the capital of the State of Israel in 1948.

Jerusalem's terrain, as varied as its inhabitants, reflects the city's turbulent history, with vestiges of buildings constructed during one occupation to be destroyed during the next. The city is built on a series of rocky hilltops surrounded by the Judean Desert; Jericho and the Dead Sea are twelve miles to the east, Tel Aviv is twenty-eight miles to the west, Bethlehem is five miles away by the road to Hebron and Eilat to the south, and Nablus and Ramallah lie to the north on the road to Galilee. These are still the main roads leading directly to the seven gates of the Old City, which until the late nineteenth century was the entire city. The central Jaffa Gate led out of Jerusalem toward the Port of Jaffa, adjacent to Tel Aviv, the Zion Gate to Mount Zion, and the Damascus or Nablus Gate toward Nablus (the biblical Shechem) and the road to Damascus.

Surrounded by walls built by Suleiman the Magnificent in the sixteenth century, the Old City covers 817 acres and theoretically is divided into four quarters — the Armenian, Christian, Jewish and Moslem. In reality, the populations, like the many styles of architecture, spill over into one another. The Old City is today as it has always been, a series of winding narrow streets, a marvelous maze for the curious. Although a narrow road for donkeys and cars runs inside and parallel to the outer walls, it is best to meander on foot through the four quarters, entering near the Armenian Quarter by the Jaffa Gate to the west. Inside to the right, is the site of the palace of King Herod, with the Tower of David at one end. Directly across and farther inside is the Anglican church. Within the Armenian Quarter on Mount Zion, there is an entire community of over four thousand Armenians, many of whom are refugees from the Turkish massacres in 1915, with others whose families have lived in Jerusalem for centuries, this being the oldest Christian community in the city.

Adjacent to this quarter, to the east, is the Jewish Quarter, now rehabilitated from its destruction between 1948 and 1967. As the road slopes downward, the Western Wall (or Kotel), the remaining outside wall of Herod's Temple, looms ahead with two stately Moslem shrines in the background. Since this wall, the so-called Wailing Wall, is all that remains of the twice-destroyed Temple, this is the central most important holy place for Jews throughout the world and is in a sense the center of Judaism. On the other side of the wall, on the Temple Mount within the Moslem Quarter in the Haram es Sharif, stand the seventh-century Dome of the Rock and the El Aksa Mosque. The Temple Mount, then, is holy also to the Moslems. After Mecca and Medina, this is the third most sacred place in the world to Moslems, for inside the Dome of the Rock is the rock from which Mohammed departed on his Nocturnal Journey to Heaven. For Christians, too, the area surrounding the Mount — the Via Dolorosa and Golgotha — is holy, since it is associated with the major events in the death and resurrection of Jesus. Since this area is so significant to all three religions, it can be thought of as the crux of the Middle Eastern conflict over Jerusalem. While Moslems pray five times a day on the Haram (Mount Moriah), religiously strict Jews pray at their feet just outside at the Western Wall and Christians pray in the many chapels lining the Via Dolorosa.

The Via Dolorosa borders on the northern wall of the Temple Mount perpendicular to the Western Wall and twists and turns through a domed-roof area of residences, schools, churches and a vast *souk* (marketplace) until it reaches the Church of the Holy Sepulchre. The Tomb of Christ is located within this church, said to be the center of the Christian world and located diagonally across from the mount on Golgotha. In 1852 the Turkish rulers decreed that ownership of the Church of the Holy Sepulchre be divided among six communities. The three

It sometimes snows in Jerusalem

ALIZA AUERBACH

major holders are the Latin (Roman Catholic), represented by the Franciscan Order, the Greek Orthodox, and the Armenian Orthodox; the minor holders are the Syrian (Jacobite), the Coptic, and the Ethiopian churches. Not only do these churches have use of the Holy Sepulchre, but they must also take care of the administration and upkeep of the church.

In a sense then, there are three religious focal points in Jerusalem — the Haram es Sharif (Temple Mount), the Western Wall, and the Church of the Holy Sepulchre — all within a circumference of approximately fifty acres. Many of the people we describe in the following pages live, work, pray or just enjoy strolling within the four quarters of the Old City.

Until the middle of the nineteenth century Jerusalem was confined within the walls and few people needed or dared to live outside the protection because of the danger of robbers. In 1843, the Englishman Sir Moses Montefiore, realizing the need for additional housing and a larger economic base for the Jews of Jerusalem, bought land, built a flour mill and created Yemin Moshe, the first Jewish settlement outside the protective walls, near the Jaffa Gate and across from Mount Zion. It seems that in the beginning the volunteers worked there during the day and returned to the Jewish Quarter at dusk. But as the population increased some individuals did eventually venture outside to live. Toward the decline of the Ottoman Empire in the late nineteenth century, many European countries also wanted footholds for their faithful in Jerusalem, and so the Turks allowed outside governments to build for religious purposes only. Consequently, German, Russian and English spires sprang up on hilltops surrounding the Old City, with a few inside as well. Both on Mount Zion and the slopes of the Mount of Olives there are series of magnificent Christian shrines, including the Dormitian Abbey, the Church of St. Andrew, the onion-domed Russian Ecclesiastical Church of St. Mary Magdalene as well as their Church of the Ascension and the Russian Orthodox Cathedral in the Russian Compound, all built in the late nineteenth and early twentieth centuries. Above and around the shrines is the age-old sprawling Mount of Olives Jewish cemetery, where some graves date as far back as 3000 B.C.E. Between the Mount of Olives and Mount Scopus is the Augusta Victoria Hospital, constructed after Kaiser Wilhelm's visit in 1898. It was followed by the Hebrew University, its foundation stone laid by Chaim Weizmann on Mount Scopus in 1918, and the original Hadassah Hospital, built in the 1920's, with recent additions constructed after 1967, when Mount Scopus was again accessible to Jewish Jerusalemites.

In fact, since the time of Sir Moses Montefiore, colonies associated with either Christian or Jewish sects and Moslem communities have sprung up all over the hillsides: the Ethiopian Quarter near the Ethiopian Church, the Asiatic Russian Jewish Bukharan colony, Eastern European Mea Shearim, the Greek and German colonies near their convents, the ex-Hebronite settlement of Silwan, and Abu Tor and so on. In this way Jerusalem outside the walls was slowly settled.

A hill closer to Bethlehem but still opposite the Old City is the Hill of Evil Counsel, or Government House Hill. The building today houses the United Nations but was built for the British High Commissioner during the British Mandate after 1917. Nearby is Jerusalem's only kibbutz — Ramat Rachel, built in the 1920's. From these four hilltops there are spectacular views of the dividing line between desert and civilization. On one side are the Judean desert and the Arava toward the Dead Sea and Jericho — all barren as far as the eye can see except for wandering Bedouins in the distance and scattered Arab villages built within the last fifty years. On the other side is the jewel-like Old City with the glistening Dome of the Rock and the El Aksa Mosque. At sunset and sunrise these views are truly extraordinary.

Going "up" to Jerusalem on the opposite side of the city from Tel Aviv one enters Jaffa Road, which eventually leads to the Jaffa Gate winding through the Mahane Yehuda, the Jewish marketplace, which grew up as the city expanded outside the confines of the Old City. Soon one passes through the central business district, which despite its apparent bustle is rather sleepy, not a city like Tel Aviv with its fast-paced commercial activity. At the end of Jaffa Road, close to the walls, is the bullet-holed Jerusalem Municipality, which now serves all the populations of the city. Skirting the walls in the direction of the Damascus Gate is the central business district of the Arab sector. Extending from this center are the American Colony, Sheik Jarrah, Shuafat and Wadi Joz, all residential areas.

The second central focus of Jerusalem, after the Old City, is not the central business district but rather the complex which includes the Israel Museum, the Knesset, the Hebrew University and the Kirya (government office buildings). After the 1948 division of the city, this site, about a mile from the Old City and relatively protected on all sides from occasional Jordanian shellings, was chosen for government institutions. Jewish settlement had risen around this area from the 1930's onward, since there was no other area in which to expand; across the border to the east was Jordan. Many of the Israelis we interviewed, including Mayor Teddy Kollek, live here or on the road to Hadassah Hospital above the quaint village of Ein Kerem, birthplace of John the Baptist. Kurdish, Rumanian, Brazilian and Russian neighborhoods have sprung up all over — reflecting successive waves of immigration.

Until the beginning of the twentieth century everyone in Jerusalem shopped in the Old City; many housewives still remember how donkeys led by young boys brought the purchases home from the marketplace. As the city expanded, other marketplaces sprang up, such as the ones in Mea Shearim and the Bukharan Quarter and the large Mahane Yehuda. After the War of Independence in 1948, when the Old City was controlled by Jordan and closed to Jewish Jerusalem, Mahane Yehuda was enlarged so that its small stalls and niches covered an even wider area at the crest of Jaffa Road. At the same time, the Arab wholesale vegetable market expanded with products brought into Jerusalem from the East Bank across the Jordan River. And now, ever since the Six-Day War, every Jerusalem housewife has an even richer variety of marketplaces to choose from: the wholesale Arab fruit and vegetable market, the many small shops in the centers of east and west Jerusalem, the Mea Shearim market, Mahane Yehuda, the Arab *souk* inside the Old City, a German delicatessen with real salami and liverwurst in the west city center and the many *supersols* (*sol* means "shopping basket" in Hebrew) located throughout west Jerusalem, where everything including blintzes is packaged as smartly as in an American supermarket.

Besides a variety of shopping facilities, there is great diversity in all customs, especially eating and drinking. Some people drink arrack (a kind of Pernod distilled from raisins), others prefer whiskey, others tea with mint, others coffee and still others tea first and coffee later. The ever-present *mitz* (orange juice) is popular in the land of the Jaffa oranges as one would expect, though it has to compete with the West's sinister tool of imperialism, Coca-Cola.

In contrast with many American cities, Jerusalem seemed to us at first to be unusually small. The longer we lived here and the more people we interviewed, however, the broader and more complex the city appeared. The nicest part about our research for this book was that it provided us with the extraordinary opportunity to reach the heartbeat of the city, the people who live here. Each one was hospitable and helpful, and they warmly revealed their personal lifestyles and backgrounds to us.

Our book is an attempt to reflect the mosaic of Jerusalem by giving examples of cookery from the various communities together with sketches or backgrounds to go with the recipes. Since there are more Jews living here than Christians and Moslems, there are more recipes from the various Jewish communities than from the Christian and Moslem.

We tried to select the recipes we liked best, but frequently it was difficult, since many persons had special ways of making the same dish — all of them good! There must be hundreds of Eggplant Salads and Stuffed Zucchinis in Jerusalem, not to mention all the Falafels, Hummuses and Kubbehs. Rice and lamb may be the staples in Jerusalem, but how many ways of cooking them there are!

The recipes here are original, either created by the cook or handed down through his or her family or the community, perhaps worked from handwritten, lovingly smudged heirloom notebooks. In collecting the recipes, besides struggling with the problem of a different language in almost every household, we had to learn to translate such personalized quantities as a "pinch of this" and a "good handful of that" into standard measurements. Another translation problem was that of identifying the English names of such exotic ingredients as "those white beans we buy in a sack" or "the oil I buy in the *souk* on Thursdays." Once we worked out these problems we faced the trying out of the recipes; we tested each several times, in Jerusalem and the United States, since consistencies of ingredients are different in the two countries. We stirred, kneaded, sautéed, chopped, baked, beat, simmered and chilled — then tested and tasted as we followed the itinerary of our cooks' tours. We hope that you will feel the special flavor of the city of Jerusalem, not only through our recipes but also through the personal profiles of the talented cooks who supplied them.

Breakfasts
and Brunches

"How could I wake up each morning without seeing Jerusalem?"
A feeling all Jerusalemites share

Ramat Rachel — Jerusalem's Own Kibbutz

Jerusalem has everything, even a kibbutz — the only one in the whole country of Israel located within the limits of a city. Kibbutz Ramat Rachel ("Heights of Rachel") sits on a hilltop overlooking the Old City of Jerusalem to the north, the Judean Desert and the Dead Sea and Jordan to the east and Bethlehem to the south. The hill was named after Jacob's second wife, Rachel, who died in childbirth when she and Jacob were traveling to nearby Hebron. Ramat Rachel is a significant name for this border kibbutz, because Jeremiah foretold, "Thy children shall come to their own border," as did Rachel's and Jacob's twelve sons. In 1948, during the War of Independence, the kibbutz helped defend Jerusalem but lost many of its members in the fighting. When the borders between Jordan and Israel were finally settled, Ramat Rachel remained within Israel, although right on the border.

A kibbutz is a collective settlement with common eating and sleeping arrangements. Children live together in communal houses and visit with their parents in the late afternoon or early evening, depending on the parents' or children's work schedules. No cash payments are distributed among the members, and profits from the crops or factory go into the further development of the common kibbutz. Meals are eaten in the common dining room and members take turns cooking and cleaning up.

Since 1926, when Ramat Rachel was settled by Russian pioneers, this kibbutz has had to help defend Jerusalem. During the civil disturbances of the twenties, the majority of Jews in Jerusalem were strictly Orthodox and did not know how to defend themselves. Forty new pioneers volunteered to live on this sandy hilltop lookout, which was open to the enemy on three sides. During the day one member worked the ten acres of land growing fruits and vegetables, with the rest helping in the late afternoon. The others traveled to the Dead Sea each morning, where they worked in the potash quarries to help provide an income for their new settlement. At night everyone took turns guarding the kibbutz. Food was so scarce that the volunteers played games in order to forget how hungry they were.

Later, Ramat Rachel became the first kibbutz to attempt combining agriculture with urban services. The members not only grew fruit and vegetables, but also provided a laundry service and bakery for the city of Jerusalem.

Today, with guard duty unnecessary, life is much easier for the more than two hundred members and volunteers, who come from all over the world. Taking care of the cows and chickens as well as the orchards with their apple, plum, peach and cherry trees keeps the members busy from 4 A.M. until nighttime.

When we arrived at 7:30 in the morning to sample their famous kibbutz breakfast, some of the *chaverim* (members) had just returned from three hours of gathering apples. Others were just leaving for town, where they hold outside jobs — a recent concession to the kibbutz way of life.

The kibbutz breakfast has become so famous in Israel that the country's hotels have adopted this casual but nutritious buffet for their guests. Whatever the season, this breakfast includes homegrown products such as fresh Jaffa orange juice, platters of attractively arranged cucumbers, tomatoes, salami, cheeses, pickles, hard-boiled eggs, yoghurt, sardines, jelly, honey, butter, pickled herring, green peppers, onions, hummus, not to mention piping hot coffee. Milk products such as yoghurt, *leben*, and sour cream are served instead of milk for breakfast. Since this kibbutz is no longer kosher, the kitchen mixes meat and milk products for all meals. Each kibbutznik creates his own combination of breakfast goodies. Sometimes this is salad and sometimes it is a sandwich containing any number of ingredients. No matter how he decides to prepare his morning meal, one thing is certain — his choice will be healthful enough to carry him through many more hours of apple picking. The breakfast salads which follow can also be used for brunch, accompanied by any or all the ingredients mentioned above.

KIBBUTZ BREAKFAST SALAD

4 large firm tomatoes
2 medium cucumbers; 1 peeled,
   1 unpeeled
1 large green pepper

Lettuce leaves (optional)
1 carrot (optional)
Green cabbage leaves (optional)
¼ cup olive or salad oil

2 tablespoons fresh lemon juice or citrus vinegar	Salt and freshly ground pepper to taste

Vegetables should be well chilled before preparation.

Chop tomatoes, cucumbers and green pepper into small even dice. If lettuce is used, tear it into small bits; carrots and cabbage should be grated coarsely. Combine the olive oil and lemon juice; toss with the vegetables and season with salt and pepper. Serve immediately. *Serves 4–6.*

SALAT CHATZILIM (EGGPLANT SALAD)

Tastes best with hot Pita (see p. 36).

1 medium-size eggplant	2 tablespoons lemon juice
½ cup finely chopped onion	Salt and freshly ground pepper to taste
¼ cup finely chopped green pepper	Black olives
2 tablespoons mayonnaise	

Preheat the oven to 450°. Place the eggplant on a cookie sheet or other flat pan and bake it for 30 minutes or until charred and tender.

Remove the eggplant and let it cool slightly. Slice it in half lengthwise and scoop out the pulp with a spoon. Mash with a fork (do not make it too smooth); mix in onion and green pepper. Blend in the lemon juice and mayonnaise; season with salt and pepper. Chill well and serve garnished with black olives. *Serves 4–6.*

SALAT GEZER (CARROT SALAD)

4 carrots	¼ cup fresh orange juice
1 handful raisins	½ teaspoon sugar

Peel and grate the carrots. Mix in a bowl with the raisins, orange juice and sugar. Add more or less sugar, according to taste. *Serves 4–6.*

Sephardic Sabbath Morning Specialties

If anything in Jerusalem is holy it is Saturday morning. No buses operate; store shutters are closed: the usually noisy and crowded streets

*June 1967. Then army Chief of Staff (now Prime Minister)
Itzhak Rabin visits the Church of the Holy Sepulchre
for the first time since 1948*

are hushed and peaceful as people dressed in their Shabbat best take advantage of this day of rest. A pleasant quiet reigns throughout the city. Some people sleep late, others go to the seashore, others hike in the nearby hills and still others walk to their synagogues to pray.

Rachel Molho was born in the Jewish Quarter of the Old City of Jerusalem. Her grandparents had come to Jerusalem from Greece and Yugoslavia during the Ottoman Empire period. Rachel remembers the Old City so well that it was natural for Mayor Teddy Kollek to ask her and her husband, Rafi, on June 9, 1967, to accompany him into that part of Jerusalem which none of them had seen for nineteen years. With a warm smile, Rachel told us of the experience. "Without thinking about it, I knew my way through the winding alleys. All of a sudden we were at the Western Wall. We cried with joy. One other person stood by the wall, a rabbi; he cried too. I returned home to cook for the soldiers — it took my mind off my worry about my son in the army. I couldn't get over the fact that I had just come from the city of my childhood." In the midst of her reverie of 1967, Rachel told us, a taxi driver entered with a note from her son — it turned out that he had been one of the very soldiers who had helped recapture the Old City, and he was safe.

Today Rachel reminisces about life in the Jewish Quarter. "On Shabbat everything was clean and shining in the Jewish Quarter. All day Friday was spent scrubbing and whitewashing. Special foods were prepared for the holy day. There was a communal oven, and it was a grand event when the bread and Burekas were pulled out crisp and golden. As a child I was frightened by the man in the room with the oven who roared loudly when the door was opened.

"Very early on Saturday morning, about six A.M., my father went to the synagogue. When he returned, about nine-thirty or ten A.M., we children were dressed and ready for his arrival and would then have our Shabbat breakfast, which you might call brunch. In the winter we ate *hamin*, which means 'hot' and is similar to the Ashkenazic Cholent, a robust stew, while in the summer we ate *hamindavo*, eggs cooked for so long they turn brown; *soutliash*, a rice porridge; and Burekas, cheese, spinach or eggplant pastries.

"The Saturday morning meals were such a treat — especially the homemade Burekas. Cooking is not permitted on the Sabbath, so the meal had been kept hot over a low flame all night long since its preparation the day before. In fact, the long cooking gave an extra flavor to the foods as well as to the coffee," said Rachel nostalgically.

Today the Molho family frequently takes walks to the Old City on Saturday mornings; Rachel is eager for her grandchildren to be old enough for her to show them the places where she played as a child. Although Rachel and her family are not as religious as her parents were, the entire family still looks forward to the traditional Sabbath morning breakfast, now eaten at her mother-in-law's.

Rachel Molho has become so famous throughout Jerusalem for her Balkan cooking — especially the Burekas — that she herself is writing a Balkan cookbook. We were delighted that she would share her Shabbat morning recipes with us — recipes which can be used throughout the day.

CHEESE OR SPINACH BUREKAS (ORIENTAL TURNOVERS)

Well worth the time spent rolling the leaves. Can be prepared ahead and frozen before baking or after.

½ pound fillo leaves or strudel-leaf pastry
⅔ cup melted butter
1 egg yolk for glaze
Sesame seeds

Cheese filling
½ cup farmers cheese
1 large or 2 small eggs, beaten lightly
1 cup finely grated Swiss cheese

2 tablespoons cream cheese
⅛ teaspoon salt
Generous sprinkle of pepper

Spinach filling
1 pound fresh or 1 package frozen chopped spinach
1 egg, beaten lightly
1 cup finely grated Swiss cheese
¼ teaspoon salt
Generous sprinkle of pepper

Remove the fillo leaves from the refrigerator 2 hours before beginning.

Cheese filling: Mash the farmers cheese with a fork until crumbly. Blend well with egg, Swiss cheese, cream cheese, salt and pepper. You may want to use the blender for this.

Spinach filling: Wash the spinach well, rinsing two or three times. Place in a saucepan with just the water that clings to the leaves after washing. Cover tightly and cook over a medium heat until tender, about 4 or 5 minutes. Remove, place in a sieve and press out the remaining water. Chop fine. Blend well with egg, cheese, salt and pepper.

Preparation: Preheat the oven to 350°.

Taking one leaf of fillo at a time, cut each into a strip about 6 inches by 12. You may want to vary the size depending on how large you want the Burekas to be. Butter the leaf with a pastry brush and then fold in half so that the leaf will then be 3 inches by 12. Butter again and place one heaping tablespoon of either filling mixture at the bottom of the leaf. Fold over to make a triangle, continuing until the end of the leaf, buttering after each fold. Place the completed triangle on a greased cookie sheet. Do the same with all the strips and with both fillings.

When the cookie sheet is filled, brush the tops of the triangles with butter and then beat the egg yolk with a little water and brush the top of each triangle with the egg mixture. Sprinkle with sesame seeds and bake for 25 to 30 minutes, until golden brown and puffy.

Serve warm or cool, not hot. You may want to take them out 5 minutes early and finish baking just before you are ready to serve. *Makes 16–20 Burekas.*

QUESADO DE ESPINACA (CHEESE AND SPINACH PIE)

Crust
12 fillo leaves or 1 9-inch frozen prepared double pie crust or any double crust

Filling
1 pound fresh or 1½ packages frozen whole leaf spinach
3 stalks scallions, chopped fine with green part

1 small onion, chopped
2 tablespoons olive oil
6 ounces feta cheese
2 ounces pot cheese
2 eggs, beaten
¼ cup fresh dill, finely chopped
¼ cup fresh parsley, finely chopped
Freshly ground pepper
¾ cup melted butter

If using fillo leaves, take from refrigerator 2 hours before beginning.

Wash fresh spinach several times and chop coarsely. Thaw frozen spinach.

Preheat oven to 350°.

Sauté onions and scallions in olive oil until golden and then add spinach. Cook until just wilted, about 5 minutes. Remove from heat, and stir in cheese, eggs, dill, parsley, and freshly ground pepper to taste.

Cut all 12 fillo leaves in half across the width. Butter a 12-by-7-by-2-inch pan with pastry brush and line with half the fillo leaves, brushing each leaf with melted butter. Pour in cheese-spinach mixture and cover with the remaining twelve leaves, brushing with butter as each leaf is added.

With a sharp knife, cut the pie into 15 pieces and bake one hour until golden and puffy. Serve hot or cold. *Serves 6–8.*

NOTE: If using prepared crust, place mixture inside it and cover with remaining crust. Bake for 45 minutes.

Hadassah Herring

When the Hadassah Medical Center opened on its present site in Jerusalem in 1961, the dietetic staff found it difficult to prepare food for their patients, who came from many different ethnic backgrounds, with many of them holding to strict religious dietary laws. When a hospital is serving over four thousand meals daily, it seems rather impossible for it to have special kitchens for Kurds, Arabs, western Europeans and Americans; the staff has enough to do preparing special medical diets without adding cultural diets. "There must be something about food," commented Dr. Jack Karpas, Associate Director General of Hadassah, when we approached his wife, Jessie, for her well-known herring recipes from their native South Africa. "All the patients seem to be particular about one thing — eating."

The staff is continually besieged by patients' special requests for food. Typical are the men who ask for "just a little bit of my wife's chicken for Shabbat." The nurses explain that no one can bring in his own food, no matter "how kosher," because some people might bring just a little of non-kosher chicken, thereby offending more strictly observant patients. Billy Rose was once a patient at Hadassah, and he wanted to bring his own cook from France because he insisted there was one way, and only one way, to fry an egg, and that only his cook could do it properly. Mr. Rose took his leave when the hospital could not accommodate his request.

Dietary restrictions may be difficult on Shabbat, but they are impossible on the Jewish fast day of Yom Kippur. At least 500 of the 600 patients request permission to fast, and for at least 200 of them, medical reasons prohibit fasting. On the first Yom Kippur at the center, Dr. Karpas asked a learned rabbi for advice. The rabbi considered for a few minutes and consulted his Shulhan Arukh (the authoritative commentary on the Talmud). Then he said that very sick patients could each receive 25 grams of food every eight minutes throughout the fast day — thus ensuring that the patients would be eating on an empty stomach (a requisite for strict observance of the fast day) and still be getting the nourishment they would need. Dr. Karpas protested that it would be quite impossible to weigh and measure 25 grams every eight minutes for 200 people on an ordinary day, much less on the Day of Atonement with a skeleton staff. The rabbi answered that he had explained how to carry out the order and thus had done his rabbinical duty. "Now do what you want," he said with a wink, and left.

Jessie Karpas is accustomed to listening to stories like this as she prepares her own delicacies for the Karpases' many friends. Like all Jerusalem housewives, Jessie never knows when a visitor will "drop in";

telephoning to warn a hostess has not yet become a custom in Jerusalem. Since the Karpases' house is open to doctors, patients and visiting representatives from Hadassah in the United States, in addition to the South African immigrants who consider this home their link with their native land, Jessie always has her favorite herring dishes available in her freezer. Typical of so many Jewish recipes found in Jerusalem today, these herring specialties came to Jerusalem via Cape Town from Lithuania, the original homeland of Jessie's mother and most other Jews who wandered their Jewish way to Jerusalem via South Africa.

CREAMED HERRING

Store in refrigerator. Keeps well.

1 cup heavy cream	night and filleted, with each
2 tablespoons sugar	fillet cut into 5 or 6 pieces)
2 tablespoons wine vinegar	1 medium onion, sliced thin
10 herrings (cleaned, soaked over-	

Whip cream with sugar, fold in vinegar. Layer fillets and onion slices in glass jar and pour cream mixture over. Cover. *Serves 20.*

HONEYED HERRING

Improves with time; store in refrigerator.

6 salt herrings (cleaned, soaked	½ cup sultana raisins
overnight and filleted, with each	2 tablespoons liquid honey
fillet halved)	Dash of cinnamon
1½ to 2 cups water	Dash of ground ginger
2 large onions	1 lemon, peeled and sliced thin

Soak herrings again while preparing sauce. To make sauce: bring water to boil, add onions and raisins, and simmer slowly for 2 hours, adding more water if necessary. When the onions are tender, add honey, spices and lemon slices. Cook for 10 minutes. Remove lemon slices. Drain fillets, roll up and fasten with toothpicks. Carefully pack into glass jar. Pour cooled sauce over and seal. Leave toothpicks in. *Serves 10–12.*

Freezes well.

2 apples, peeled and chopped into small squares	2 small cans tomato paste
2 onions, peeled and chopped coarsely	6 herrings (cleaned, soaked overnight and filleted, with each fillet cut into 5 or 6 pieces)

Put apples, onions and tomato paste into a small saucepan and bring to a boil. Lower heat and cook 2 minutes. Pour over herring and chill before serving. *Serves 10–12.*

A Wandering Dane's Smørrebrød

We have all heard of the wandering Jew, but what about the roaming Christian? One of Jerusalem's leading architects today is a Christian immigrant to Israel, blond, blue-eyed, Danish Ulrik Plesner — the antithesis of the melancholy Dane! The son of a Scottish painter and a Danish historian, Ulrik was born in Florence, where his father fell in love with and married his artistic mother. When Ulrik was two years old, the family moved to Copenhagen and he grew up there under the German occupation during World War II.

Throughout the war the Danes heroically supported the persecuted Jews of Europe, saving virtually all of the 8,000 Danish Jews from the Nazis. Living on the Copenhagen seashore, young Ulrik often watched the fishing boats smuggling Jews across the sea to neutral Sweden. His next-door neighbor, disguised as a fisherman, operated such a boat on moonless nights. One evening the disguised fishermen were stopped by a German patrol boat. "What have you there?" demanded the German captain. "Fish," replied a "fisherman" as he opened the hold only to reveal fifty Jewish heads. "*Ach so*, fish," was the German's miraculous misconception as he sailed away in what must have been a fairy tale come true in the land of Hans Christian Andersen. Two memorials in Jerusalem to the Danes' courageous efforts are the brand-new Denmark High School and an artistic plaza called Danish Square, the focal point of which is a stunning iron sculpture symbolizing the small boats in which Jewish refugees were smuggled to safety by the Danes.

After the war, Ulrik was selected to represent Denmark at the *Herald-Tribune* Youth Forum in the United States, where he met and fell in love with another participant, Tamar Liebes from Israel. Ulrik returned to Denmark to finish his architecture studies, only to win a competition which brought him to Ceylon, where he stayed for nine years. In Ceylon the Plesner-style house, with its use of natural local building materials and huge roofs, eaves, fountains and gardens, became well known. Later, when Ulrik went abroad to study Hilton hotels before designing one in Ceylon, his research included a Hilton in Tel Aviv, and while he was there he visited the girl from Jerusalem whom he had met many years before. Ulrik and Tamar married and lived on a tiny Ceylonese island before moving to England. After several years in London, both Ulrik and Tamar decided that it was "no good living in a place with no roots. We had to take Tamar's or mine. Since Jerusalem is such a marvelous place, we decided to move here."

Like other new immigrants Ulrik has been struggling to learn Hebrew — a language he finds more difficult than his eight others, which include Singhalese. Ulrik's and Tamar's three small children already speak perfect Hebrew and have forgotten most of their English, the common language used by their parents.

"Food, like building, has a mythology of its own. Danish cooking is basically peasant food. Denmark's great and only contribution to gastronomy is Smørrebrød. A splendid food world of its own, it varies from simple robust sandwiches to rich complicated ones. Because foreigners really do not understand it, you just do not get a proper Smørrebrød outside Denmark, but rather a misunderstood open-faced pale tea sandwich, or a cocktail sandwich version. In reality it is a rich tradition: one meal using many kinds of bread — black, brown, white, full grain, crackly; and many kinds of tastes — salt fish, smoked fish, straight fish, pickled fish, salamis; smoked, salted, spiced, raw meats; greenery; cheeses; sweets; etc., and usually served with beer to wash it down and schnapps to wash down the beer. Least understood by outsiders is the basic importance of the sequence of tastes, from salt fish and meat to sweet dessert, from the hard black bread to soft white bread.

With the same gusto which he applies to his work in Jerusalem, Ulrik prepared for us his typically Danish Smørrebrød (he prefers the simple kind, spicy), perfect for people with hungry appetites — ideal for brunch or midday luncheon.

SMØRREBRØD (DANISH OPEN-FACED SANDWICHES)

Round 1: Smoked Herring Sandwich

1 slice whole grain rye bread	Chopped scallions
1 pat sweet butter	1 onion, sliced in rings
1 whole smoked herring	Salt and pepper to taste

Spread one slice of whole grain rye bread with butter. Place one whole smoked herring about 6 inches long on top. The herring should be freshly smoked. Open up the herring, turn it upside down and pat it with a knife to loosen the skin. Remove skin and gently place the herring on top of the bread.

This whole procedure must "happen" on your plate in front of your very eyes. Sprinkle chopped scallions and 1 or 2 onion rings on top of the herring. Add salt and pepper to taste.

Drink one swig of schnapps, swallow one bottle of pilsner beer and you are ready for the second round of Smørrebrød.

Round 2: Salami Sandwich

1 slice whole grain rye	with garlic
1 pat sweet butter	8 or 9 peppercorns
1 or 2 pieces Italian salami smoked	1 slice green pepper

Spread another slice of good fresh whole grain rye bread with butter. Cover with 1 or 2 slices of salami, making sure the salami hangs over the edge of the bread. Shove about 8 or 9 whole peppercorns into the meat. Top the sandwich off with a slice of green pepper and dig in. Take another swig of schnapps and another bottle of pilsner beer.

Round 3: Cheese Sandwich

1 slice French or Danish white bread	½-inch-thick slice Camembert cheese
1 pat butter (be generous this time)	3 or 4 large radishes

Spread a thick slice of white French or Danish bread with a generous pat of butter. Add a thick slice (½ inch) of Camembert cheese so that it droops over the sides. Next to the bread place several large radishes attractively arranged. Drink yet one more swig of schnapps and half a bottle of pilsner beer and you are ready for the final portion.

Round 4: Sweet Smørrebrød

1 slice cracked Vita bread	Generous spoonful honey
1 pat butter	

Spread the cracked Vita bread with butter and an equal portion of honey until it runs off on your fingers — if it is not all over your hands. This sandwich should be greasy and sticky up to your wrists. Arrange beautifully and eat!

There are over a hundred additional varieties of Smørrebrød, but these are Ulrik's favorites.

A Black Moslem Commune near the Dome of the Rock

A visitor to Jerusalem is often struck by the apparent oddity of a black community in an enclave outside the Prison Gate, the northwest corner of the Temple Mount, the thirty-six-acre complex housing the Dome of the Rock and the El Aksa Mosque. Actually, this community is descended from the very first guards of the thirteen gates leading to the Moslem shrine.

Beginning in the late thirteenth century, when the Egyptian Mamelukes were extending their rule over the Holy Land, all Jewish and Christian holy places were guarded by local Moslems, and Moslem mosques were guarded by black Moslems from Africa. The Africans were enlisted for this first by the Mamelukes and later by the Turks. The black guards, respected for their loyalty and trustworthiness, would not allow a Christian or Jew to enter the Moslem shrines without special written permission from the sultan. And so on one occasion the Governor of Jerusalem imprisoned all the guards because he wanted a visiting Christian duke and duchess to be free to enter, and while the guards wailed, the Christian visitors made their way through the Haram. By the late nineteenth century, however, the authorities had begun to realize that not all visitors would desecrate the holy shrines, and today the vast area is open to everyone except during the special five-times-daily prayers and all day Friday, the Moslem Sabbath.

The community, consisting of about sixty families and numbering about five hundred people, is still very black, despite intermarriage through the years with the local Arab community, because throughout the centuries African Moslems on *hajj*, or pilgrimages to Mecca, returned by way of Jerusalem and often remained there, never to return to their distant homeland. They then settled and intermarried with this community. With ancestors from Chad, Nigeria, Senegal and Sudan, these Africans all live in a large family commune and share facilities. Their customs are similar to those of other Moslems in Jerusalem, except that each Friday after the noonday prayer in the El Aksa Mosque the men gather together in their own tiny mosque next to their home to cook their meal and discuss community affairs.

We visited the community during the month of Ramadan, while the women were preparing a sweet and coffee, the traditional break in the daily fast which lasts throughout the month. All the men were seated on the floor, eating from a large platter in the traditional manner by scooping rice and meat up with their right hands. We joined them in savoring Katayif, fruit- and nut-filled pancakes, which we thought would make a novel brunch treat, breaking a Saturday night fast.

KATAYIF (FRUIT- AND NUT-FILLED PANCAKES)

Pancakes can be prepared and filled in advance. Heat and pour warm syrup over just before serving.

Pancakes
2 cups flour
1 teaspoon salt
2 teaspoons baking powder
½ cup cornmeal
½ cup sugar
2 eggs, beaten well
3 cups milk
Vegetable oil for cooking

Filling
1 cup finely chopped walnuts
2 tablespoons brown sugar
1 teaspoon cinnamon
1 cup raisins
1 apple, peeled and grated
Warm water, orange juice or
    applesauce

Honey Syrup
¾ cup water
¾ cup honey

Pancakes: Sift flour with salt and baking powder. Add cornmeal and sugar and blend well. Add the eggs and finally the milk mixing well each time, until batter is smooth.

Barely cover the bottom of a 6-inch or 7-inch skillet (a crêpe pan is best) which has a cover with oil and heat until hot but not smoking. Pour in a small amount of batter to thinly cover the surface of the pan — pancakes should be thin — and cook, covered, over medium heat for a few minutes. Flip pancake and cook the other side (it will not brown as evenly as the first side). Repeat until batter is finished, adding a few drops of oil to heat before making each pancake. Place pancakes aside. Keep warm and moist. Preheat oven to 350°.

Filling: Mix nuts, brown sugar and spices with one or two of the suggested fruits and enough water, juice or applesauce to hold the mixture together. Spread a small amount of the filling on each pancake, fold in half and press sides together.

Syrup: Boil water and mix with honey.

Place completed pancakes slightly overlapping each other in baking dish, and dribble with some of the honey syrup. Bake in oven for 8 minutes. Serve with piping hot remaining syrup. *Makes 12–14 pancakes.*

Variation: 1 cup dried apricots, chopped coarsely can be used instead of the apples or raisins.

Russian Blintzes and Trees Transplanted in Jerusalem

"When I first arrived in Jerusalem from Russia in 1921 as a young bride, my husband and I moved into a two-family house in a suburb of Jerusalem," related Miriam Granott. "Expecting the worst, we were delighted with the large airy rooms with the garden adjoining. There was one thing wrong, though, and that was the lack of a kitchen in any form. My landlord assured me that this was not a problem, since a table and chairs could be placed in the middle of the back room, water could be pumped from the well in the garden, and all would be fine." After several years with this makeshift kitchen arrangement, the Granotts moved to their present home in Rehavia. At that time Rehavia was a desert area with no trees and only four houses. Now it is the home of many better-known Israeli citizens (among them Miriam's next-door neighbor, the Israeli Prime Minister), and its sidewalks are bordered with towering trees and private gardens filled with exotic flowers and shrubs.

Miriam, the widow of Avraham Granott, past President of the Jewish National Fund, the organization which since 1902 has been collecting money from people throughout the world to buy land and plant trees in Palestine, told us that in the twenties, trees and flowers were unbelievably scarce in what was then Palestine. She related that once when she was walking with a precious bunch of daisies in her hand, an elderly woman approached her to ask what kind of vegetable she was holding and how she planned to cook it. In 1931 she eagerly planted the first saplings near her home, and today they tower between her property and the neighboring building, the Prime Minister's official residence.

While visiting Miriam in her lovely home we asked her how she learned to cook. "I am Russian, the daughter of the Chief Rabbi of Odessa. We Russians don't like to cook, but I can make gefüllte fish and knishes well because I watched my mother do it." Miriam gave us her recipe for cheese blintzes, which certainly taste as though daughter, if not mother, enjoyed cooking them. Candied grapefruit peels, another of Miriam's specialties, can be found in the Cookies and Sweets section.

BLINTZES (CHEESE-FILLED CRÊPES)

Pancakes	*Filling*
2 cups milk	1 cup cream cheese
1 egg, slightly beaten	½ cup cottage cheese, drained, or
1 tablespoon cooking oil	farmers cheese
2 teaspoons brandy	1 egg yolk, slightly beaten
1¼ cups flour	1 tablespoon sugar
¼ teaspoon salt	½ teaspoon vanilla

Pancakes: In deep bowl, mix milk, egg, oil and brandy. Sift flour with salt and add to milk mixture. Beat with rotary beater until smooth.
   Preheat oven to 350°.
   Grease a 6-inch frying pan by putting a little oil on a paper napkin and wiping the pan lightly, bottom and sides. Place over medium heat — pan is ready when drop of water skitters over the surface. Pour the batter from the bowl into a small glass for easier handling. From the glass, pour small amount of batter over the surface of the pan, tilting immediately so that batter covers complete surface thinly and evenly. This takes a little practice if you are making blintzes for the first time, and the first one or two might not work out properly. If any brown pieces remain, scrape off before starting again. When large bubbles appear on surface of pancake and edges pull away slightly, run metal spatula around edge and turn pancake over. The pan usually does not have to be greased after the first pancake is made, but until about six or eight are made. (It takes about 1½ minutes for bubbles to appear). Cook other side for about half a minute. Turn out onto counter top, making piles of about four each.
   Filling: Mix ingredients together until blended. Place heaping table-spoonful of filling in center of pancake. Fold one side over filling, then the other, and then fold over the ends. Set aside, folded side down, on a cookie sheet. Bake for 20 minutes or until nicely browned. Can be served warm or cooled. Serve with sour cream, fruit compote, apple-sauce, stewed plums, fruit preserves or jam. *Makes 14–16 Blintzes.*
   Variations: Add to the cheese filling any one of the following: grated lemon rind, cinnamon, nutmeg, raisins or small amount of chopped apple.

Breads

*Pita prepared in the bedroom — "the best place for the
dough to rise," the cook explains*

A TV Star Prepares Pita

Gloria Stuart Sofer was born in Amman of an Italian mother and a Scottish father who was serving under Colonel Peake (popularly known as Peake Pasha) with the British army. Soon afterward, the family moved to the oasis town of Jericho near the Dead Sea, where Gloria's father, Alexander, opened the first supermarket. Regrettably, the venture did not succeed because the local community was accustomed to shopping only in open-air markets and no one could get used to the packaged, imported foods.

Until she was a teenager, Gloria attended the Franciscan School, then the American Friends School, a Quaker establishment in nearby Ramallah. Afterward she went off to study Arabic, economics and history at the American University in Beirut. As a result of this varied educational and social background Gloria speaks Italian, English and Arabic with equal fluency.

Working in Amman to help pay her college tuition, Gloria became interested in the "sport of kings," horse racing. Her enthusiasm led her to buy her own horse, who turned out to be a prizewinning champion for six consecutive years. In fact, the horse, which she named Glorious Lion, became so famous that King Hussein himself expressed his personal admiration. Arab tradition says that when a friend shows a strong interest in a possession of yours, you should offer it as a gift. She did.

Gloria commuted to work from Jericho to Amman until the end of 1966, when a Jordanian law came into effect: British passport holders were no longer allowed to work in government offices. So Gloria went to work for Kuwait Airlines in Jerusalem, Jordan. After the Six-Day War, Gloria found that any job she applied for required that she speak Hebrew. Undaunted, she bought a basic Hebrew language book and taught herself enough to converse with her new Israeli friends. During an interview with Israel radio, a television director who happened to be present "discovered" her for the Arabic news program on the newly instituted Israeli network. Her face and voice proved so attractive that Israelis who did not even speak Arabic used to watch her news broadcasts. She made her own news story when she resigned over what she considered unfair work conditions and won her point with a special contract, under which she works today.

Gloria made her own news again when she married an Israeli Jew, Eddie Sofer — first in Cyprus in June of 1970, since Israeli religious law prohibits a Jew and a non-Jew from marrying in Israel, and then in December of the same year in Jerusalem, after her conversion to Judaism. Eddie had come to Israel from Baghdad, Iraq, after the Six-Day War and was working in news broadcasting for radio and television.

Gloria and Eddie speak Arabic to each other. Their little girl, Hazel, speaks Italian with Gloria, English with Eddie; she has learned Spanish from her nurse and Hebrew from her playmates! Both being from Arabic cultures, Gloria and Eddie prefer Arabic cooking to all others. Even though she leads a busy life, Gloria enjoys making most of their meals from the basics, including Pita — the Middle Eastern flat bread which has become so popular in the United States. (The Arabic word for this bread is *kimaje,* meaning "open bread.")

PITA (KIMAJE — MIDDLE EASTERN FLAT BREAD)

1 tablespoon dry active yeast	2⅓ to 3 cups warm water
1 tablespoon salt	5 to 6 cups flour
2 tablespoons honey	

Place the yeast, salt, honey and ½ cup warm water in a small bowl and let stand 10 minutes in a warm place. Place 4 cups flour in a large mixing bowl. Add the yeast mixture and 2 cups warm water. Mix vigorously for 1 minute and add 1 more cup of flour. On a floured board, knead the bread for 10 minutes, adding more flour if necessary to make a medium stiff dough. Clean and lightly grease a bowl. Return the dough to the bowl, making sure all sides are greased. Cover with a clean damp towel, place in a draft-free warm place, and let rise until doubled in size (about 1 hour).

Preheat oven to 450°.

Punch the dough down and knead a little. On a floured board, divide the dough into 12 pieces, form each into a ball, cover and let rise 10 minutes. Roll or pound the balls of dough into flat circles about 5 inches in diameter, and ¼ inch in thickness. Do only 5 or 6 at one time. Place these rounds on an ungreased cookie sheet and bake on the bottom of the oven for 8 minutes, or until the bottoms are browned. If the tops remain pale, let brown under broiler briefly.

Let cool, then place in plastic bags and refrigerate or freeze.

To serve, place in 350° oven about 3 minutes until the Pita is warm. Be careful not to keep the bread in the oven too long, as it becomes rock-hard. Serve immediately as Pita hardens quickly if left uncovered.

Pita can be eaten many different ways and at every meal. For breakfast, toast and fill with butter and honey. For a sandwich, open by tearing one edge apart half way down and fill with Falafel (Page 53) and salad. For an accompaniment to an array of hors d'oeuvres, cut into small wedges and dip in all the traditional *maza* salads, such as Tahina and parsley (Page 47), Hummus (Page 46) and Baba Ghanouj (Page 46). *Makes 12 "loaves."*

The Bathtub Would Be Best — The Ingenuity of an American Immigrant

The notice tacked up in the hallway announced that Giveret (Mrs.) Shosh's challah, with or without raisins, was for sale in Apt. 21. Orders were to be given no later than Thursday evening. Penciled in at the end of the notice was the stipulation: "Because of the egg shortage, please bring one egg for each challah ordered." (This was one of the shortages which occurred during the Yom Kippur War.)

Shoshanna (Hebrew for Rose) officially changed her first name when she and her husband Sid, a high school teacher, arrived in Israel three years ago with their two young children. Unlike a move from one city to another in the United States, it has not been easy for them. There is no comparison between their four-bedroom home near Boston and their four-room apartment in Jerusalem, to say nothing of the unheated, overcrowded absorption center where they studied Hebrew for six months. Adjustment was not easy.

"I lived in Israel for one year and then I went back to the States to visit. After having devoured as many hot fudge sundaes and pancakes as I could, I began to miss Israel. Something seemed wrong with my friends' lives in Boston — no definition, no goals. I realized what an honor it is for a Jew living in the twentieth century to be in Jerusalem. It's worth staying here even with all the hardships; worrying about wars; paying the highest taxes in the world. Here I have a Jewish identity which is far more than my once-a-week Sunday school visit gave me in the States. Moses and Abraham are alive for my children. Israel represents a continuity in our lives."

Sid and Shoshanna came to Israel for the first time on their honeymoon, just after the Six-Day War. "We then decided to give life here a try; Sid felt he could make a contribution in education and I felt that this was where we belonged. We talked about it for two years and then planned for two more.

"I am baking my way to Switzerland," laughed Shoshanna, who began catering friends' parties to help out financially and then decided to begin a business selling home-made challah (braided bread eaten with the Shabbat meal). On Rosh Hashanah, the Jewish New Year, the challah is round — to pray for a good year "all year round."

On Friday morning Shoshanna gets up at 3 A.M. to prepare the large batches of dough. Her friends have donated their largest cooking pots for the operation — Shoshanna still says the bathtub would be best but might scare off her customers! By 7:30 the neighbors' children are knocking at her door to pick up their orders, encouraged by the delicious aroma of homemade bread wafting through the corridor. As we left Shoshanna's apartment smelling the bread, we wondered how many challahs actually last until the Sabbath blessing is made over the bread.

CHALLAH (SWEET BRAIDED BREAD FOR THE SABBATH)

Traditionally 2 loaves are served for the Sabbath.

2 packages active dried yeast	1½ teaspoons salt
½ cup warm water	9 cups of flour (used in varying
1 teaspoon sugar	amounts)
3 eggs	2½ cups raisins (optional)
½ cup sugar	2 eggs beaten with 2 tablespoons
1½ cups warm water	water
½ cup vegetable oil	Sesame or poppy seeds

Combine the yeast, water and sugar; set aside. Beat the eggs with sugar; add the warm water, oil and salt. Blend in the yeast mixture, beat well. Using 5 cups of flour, add 1 cup at a time, beating well after each addition; the dough will be sticky. If raisins are used, add them now. Now add 2 more cups of flour, beating well (wooden spoon is best), until the dough leaves sides of bowl. Place the dough on a surface onto which you have shaken an additional 2 cups of flour and knead until almost all the flour is absorbed into batter. Return to bowl. Cover with a towel and let rise until double in bulk (usually 1 hour in unheated oven with door closed or 2 hours on counter top). Punch down.

Divide the dough into three parts and divide each part into three again for braiding. Braid on a greased and floured cookie sheet, cover with a towel and let rise until double in size — about 1½ to 2 hours.

Preheat the oven to 400°. Before baking, brush with the egg-water mixture and seeds. Bake for 15 minutes, tap the loaves, which should have a hollow sound; if not, then bake 5 more minutes. Cool on a wire rack. *Makes 3 loaves.*

PUMPKIN BREAD

Pumpkin Bread keeps well stored in refrigerator or freezer.

4 eggs	2 teaspoons baking soda
2 cups canned or fresh pumpkin	1½ teaspoons salt
(not pie filling)	1½ teaspoons cinnamon
1 cup cooking oil	1½ teaspoons nutmeg
⅔ cup cold water	3 cups sugar
3¼ cups flour	

Preheat the oven to 350°.

Beat the eggs until frothy. Add the pumpkin, oil and water; blend well. Sift together all the remaining ingredients and add to the egg-pumpkin mixture. For this batter use two 5¾ inch x 9¾ inch x 2¾ inch or three small loaf pans. Grease and flour the pans, pour the batter in and bake 50 to 60 minutes, or until the edges shrink from the sides of the pan and a knife blade inserted in the center comes out clean. *Makes 2–3 loaves.*

An Archaeologist Who Digs Cooking

A favorite Israeli pastime is archaeology. Priceless treasures have been unearthed in backyard vegetable patches; ancient buildings have been uncovered while workers dug the foundations for new ones. Everyone here considers himself an amateur archaeologist and it is not surprising to find many professionals as well. Magen Broshi is a good example. He is the well-known curator of the Shrine of the Book at the Israel Museum, where the Essene parchments discovered at Qumran near the Dead Sea, known the world over as the Dead Sea Scrolls, are located. The discovery of the scrolls in 1948 revised traditional thought about the origins of Christianity.

Magen also digs a good meal. "I began cooking last year when my wife stopped," joked Magen while he showed us some fragments of pottery found on his current dig at Mount Zion. Under the auspices of the Armenian Orthodox Church and the Israel Department of Antiquities, Magen and his team of archaeologists and volunteers from all over the world are excavating a part of Jerusalem which flourished at the time of Jesus. When we were interviewing Magen, we were actually standing on the site of the house of the High Priest Caiaphas. It is here that tradition places the room in which Jesus spent the night after he was betrayed in the Garden of Gethsemane. "If this tradition is accurate, the square in front of the palace where Pilate would have faced the crowd must be under the main buildings of the Armenian Patriarchate — and it is therefore physically impossible to excavate now." During the first decades of the Christian era the area around Mount Zion was covered with aristocratic and priestly residences not far from Herod's palace. In 70 C.E., with the Roman destruction of Jerusalem, the area was covered up and subsequent civilizations were built upon it.

"In the past four years we have learned more about ancient Jerusalem than had been known during the last century's excavations," commented Magen. When we asked how the excavation got started, Magen's answer brought us abruptly back to the present. The Armenian Patriarchate is building a new seminary for priests. As with every new construction in Jerusalem, the archaeologists must be allowed to excavate before the past is sealed off even further by the builders' bulldozers.

Like most archaeologists, Magen is fascinated with fitting together the jigsaw puzzle of the past. "This is probably why I enjoy cooking so much — it's a challenge to see what you can create out of a mixture of unknown ingredients."

BAGELES (ISRAELI BAGELLIKE PRETZELS)

Sold on every street corner, Bageles are eaten for snacks.

1 package active dried yeast	7/8 cup margarine
1/4 cup warm water	1/2 cup vegetable oil
4 cups flour	1 egg, beaten
1 teaspoon ground caraway	1 teaspoon water
1 teaspoon salt	Sesame seeds for topping

Dissolve the yeast in water; set aside. Sift together the flour, caraway and salt. Blend in the margarine and oil. Make a hole in the center of the batter; pour in the yeast-water mixture and combine well. You may have to add more lukewarm water to make a firm, but not stiff, dough.

Cover the bowl with a towel and place in a warm spot for one hour so that the dough can rise.

Preheat the oven to 375°. Shape the dough into crescents about three inches long. Brush each with some of the egg-water mixture and sprinkle with the sesame seeds. Place on an ungreased baking sheet and bake for 20 minutes or until lightly browned. *Makes 4 dozen.*

They are especially good warm from the oven.

Appetizers

An Actor's Appetizing Performance

"I was born an actor and so was my younger son, who once appeared on a German television program," commented Abu Hamdi Zaud. "In fact, all Arabs like acting. Many years ago I began my career with the Arab Legion as Julius Caesar in the ruins of Jerash." Recently Abu Hamdi completed a successful run as Kishkish, the gypsy looking for food, in an East Jerusalem performance of Hans Christian Andersen's *Red Shoes*. Abu Hamdi was born in the Old City and worked as a policeman in Amman until 1967. At that time he left the police force and began working as a teacher and also as an actor for both the new Jerusalem Arabic theater, created by Mayor Teddy Kollek, and Israel's most popular children's program in Arabic on Israeli television.

Despite his busy schedule, Abu Hamdi believes that he and his wife should share in the chores of bringing up their seven children. However, the scene is not as pro-feminist as it might appear. Even though Abu Hamdi's oldest child is a daughter, his friends call him Abu Hamdi, "Father of Hamdi"; Hamdi is the name of his oldest son. "Women don't count," he explains, and although he takes a certain pride in his wife's modern clothing — a new wig and short dresses — he prefers the traditional long dress of Arab women.

At the Zaud home we sat down to an elaborately prepared meal beginning with arrack and water to soothe our appetites and then continuing with the traditional *maza*, a huge array of hors d'oeuvres. Commenting on the delicious Hummus and Tahina on the hors d'oeuvres table, Abu Hamdi said that every Friday, the Moslem Sabbath, it was his chore to prepare Hummus for the family. He described how he soaks chick-peas in water the night before and then grinds them in a mortar, pausing frequently for rests until the mixture reaches the right consistency. Finally he adds other ingredients until the Hummus reaches the perfection he wants. When one guest commented on the amount of work involved, Abu Hamdi admitted that what he actually does is open a can of prepared tahina and chick-peas and then makes a few additions, thus doing away with the laborious grinding procedure. Abu Hamdi's recipes for Hummus, Eggplant, Tahina and Cucumbers offer means for producing simply prepared but very interesting hors d'oeuvres.

HUMMUS (CHICK-PEA DIP)

Hummus freezes well. Tastes best with Pita.

2 cups canned chick-peas, drained
⅔ cup tahina paste (ground
  sesame seeds)
¾ cup lemon juice

2 cloves garlic, mashed
1 teaspoon salt
¼ teaspoon cumin
Parsley for garnish

Place all the ingredients in a food mill or blender, mix until the chick-peas are smooth. Store the Hummus in a covered container in the refrigerator. Serve well chilled, and just before serving sprinkle chopped parsley on top. If desired, reserve ¼ cup unmashed chick-peas and sprinkle on top of the dip before serving.

More garlic may be added, if desired. Also, if a thinner consistency is required, for instance when serving as a dip with potato chips, the mixture may be thinned with lemon juice. If Pita is not available, crackers or thick slices of French or Italian bread may be used. *Serves 4.*

BABA GHANOUJ (EGGPLANT WITH TAHINA)

1 large eggplant
1 medium onion
½ bunch parsley
½ cup tahina (sesame seed paste)
2 tablespoons lemon juice

2 garlic cloves, crushed
2 teaspoons water
1 teaspoon salt
Dash cayenne pepper

Place the whole unpeeled eggplant directly on gas burner with the flame set at medium, turning it as the skin chars and the inside becomes soft, or bake in a pan in 450° oven until it is charred and tender, about 30 minutes. When done, let cool slightly, cut in half lengthwise and scoop out the eggplant pulp with a wooden spoon (the wooden spoon preserves the flavor). Chop fine in a ceramic or wooden bowl. Grate the onion on the largest holes of a grater. Squeeze out juice from the onion. Chop parsley fine and blend with the eggplant and onion.

Blend the tahina thoroughly with lemon juice and garlic, stir in small amount of water until the mixture is white in color. Stir into eggplant mixture, add salt and a dash of cayenne pepper. More lemon juice may be added for extra flavor. Garnish with parsley. *Makes 2½–3 cups.*

CUCUMBERS WITH DILL AND SOUR CREAM

3 cucumbers
2 teaspoons salt
½ cup vinegar, cider or white
2 tablespoons cold water
1 teaspoon sugar

3 tablespoons chopped fresh dill
Freshly ground black pepper to
  taste
Sour cream

Peel the cucumbers and slice them very thin. Place in a colander, sprinkle with salt and set aside for one half hour. Mix the vinegar, water, sugar and dill, combine with the cucumber slices and mix well. Sprinkle the mixture with pepper and chill until icy cold. Serve with a large spoonful of sour cream on each portion. *Serves 4–6.*

TAHINA-PARSLEY DIP

A good dip with Pita, potato chips or fresh vegetables.

1 cup tahina
1 cup fresh lemon juice
4 cloves garlic, mashed
1 teaspoon salt

1 cup finely chopped fresh parsley
½ cup finely chopped mint
  (optional)

Mix the tahina and lemon juice. Mash the garlic cloves with the salt. Then add to the tahina mixture. Stir in parsley. Taste the mixture for seasoning; you may also want to add a little more lemon juice. A nice variation is the addition of ½ cup finely chopped mint. *Serves 4–6.*

Next Year in Jerusalem

"*Hashana haba'a b'Yerushalaim* — Next year in Jerusalem" is the wish recited by Jews all over the world on the first night of Passover during the *seder* (order) meal. This celebration of the exodus of the children of Israel from Egypt over 2,000 years ago is one of the most ancient continually observed festivals known to man. The Jewish historian Josephus, in the *Jewish War*, estimated that the participants who gathered in Jerusalem to perform the sacrifice during the "Feast of Unleavened Bread" in the year 65 C.E. were "not less than three million." Passover is also one of the three pilgrim festivals, originating from the time of the First and Second Temples when every male Israelite was to make an annual pilgrimage to Jerusalem to offer a sacrifice. Today Jews still perform the *seder* prescribed in Exodus, and thousands continue to make the annual pilgrimage to Jerusalem.

To us Jerusalem is at her most glorious during this springtime holiday. The sweet smell of almond blossoms, the patches of red poppies, and the budding greenery create the fresh atmosphere in which the special Pesach (Passover) preparations begin. For one week, most families use an entirely separate set of dishes, cutlery and cooking utensils — all of which are kept carefully packed away during the rest of the year. Ultra-Orthodox families may even have a separate kitchen which is used only at Passover. Poorer families bring their everyday dishes to locations specially set up by the Ministry of Religious Affairs for their purification. "Kosher for Passover" is stamped on all those packaged food products which have been prepared according to religious dietary laws for the occasion. Schools are out for the holiday and businesses open only half a day. This is the time for many Jerusalemites to take *teulim*, trips throughout the country.

During the week of Passover, no food containing leavening may be eaten. This is to remind us that when the Jews had to flee from Egypt in great haste, there was not enough time for their bread to rise. Before the holiday Jewish homes are spring-cleaned to remove any trace of leavening, and the day before the *seder* feast, children search for *humitz* (breadcrumbs or leavened bread). Mothers hide something made with flour for the children to find, and then, as tradition dictates, it is swept up with a feather and then burned so as to be thoroughly destroyed. All over Jerusalem small bonfires can be seen burning on the morning of the beginning of Passover.

The eating of *matzah*, unleavened bread, is the main custom of the *seder*. The wheat for its preparation is under observation from the time of reaping, and care is taken that the whole process from kneading to final baking does not take more than eighteen minutes, so no rising can take place. In search of a special handmade *shemurah matzah*, we wandered into a Chassidic shop in Mea Shearim. (These *matzot* differ from the packaged variety to which we are accustomed in that these crisp crêpelike crackers are pierced with holes by hand and are carried to the oven by a man who yells, "Matzah!") Because we were women — al-

Stocking up on matzot for Passover

though we were dressed in the obligatory long skirts and sleeves — the bakers quickly turned their backs, refusing to wait on us. After asking a Chassidic male friend to intercede, we happily procured two *shmurah matzot*, which we proudly used in our own Passover *seders*.

The central event of the week is the *seder*. The first-night feast is so meaningful in the Jewish year and in family life that everyone makes a special effort to gather together from near and far. It is also a special *mitzvah* (duty) to have as many guests as possible at the table. No one is left out — *seders* are held in hotels for tourists, with the city of Jerusalem sponsoring public ones. A quiet and happy hush falls peacefully over the city as every resident is seated at the *seder* table, celebrating Passover the same way it has been done for hundreds of generations.

In answer to the four questions (asking why this night is different from all other nights), traditionally read by the youngest child, the father lifts each food item and recites the *Haggadah* (narration of the exodus) as he fulfills the Biblical obligation of informing his children of their deliverance from Egypt. Many Orientals act out the story of the exodus while Ashkenazis often recite the Song of Songs.

Tables are set according to custom, each reflecting the cultural background of the family. The central object of every table is the *seder* plate arranged with the symbolic foods of the ritual. Among these are *charoset* (clay) and *maror* (bitter herbs), symbolizing respectively the mortar used by the Jewish slave-builders and the bitterness of their enslavement. Charoset is a pleasing blend of sweet ingredients, and the combination of this dish with the bitter herbs, often eaten in the form of horseradish, is unusual and delicious. We have included a special Sephardic Charoset (sweeter than the Ashkenazic) from the island of Rhodes as well as a Ukrainian Gefüllte Fish, the traditional beginning of an Ashkenazic *seder* meal.

CHAROSET (SEPHARDIC STYLE FROM RHODES)

This version is from the island of Rhodes. The neighboring island of Salonica adds raisins.

2 cups pitted dates
1 cup walnuts
½ teaspoon ginger

2 tablespoons sweet red wine (or to taste)

Soak the dates for 3 to 4 hours and then simmer for 20 minutes. Grind the nuts in a Mouli grater or a blender. Combine the dates and nuts and then blend well. Mix with ginger and a little wine.

Spread on matzah at Passover with romaine. Good as an hors d'oeuvre throughout the year. *Makes 2½ cups.*

GEFÜLLTE FISH (ASHKENAZIC STYLE FROM THE UKRAINE)

Stock
4 stalks celery, cut in 4-inch slices
2 onions, quartered
1 green pepper, cut in chunks
3 carrots, halved
8 cups water
Bones of fish (and heads, if desired)
1 tablespoon salt
½ tablespoon freshly ground pepper
12 sprigs parsley
2 teaspoons sugar

1 bay leaf (optional)

Fish
4 pounds pike
1 pound whitefish
1 pound carp
1 tablespoon salt
2 medium onions, finely grated
6 eggs
1 tablespoon vegetable oil
1 teaspoon sugar
½ cup matzah meal

(The ratio of fish can be adjusted according to taste. The less carp and the more whitefish, the more delicate the flavor. Depending on price and availability of fish, each fish market will have its own suggestions. Today most markets will grind the fish for you and give you the heads, bones and skins in a separate package.)

Place all the stock ingredients in a large kettle with a cover. Bring to a boil, then cover and reduce heat to simmer. While waiting for the pot to boil, begin preparing the fish.

In a wooden bowl, add to the ground-up fish all the ingredients listed under Fish, carefully chopping and blending. Wet hands and form fish mixture into fat oval-shaped patties, carefully sliding each into the simmering stock. Cook slowly for 2 hours. Allow to cool slightly in pot and carefully remove all the patties, placing them on a platter. After the fish has been removed, strain off the vegetables and loose fish. This stock should then jell when chilled; however, if it does not, simply add a small package of unflavored gelatin.

Serve the chilled Gefüllte Fish with a carrot slice, horseradish and the jelled fish stock. *Makes 36 large pieces.*

"Marry Her If She Can Cook Kubbeh . . . ."

One day we visited Katamon, a neighborhood in Jerusalem which is home to the immigrants from Kurdistan; Kurdistan was at one time a rural area that included parts of present-day Turkey, Persia and Iraq. When we entered the home of Hannah Nehemia, we noticed that she seemed somewhat embarrassed by our presence. She quickly put aside her notebook and blushingly explained that she had been doing her "homework," which was learning to read and write Hebrew.

We would have thought that Hannah probably had enough "homework" with her ten children, but she told us that she was pleased now to be able to spend some time studying. She explained that she had married at the age of fourteen, according to the custom in Zacho, their village in Kurdistan, which they left in 1952. She is now in her late thirties and can let her older children take care of the younger ones. "Reading and writing were always secondary to a woman's role as wife and mother where I come from," she explained. And she asked Joan, "Why aren't you married? I'll find you someone. It just isn't right for a woman not to get married and have children."

During our chat with Hannah, her husband came home after a tiring day of construction work. The Kurds are well known in Jerusalem as the builders of roads and buildings — always working together in groups. We had previously learned that Kurds were in fact so clannish that even today in Jerusalem people from the same village of Kurdistan tend to marry one another. Over a glass of tea we asked Ovadia if he would mind if his son chose to marry a non-Kurdish woman. His reply was rapid: "As long as she can make Kubbeh, I don't care who my son marries."

The main ingredient in Kubbeh is burghul (cracked wheat), originating thousands of years ago in Kurdistan. Kubbeh consists of a meat or rice filling inside a dough made with burghul and is formed in the palm of one's hand into torpedolike shapes before being cooked. Hannah insisted upon giving us a lesson in the many ways of making this delicacy. Even Ovadia was relatively pleased with the results, although he still thinks that no one can make Kubbeh as well as a woman from Kurdistan.

KUBBEH (BURGHUL AND BEEF HANDFULS)

Outer Shells
½ pound #3 burghul (cracked wheat)
½ pound ground beef or lamb
1 medium onion, finely grated
½ teaspoon mint leaves
Salt and pepper to taste
¼ teaspoon cumin
½ teaspoon cinnamon
½ cup cold water
¼ cup margarine

Vegetable oil

Filling
1 to 2 large onions, very finely chopped
Olive oil
¼ pound chopped beef or lamb
⅛ cup pine nuts (pignolias)
Salt and pepper to taste
Pinch of cumin
Pinch of cinnamon

NOTE: A meat grinder or food mill is required for this recipe.

Shells: Place the burghul in a bowl and pour boiling water over; let sit for one half hour. Then squeeze the water out. Add the burghul to the meat and, using the fine blade of the grinder, put the whole mixture through the grinder twice, the second time adding the onions and mint leaves. Season with salt, pepper, cumin and cinnamon. Then, working with your hands, add enough water to make the mixture into a smooth dough. Place in the refrigerator.

Filling: Sauté the onions slowly in olive oil until soft. Add the onions to the meat and cook until the meat is browned. In a separate pan brown the pine nuts in oil until golden. Season with salt, pepper, cumin and cinnamon.

Preparation: Wet your hands with cold water. Take a small lump (about the size of a walnut) of the shell mixture in one hand, smooth into a ball, then form a cone over your thumb. Press the sides to make a thin wall. Place about a tablespoonful of the filling into the opening and smooth the outer mixture over it, using cold water to seal any cracks. Now, using the palms of your hands, shape the filled lump into an elongated egg shape, something like a torpedo.

In a deep pot, heat vegetable oil until very hot and deep-fry the Kubbehs until dark brown in color. (If your outer shell is thin enough and properly fried, you will be able to hear the nuts rattling inside.) Place on paper towels to drain. Serve hot as cocktail snacks. *Makes 26–30.*

Variation: You can also prepare this dish the following way as a main course for 3 to 4. Preheat the oven to 350°. Grease a 9-inch round or square baking tin. Spread half the shell mixture over the bottom, place the filling on top and cover with the rest of the shell mixture. Melt ¼ cup margarine and trickle it over the surface. Bake for 1 hour until dark brown and crisp on top. Slice diagonally in both directions to make diamond-shaped pieces.

FALAFEL (CHICK-PEA PATTIES)

1 pound can chick-peas (drained)	1 teaspoon garlic powder
1 large onion, chopped	1 teaspoon ground coriander or
2 tablespoons finely chopped	cumin
parsley	½ to 1 cup breadcrumbs or fine
1 egg	burghul (crushed wheat)
1 teaspoon salt	Vegetable oil
1 teaspoon dried hot red peppers	

Mix the chick-peas and the onion. Add the parsley, lightly beaten egg and spices. Whirl in a blender. Add breadcrumbs until the mixture will form a small ball without sticking to your hands. Form the chick-pea mixture into small balls about the size of a quarter (one inch in diameter), or use a "falafel measuring gadget." Flatten the patties slightly before frying them in deep hot fat until golden brown on each side. Drain the falafel on paper towels.

Serve individually with toothpicks as an hors d'oeuvre or as a sandwich filling with chopped tomato, cucumber, radish, lettuce, onion and/or tahina inside Pita (page 36). *Makes about 24.*

A Teacher-Chef Who Cooked for King Abdullah

Many great cooks have come into their own not as a result of formal training but rather as a result of many years of hard work and experience. Such is the case with Salah El Sharif, who began his career at the age of fourteen, working as a cook's apprentice in a small restaurant in the Old City's *souk* near Damascus Gate. Soon realizing that he wanted to make cooking a profession, the young boy journeyed to Egypt, where he luckily became an assistant to the chef of the late King Farouk. Today, boasts Salah, late in his seventies, "Most of the young cooks around have learned from me." This seemed apparent when we saw no fewer than seven assistants surrounding him in the kitchen of his family restaurant. Until last year when Salah's sons expanded the Ummayyah restaurant, there was no menu, and hungry customers went into the kitchen to select what looked most appetizing from the huge pans simmering on the stoves. Even today the printed menus do not daunt the regular customers, who act as if they do not exist.

"You don't need talent to make kebab," says Salah El Sharif

Until 1948 Salah's restaurant, which he had opened on his return from Egypt, was a favorite gathering place for Jews, Christians and Moslems alike — especially those involved in city politics. When the city was divided, Salah reopened his restaurant in the main business street of the

Jordanian sector outside the city walls. His culinary skills became renowned in Jordan and reached the ears of the late King Abdullah,
grandfather of King Hussein. Until his assassination in the El Aksa
Mosque at noonday prayers in 1951, the King came from Amman every
Friday to pray, never leaving Jerusalem without a meal of roast whole
lamb prepared by Salah.

It is great fun to sip Turkish coffee or mint tea while watching Salah
cook and direct his assistants. Every possible Arab dish is prepared
here — this being the most popular restaurant in East Jerusalem. Salah
mixes all the fresh ingredients with his hands, the only canned product
being tomato paste, which has only recently become a concession to
modern methods.

"You don't need talent to make Kebab," Salah quickly commented
about the skewered meat so popular with us Westerners. Instead he gave
us a recipe for Arab hors d'oeuvres which appeal to both Easterners and
Westerners.

SFEEHA (JERUSALEM PASTRY HORS D'OEUVRES)

Dough
1½ cups flour
½ teaspoon salt
½ cup margarine
4 tablespoons plain yoghurt

Cheese Filling
½ cup feta cheese, crumbled or
    mashed
1 egg, separated
1 tablespoon finely chopped fresh
    parsley
Freshly ground pepper to taste

Meat Filling
½ cup uncooked chopped beef

1 green onion, chopped fine
1 tablespoon finely chopped fresh
    parsley
1 egg yolk
Salt and freshly ground pepper to
    taste
½ teaspoon cumin
1 tablespoon chopped pine nuts
    (pignolias)

Tahina Filling
4 tablespoons tahina
2 tablespoons fresh lemon juice
2 tablespoons finely chopped fresh
    parsley
Juice of 1 pressed garlic clove

Dough: Blend flour and salt. Cut in margarine with two knives or
pastry blender until mixture is crumbly. Mix in yoghurt with fingers
until well blended. Divide dough into three equal parts and place in refrigerator while preparing fillings.

Cheese Filling: Mix cheese, egg yolk, and parsley and season with
pepper. Save egg white for glaze.

Meat Filling: Mix the chopped beef, onion, parsley and egg yolk.

Season with salt and freshly ground pepper. Save cumin and pine nuts for topping.

Tahina Filling: Combine the ingredients and season with salt and pepper.

Preparation: Roll out one part of the dough as thin as you would for piecrust. Cut out twelve 2-inch circles and place them on an ungreased cookie sheet. Divide the meat mixture evenly among the circles, spreading it almost to the edges. Sprinkle each with cumin and stick a few pine nuts into the top. Set aside.

Roll out the second part of the dough and cut out twelve circles. Place them on an ungreased cookie sheet. Spread a spoonful of tahina mixture on each circle, covering each right to the edge. Set aside.

Roll out the third part and cut out twelve circles. Place six circles on an ungreased cookie sheet, divide the cheese mixture evenly among them, spreading it not quite to the edges. Place the remaining circles on top of each and seal well with water. Make a small X in the top of each with a sharp knife. Brush the tops with reserved egg white mixed with a little water.

Preheat the oven to 400°. Place the cookie sheets in the oven, the meat hors d'oeuvres on the top rack. Bake tahina pastries about 15 minutes until lightly browned, meat pastries about 20 minutes until nuts and meat are browned, cheese pastries about 30 minutes until pastry is golden. *Makes approximately 6 cheese, 12 meat, 12 tahina pastries.*

The Jerusalem Post: The Editor's Wife Entertains

"The State of Israel Is Born," the *Palestine Post* announced in a banner headline on May 16, 1948. To reflect this momentous change in the country's status and to demonstrate faith in the capital of the new state, then a sleepy little town, young American-born Ted Lurie, the assistant editor, suggested changing the name of the paper to the *Jerusalem Post.*

Founded in 1932 by the well-known American Zionist Gershon Agron, the *Palestine Post* was able to stay on its feet by virtue of a gambled investment of £250 made by the late Mr. Lurie. His new sabra (Israeli-born) wife, Tzila, a Jerusalem beauty, quickly learned that marrying Ted meant marrying the *Jerusalem Post* as well.

On February 1, 1948, during the disturbances just prior to the creation of the state, the *Jerusalem Post* building was bombed. "At that time there was a curfew on all the citizens of Jerusalem. I had a pass to pick up my husband at night," recalled Tzila recently as she was preparing hors d'oeuvres for an unexpected guest from India. "Ted had not had supper, so at 10:50 P.M. we decided to leave the *Post* for a cup of coffee. I remember that it was so terribly cold that we were hugging each other as we ran to Café Atara on Ben Yehuda Street. Halfway there we saw a British covered truck going fast over the sidewalk. 'I wonder what he's doing here at this time of night,' commented my husband. As we reached Jaffa Road we heard an explosion. Two seconds later we heard that the *Post* had blown up. We ran back, to learn that three people had died and over thirty-seven were wounded. The press and the archives were completely burned.

"We all decided that the paper had to come out. We made arrangements to print on another press, and all kinds of people volunteered to help. The *Palestine Post* was on sale in the morning as usual. And somebody even remembered to buy us sandwiches and coffee."

From an initial daily circulation of eight hundred the paper has grown to a daily circulation of thirty-one thousand with thirty-five thousand for the new weekly overseas edition. With the fourth largest circulation in Israel, the *Jerusalem Post* is a key item for tourists, diplomats and English- or German-speaking Israelis.

Knowing about newspapermen's erratic hours from our own experience in Jerusalem, we asked Tzila how she had adjusted to irregular meals. "I never have. While the children were growing up I kept their hours and Ted's. You become entirely absorbed and involved in the newspaper world. There was such excitement in helping to make a new state and prestate."

Accustomed to the unexpected, Tzila gave us several hors d'oeuvres recipes, some of which incorporate her now-famous Mayonnaise.

MAYONNAISE LURIE

2 whole eggs
1 tablespoon salt
1 tablespoon pepper
2 tablespoons sugar
2 heaping tablespoons Dijon
   mustard

½ teaspoon paprika
4 cups vegetable oil (do not use
   olive oil)
½ cup fresh lemon juice (or to
   taste)

Beat together all ingredients, except the oil and lemon juice, with a rotary beater or blender. Add the oil, ¼ cup at a time, beating well after each addition. When all the oil has been thoroughly beaten in, add lemon juice to taste. The mayonnaise should have a sweet and sour taste. Store it in covered jars in the refrigerator; use it in the following recipes. *Makes 4 cups.*

AVOCADO DIP

1 avocado	Salt and pepper to taste
1 crushed garlic clove	1 tablespoon Mayonnaise Lurie

Mash the avocado, then blend in garlic, salt and pepper to taste. Then stir in Mayonnaise until the mixture is of the desired consistency. Chill to serve.

Eat it with crisp crackers, chips or small buttered crisp-breads. Crumbled fried bacon bits may be added. If the avocado dip is made much before serving, it gets dark on top. Skim this part off and stir again. *Makes 1 cup.*

EGG CURRY DIP

4 hard-boiled eggs	1 teaspoon curry powder (or to
Mayonnaise Lurie	taste)
Salt and pepper to taste	

Grate the eggs on medium holes of a grater. Add enough mayonnaise to give a creamy consistency, like a thin paste. Season with salt, pepper and curry powder to taste. Chill.

Variations: Add fried onion or crumbled fried bacon bits just before serving (do not add them earlier because they will become soggy). Chopped parsley, scallion, or a handful of raisins may also be added. *Makes 1⅓ cup.*

EGGPLANT ROLL

Crust	Filling
2½ cups flour	1 medium eggplant
¾ teaspoon salt	4 tablespoons tahina
1½ teaspoons baking powder	½ teaspoon salt
¾ cup margarine or butter	¼ teaspoon pepper
1 cup sour cream	Pinch of sugar
Yolk of 1 egg	2 garlic cloves, minced
Sesame seeds	1 tablespoon water
	1 tablespoon lemon juice

Preheat oven to 450°.

Filling: Place the eggplant in the oven 30 minutes until charred and tender. Let it cool. Then peel and mash it. Meanwhile, blend the tahina with salt and pepper, sugar, garlic, water and lemon juice. Mix the eggplant with the tahina and set it aside.

Reduce oven temperature to 350°.

Dough: Sift the flour with the salt and baking powder. Mix the flour and margarine with a pastry blender or your hands. Add the sour cream. Knead the dough three or four times with your hands. Place it in the refrigerator for ½ hour.

Roll the dough into a long thin rectangle on a floured board. Place the eggplant mixture down the length of one side and roll the dough one and a half times lengthwise. Place the roll on a greased cookie sheet, brush it with the yolk of one egg and sprinkle it with sesame seeds. Bake about 30 minutes, until brown. Serve it warm, cut in thin slices. *Makes 1½–2 dozen slices.*

Wear a Burmese Longyi When You Eat This Dish!

"I think there are probably as many countries represented among United Nations personnel living in Jerusalem (one thousand families) as there are Jews from different nationalities," commented Robert Myaing, retired Chief of Survey and Investigation for the United Nations in Jerusalem. Seated with the Myaings in their home, we admired the lovely *longyis*, or sarongs, which everyone was wearing. The difference between a man's longyi and a woman's is the way in which it is wrapped around the waist and tucked in, they explained.

As in Israel, in Burma women have equal status with men. "Women are in the army and police force — in fact, in many spheres, they have better positions than men," remarked Kathryn, the Myaings' daughter, who is one of nine women in a class of twenty-one studying dentistry at Hadassah Medical Center. "I feel very much at home at Hadassah, because I know everyone, male and female," she grinned. There has always been a special rapport between the Burmese people and the Israelis, because both countries attained independence in the year 1948. On a visit to Rangoon, David Ben-Gurion studied the Burmese way of meditating in absolute silence, preferably at three or four A.M. And after a visit to Israel, Burmese ex–Prime Minister Unno tried to initiate the concept of a kibbutz in Burma. To the Myaings, who have lived in

Jerusalem for the past seven years, Jerusalem and Rangoon are somewhat similar. Both have mixed populations, and this affects the so-called "typical" food of both cities. Indian, Chinese and Pakistani cultures influence Burmese cooking.

Kathryn put a platter of unusually shaped objects on the table and instructed us to eat each piece with our fingers. The "objects" were pieces of zucchini which had been cut in strips dipped in batter and deep-fried. The recipe comes from the cookbook Kathryn used in cooking class when she was a high school student in Rangoon.

NGABAUNG JYAW (SQUASH STRIPS TEMPURA)

4 medium-size zucchini or Hubbard squash	½ teaspoon ginger
¼ cup cornmeal	⅛ teaspoon saffron
¼ cup flour	½ teaspoon salt
1 cup ground rice, Cream of Rice or rice flour	1 egg
1 teaspoon chili powder	Cold water
	Vegetable oil for frying

Scrub the unpeeled squash and cut it into thin strips 3 inches long (like french fries). Mix the cornmeal, flour and ground rice with spices, add the well-beaten egg and cold water until the mixture forms a creamy paste (like a cake batter, thick but pourable). Add the squash strips and stir well to coat each piece thoroughly. In a large frying pan with deep sides place vegetable oil to a depth of 3 inches and heat it until very hot but not smoking (approximately 350°). Drop clumps of squash strips into the hot oil and cook them about 8 to 10 minutes until golden brown. (The strips are not fried separately; they are done in clumps.) Drain them on paper towels.

Since Ngabaung must be eaten hot, it can be done in an electric frying pan at a party or for a snack. Shrimp or thin onion slices can be prepared the same way. *Serves 6–8.*

BANANA CHIPS

Cooking oil	Salt
2 pounds very green bananas	

Heat the oil in a deep pot until very hot (370°). Slice peeled bananas into ⅛-inch-thick circles and fry, one cupful at a time — it takes only a few minutes. Remove them when golden brown and crisp (like potato chips), drain on paper towels and sprinkle with salt. Serve as an hors d'oeuvre or as an accompaniment to a curry dish. *Makes approximately 4 cups.*

From Georgia (Russia) with Love

We had heard so much about the clannish Georgians, the latest wave of new immigrants to Israel, that we were delighted when a new Georgian restaurant, the Gruzia, opened in Jerusalem.

Part of the Caucasus in southern USSR, Georgia, the birthplace of Stalin, is bounded by the Black Sea, northern Turkey, Armenia and Azerbaijan. For two thousand years it was a united separate kingdom until it accepted Russian sovereignty in the nineteenth century. The Jews in Georgia claim descent from one of the ten lost tribes of Israel, and some even believe they are descendants of the Jews exiled by Nebuchadnezzar from the Kingdom of Judah. In 1804, Georgia was recognized as part of the Pale of Settlement where Jews were allowed to live. By the end of the century there were thirty-five thousand Jews living in the area.

By the nature of its geography Georgia remained relatively isolated, and the Georgian Jews are less assimilated to life in Israel and less sophisticated than the other Russian Jewish immigrants. Despite their isolation, the Georgian Jews had heard of Zionism from Russian Jewish soldiers and by the 1860s dozens of them had settled in the Old City of Jerusalem.

Today twenty (or one-third) of all the synagogues in the Soviet Union are located in Georgia. Georgians are strongly family-centered; the father is a patriarchal figure whose word is law. Property is owned jointly by the family and sometimes, as in this case, by the clan, with the eldest, here Ilya Migre, as the undisputed authority.

This authority was evident as we entered the restaurant across from the famed King David Hotel. The partners were seated around a table, wearing their embroidered skullcaps, while Georgian music played in the background. When our interpreter asked which was the owner, they all deferred to Ilya, who immediately introduced himself.

While still in Georgia, Ilya Migre heeded the advice of his rabbi and prayed three times a day to come to Jerusalem. In November 1968, former Prime Minister Golda Meir received a letter from eighteen Georgian families telling her of their desire to leave Georgia and settle in Israel. These same families, all friends of Ilya, also wrote to the United Nations Human Rights Commission, requesting the right to emigrate. Eventually they received permits to leave, and by 1972 there were over fifteen thousand Georgians in Israel, among them Ilya Migre and his extended family, who were granted exit visas two years after their initial request.

Today, Ilya, his family, his friends and his local rabbi have resettled in apartments near each other in Jerusalem. Many Georgian immigrants, however, were not so fortunate as to maintain their separate community within a community, a carry-over from their life in Georgia, and are scattered all over the country.

Ilya had been the foreman of a nylon plant in Tiflis. His dream was to open a carpet factory in Jerusalem with several of his friends. Since he speaks only Georgian and Russian but not French, Hebrew or English, it was very difficult for Ilya to make the necessary arrangements for the project, and so he and his friends decided to take advantage of the culinary skills of their wives. Thus opened the first Georgian restaurant in Israel.

The tables are set with heavy antique Georgian silverware, sparkling crystal and elegant china, most of which are family heirlooms dating from before the Revolution. Hand-painted murals decorate the walls and on the counter rests an ancient abacus for adding up the bills. In the kitchen all four wives were chattering to each other in Georgian while cooking Chenagi and other Georgian delicacies, some of which had a taste very foreign to anything we had ever eaten. When we asked how to prepare this especially tasty chicken and walnut hors d'oeuvre, Ilya showed us the recipe in his old Georgian cookbook, which we naturally could not read. Watching his wife cook the Chenagi, we were able to "translate" the recipe — an exciting appetizer.

CHENAGI (CHICKEN AND WALNUT APPETIZER)

Walnut sauce, light and delicately seasoned, is a Georgian specialty.

1 small chicken, cut into six pieces	1 tablespoon finely chopped
3 cups salted water	shallots or chives
4 eggs, separated	1/4 teaspoon rosemary
1 teaspoon confectioners' sugar	1/2 teaspoon salt
1 cup finely chopped walnuts	1/4 teaspoon pepper

Simmer the chicken pieces in the water until tender. Let the chicken cool slightly, reserving the liquid. Bone and skin the chicken and shred the meat into small pieces; set aside. Beat the egg whites with the confectioners' sugar until stiff; then, using the same beaters, beat the yolks until foamy. Into the whites fold the yolks, walnuts, shallots or chives, rosemary, salt and pepper. Bring one cup of reserved chicken broth to a boil and add the egg mixture, stirring constantly. Lower the heat and continue stirring for a few minutes. Remove from the heat and stir in the shredded chicken. Serve immediately, as the broth will separate if allowed to stand too long. Chenagi is more liquid than solid, so it it best served in small bowls. *Serves 6–8.*

A Finzi-Contini in Jerusalem

Vittorio de Sica's Academy Award–winning film *The Garden of the Finzi-Continis* focused attention on the fate of Italian Jews during the Second World War. Until the time of the war, Jewish communities had flourished throughout Italy — in Rome, Florence, Venice and Milan. Little is left of these enclaves, most of the Jews having been killed by the Nazis and the others having moved to Israel and elsewhere. The wealthy and prestigious Finzi-Contini family of Ferrara, who had isolated themselves for so long in their own exclusive world, in the end suffered the same fate as their less affluent brothers.

The story of the Finzi-Continis was a fictionalization by Giorgio Bassani from his own family history. A relative of Mr. Bassani's, Hannah Fishman-Benzimra, came to Jerusalem as a young child just prior to World War II. Like the other Italians arriving in the late thirties and forties, her family and friends formed themselves into an Italian community with an Italian synagogue, created in 1940. In 1952 an authentic synagogue building was transported *in toto* from Conegliano Veneto, near Venice. While growing up in Israel, Hannah remembers seeing all the religious objects throughout the city, attesting to the rich heritage of her family.

Hannah, now married to an Israeli, teaches Italian literature at the Hebrew University of Jerusalem. Like most Israelis, the Fishman-Benzimras eat their main meal at lunchtime, but this family always adds an Italian antipasto. "Although I am the mother of two sabras and consider myself more of an Israeli than an Italian, I still have to cook with an Italian touch." Both these recipes were handed down from Hannah's and thus Bassani's family in Italy.

CAPELLINI FREDDI (COLD PASTA)

1 package (18 ounces) very thin hairlike spaghetti	3 cloves garlic, minced
2 tablespoons olive oil	2 tablespoons finely chopped parsley

| 6 tablespoons tomato paste | Pepper to taste |
| 1 teaspoon salt | |

In a large saucepan, bring to the boil enough water just to cover the spaghetti. When the water is boiling strongly, drop in the spaghetti, count to fifty-five (timing is important!) and immediately pour the pasta into a colander or strainer. Rinse quickly with cool water, stirring with a rubber spatula to separate the noodles, but do not tear them. Set them aside to drain well.

Heat the olive oil in a small saucepan and add the garlic. When the garlic is lightly browned, add parsley, tomato paste, salt and pepper. Cook and stir for about 4 minutes.

Place the spaghetti in a deep bowl and pour the sauce over it. Stir well until the sauce is absorbed by the pasta. Place in the refrigerator, chill well to serve. It is also good as an entrée. *Serves 4–6.*

MELANZANA ALLA GIUDEA (JEWISH-STYLE EGGPLANT BITS)

4 large eggplants	1 tablespoon cooking oil
2 teaspoons salt	1 tablespoon butter
4 garlic cloves, minced	

Wash the eggplants well; cut off the stems. Slice them in half lengthwise and scrape out the pulp (a grapefruit knife is good for this), leaving a half-inch shell. (Reserve the pulp for spinach fritters, Page 165). Cut the skins into one-inch squares. Place the squares in a strainer or colander and mix with salt. Place a heavy saucepan on top to crush, and set aside for one hour so that the bitter juice drains off.

Heat the oil and butter in a frying pan and cook the squares with garlic, covered, until soft. Remove the cover and fry for another 10 minutes. Drain on a paper towel. Chill before serving.

Makes a delicious and different hors d'oeuvre or light entrée for an Italian meal. *Serves 4.*

Phone Calls to Moscow — A Mother's Long-Distance Love

In 1973 alone over 33,361 Jews entered Israel from the Soviet Union. One of them is Berta Rashkovska or "Ima [Mother] Slepak," as she is

Ima Slepak receives a welcome phone call from her children,
still in Moscow

called. For those of us who remember what Helena Rubenstein looked like, Ima Slepak could be her double, and even more interesting is that Ima Slepak makes her own face creams, which she generously gives to her guests. "Better than Helena Rubenstein's," she boasts in Yiddish or Russian. This ebullient septuagenarian, who wears heavy loops in her ears and many rings on her fingers, is always active, working to bring her four children and their spouses from Moscow to Jerusalem.

Her son-in-law, Vladimir Slepak, a forty-year-old electronics engineer, has been working in the Soviet Union's top-secret industries, and consequently he and many others have not been granted the right to leave, on the grounds that their departure would constitute a security risk for the USSR. One of the foremost activists in the Jewish Movement, Vladimir has participated in virtually every effort in Moscow to ease the restrictions on Jews who wish to settle in Israel. In fact, the Slepak home was used as a center of such activity until Ima Slepak left for Jerusalem.

Reluctant to leave Vladimir alone, her children have remained in Moscow while Ima Slepak continues the campaign in Jerusalem. She lives alone in a tiny apartment which was allotted to her by the Jewish Agency's immigration-absorption department, an organ of the Israeli government. Small as her apartment is, it teems with activity as old and young alike come to chat, sip tea, discuss their problems and partake of her homemade food. Occasionally the telephone may ring with a call from one of her children in Moscow — making them seem poignantly close, yet so far away.

Although we required an interpreter to communicate with Ima Slepak, her warmth and kindness came across very clearly. With a brave smile she told us that the following are her children's favorites, Potato Knishes and Pirogen, both of which taste especially good with Borscht but are also very fine on their own as hors d'oeuvres.

POTATO KNISHES

Pastry
4 cups flour
1 cup salted margarine or butter
1 egg, slightly beaten
1 tablespoon white vinegar
¼ cup club soda

Topping
1 egg yolk, beaten
Sesame seeds

Filling
6 medium-size potatoes
1 large onion, chopped small
Cooking oil, chicken fat or
   margarine
1 egg, beaten
1 teaspoon salt
Pepper to taste

Pastry: Sift the flour and blend in the margarine or butter. Add the egg, vinegar and club soda. Knead well and form the dough into a ball. Place in the refrigerator for 2 hours.

Filling: Peel and halve the potatoes. Cook them, covered, in boiling salted water until tender, about 30 minutes. Drain and mash them well into smooth purée. While the potatoes are cooking, fry the onions in cooking oil, chicken fat or margarine until soft and golden but not crisp. Add to the purée, stir in the egg and season to taste.

Procedure: Preheat the oven to 375°.

Divide the dough into four parts. Roll it out thin and cut into small circles, about 2 inches in diameter. Place 1 teaspoon of the potato mixture in the center of each. Fold the crust in half and crimp the edges to close with a fork dipped in cold water. Place on a greased baking sheet, brush with beaten egg yolk and sprinkle with sesame seeds.

To prepare potato knishes ahead, follow the recipe until the pastry is filled and closed. Place on a sheet of waxed paper, cut into slices and wrap tightly. Store in a freezer or refrigerator. Remove ½ hour before baking, let sit. Brush the surface with egg yolk and sprinkle with sesame seeds. Bake as described above.

Variation: Take one quarter of the dough and roll out into a large circle. Place the mixture on half of dough circle, fold the other side over and crimp the edges closed with a fork dipped in cold water. Brush the surface with egg yolk and sesame seeds and bake as described above. Slice and serve hot. *Makes 4 dozen.*

PIROGEN (MEAT AND CHEESE TURNOVERS)

Make the dough for Potato Knishes (page 66) and divide it in half, using one part for Meat Pirogen and the other for Cheese Pirogen.

Meat Filling
2 slices white or rye bread
1 cube chicken or beef bouillon
    dissolved in 1 cup hot water
Margarine
2 small onions, chopped coarsely
2 cups cooked ground meat
    (chicken, veal, lamb or beef)
1 egg, slightly beaten
1 egg white, beaten stiff
½ teaspoon rosemary

Salt and pepper to taste
1 egg yolk (to brush on dough)

Cheese Filling
Margarine
1 onion, chopped fine
2 cups large-curd cottage cheese
Salt and pepper to taste
Breadcrumbs from fresh white
    bread

Meat Filling: Soften the bread in the bouillon, then drain. Heat the margarine until very hot, then sauté the onions and softened bread. Mix in the meat and cook 5 minutes. Stir in the beaten whole egg and egg white. Season with rosemary and salt and pepper.

Cheese Filling: Heat the margarine, sauté the onion until tender. Season the cheese with salt and pepper, add the onion and enough breadcrumbs to make the mixture firm.

Procedure: Roll the dough thin and cut it into 2-inch-diameter circles. Place the filling on half of a dough circle, fold the other side and crimp the edges to close with a fork dipped in cold water. Continue until the dough and filling are used up, or roll the dough into a large circle, fill it, fold it in half and crimp the edges as described above.

Preheat the oven to 375°. Place the Pirogen on a greased cookie sheet and brush the surface with the egg yolk beaten with a little water. Bake 35 minutes until golden brown. Serve warm, not hot. Cheese Pirogen may be served with sour cream. *Makes 4 dozen small Pirogen or 2 large ones.*

Life in the Armenian Quarter

It was nine o'clock in the evening and we were visiting Erya Bekarian in the Armenian Quarter of the Old City, when suddenly we heard a loud knock-knock-knock echoing up and down the small streets outside. Erya explained that the old-fashioned custom of locking the quarter gates each evening is still in effect and that just prior to their closing, one of the residents walks through the streets banging on the ground with a wooden staff to warn everyone that the gates will soon be locked.

Erya, who with her family has lived in this quarter all her life, explained to us how according to Armenian tradition St. James the Less, a disciple of Jesus and the first Christian bishop of Jerusalem, lived until his death in 62 C.E. on Mount Zion, which then became the center of Christian life. Since that time, Armenians, disciples of St. James the Less, have continued to live on Mount Zion in what has become the Armenian Quarter. As members of the leading Monophysite Church, the Armenians share major rights in all the important Christian shrines with the Roman Catholic and the Eastern Orthodox Churches. The separation of the Armenian Orthodox from the main body of Christianity dates from 451 C.E., when the Armenians rejected the doctrine of the Trinity in favor of a belief that Jesus had a composite nature. The Monophysite doctrine of the Armenian Orthodox Church hardened in 506 and 554, the latter date being the one of their final rejection of Western Trinitarianism.

A town within a town, the compound of the Armenian Monastery of St. James was originally built for priests and nuns. With the Turkish massacres of 1914, Erya's parents and other Armenians arrived homeless in Jerusalem, and the church offered them refuge in its compound, where several thousand still live today.

The residents of the compound live a life unto themselves; they speak Armenian at home and live by the Armenian church calendar. The quarter offers them everything they require: churches, schools, houses, a library, shops, and a press which prints books in Armenian. Soon students will be able to study for the Armenian Orthodox priesthood as well, when the new seminary now under construction is completed. The early closing of the quarter's gates, however, makes life rather difficult, especially for the young people like Erya. It means that she cannot have friends in to visit, nor can she stay away from the quarter after early evening — even to see a movie. "But at least our youth club with its wonderful jazz makes up for that," commented Erya with a grin. The jazz begins after the gates close, so unfortunately we could not listen.

Erya told us that for Armenians, New Year and Easter are the most important events on their religious calendar. The preparation of food (such as Topik) for festive occasions starts weeks ahead, and special utensils, put away since the last Easter, are used. The recipe for Topik is terribly involved, and listening to the detailed instructions for its preparation, we understood why it is made only once a year. After the many ingredients are cleaned, peeled, chopped and cooked they are mixed together and left to soak for several days, and the mixture must be stirred at set times throughout each day. Then it is tied up in special squares of white cheesecloth and the cooking process starts. Some families choose New Year's as their special day for this treat instead of Easter Sunday — but it is always made just once a year. While listening to Erya's mother's description of this complicated recipe we munched on Lahmajoun, Armenian pizza, which was delicious. We also could not resist tasting the marinated shish kebab enjoyed by Israel's former Defense Minister Moshe Dayan, who often enjoys it at lunch with the Armenian Archbishop. The recipe for it can be found on page 134 under Main Dishes.

TOPIK (A ONCE-A-YEAR HORS D'OEUVRE)

Outside Crust
3 medium potatoes
2 tablespoons salt
1 pound dried chick-peas

Filling
4 pounds onions
¼ cup walnuts or pine nuts
¼ cup currants

1 teaspoon salt
1 teaspoon black pepper
1 tablespoon cumin
1 teaspoon allspice
¾ pound tahina
Lemon juice
Olive oil
Cinnamon

One day before preparation, wash and soak the chick-peas in lukewarm water to cover for 24 hours. Then, drain and peel each pea. The next day cook them until tender enough to eat but not too soft. Put them through a food grinder or blender and set aside.

Boil the halved and peeled potatoes until tender, mash until smooth. Blend the chick-peas and mashed potatoes together with salt and pepper, mixing well with wet hands. (Moisten your hands to prevent sticking.) Cut the onions in round thin slices and cook until tender. Place them in a strainer for about 1½ hours, stirring occasionally, until all the liquid has run out. Blend together the onions, nuts, currants, salt and pepper, cumin, allspice and finally the tahina. Set this filling aside.

Take 8 to 10 white clean muslin squares the size of a large handkerchief, or about 12 inches square. Soak these in cold water and wring them dry. Place one cloth on the table. Take a handful of the chick-pea–potato mixture, shape it into a circle about the size of a small orange and put it in the center of the cloth. Pat it down with hands to ½ inch thickness, leaving a border of cloth about 1 inch wide. Put 2 heaping tablespoons of the filling in the center of the crust. Bring the four corners of the muslin together, tying two diagonal corners together and then the other two corners to make a small loose ball fastened at the top.

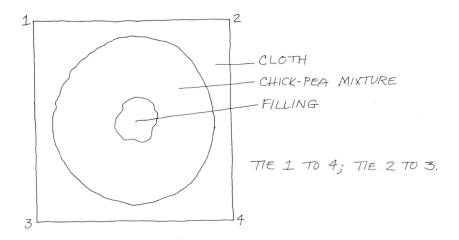

1

2

CLOTH

CHICK-PEA MIXTURE

FILLING

TIE 1 TO 4; TIE 2 TO 3.

3

4

Meanwhile, bring to a boil a large kettleful of water with 1 table-spoon of salt added. Drop the Topiks into the water and cook them about 20 minutes. Do not put more than four bundles in at a time and do not untie them until you want to serve the Topiks.

Once the Topiks are cooled, wrap each in aluminum foil so the filling will not drop out. Let sit for 24 hours. At serving time, untie the cloth bundles, one for each person, cut an X across the top, open the edges slightly and pour a small amount of lemon juice and olive oil over. Sprinkle with cinnamon. *Makes 8–10 Topiks.*

LAHMAJOUN (ARMENIAN PIZZA)

4 small loaves Pita bread, halved
   (see page 36)
½ pound ground veal, beef or
   lamb (ground twice)
½ large onion, chopped fine
3 tablespoons finely chopped

   parsley
½ green pepper, chopped
1 clove garlic, minced
Salt and pepper to taste
½ can tomato sauce
¼ can whole tomatoes, mashed

Preheat oven to 450°.

Slice the Pita in half to form two circles. Mix the other ingredients in the order given and spread them thinly on the rough side of Pita halves. Bake meat side up on a greased cookie sheet for 15 to 20 minutes.

Cut the Lahmajoun into small wedges and serve as an hors d'oeuvre or serve whole as a main dish with Cucumber Salad (see page 47). The Lahmajoun can be frozen and reheated. *Makes 8.*

Soups

The Ultimate Jewish Mother — Golda Can Cook Too

When Golda Meir was the Prime Minister of Israel, she employed no live-in servants and had no one at all working for her on Shabbat in her Jerusalem residence. Golda frequently prepared snacks herself for guests and often prepared her own evening meal. She is a good cook and considers working in the kitchen a form of relaxation. Now living in a kibbutz, the former Prime Minister has returned to these simple ways.

Golda's kitchen staff did not boast a complicated roster of servants including pastrycooks, specialty chefs and underlings to stir the soup, as do the homes of many world leaders. Housekeeping at her home was kept simple, supervised by Leah Zahiv, who with the help of only one other person managed the official residence and did the cooking as well.

Just as in every home, an occasional mishap may occur at the home of the Prime Minister. One Saturday afternoon, for instance, several friends dropped in to visit and Golda prepared coffee and a plate of cookies. Enjoying the conversation and the company, she did not notice until the guests had departed that the coffee cups were still full: no one had touched a drop. A short time later, Moshe Dayan dropped in and Golda again made coffee, using the same tray of sugar and milk. This time there was no leftover coffee because he immediately complained that there was something terribly wrong with the drink. Someone had inadvertently filled the sugar bowl with salt!

Lou Kadar, Golda's personal assistant, was with her for the better part of the last twenty-five years. She accompanied the former Prime Minister on most of her trips abroad and they have eaten together all

Israel's former Prime Minister finds her kitchen a relaxing place

over the world. "Golda is very game when it comes to foreign foods," says Lou. "And that word reminds me of an official dinner in Africa. The hosts were especially anxious to please Golda and we were served a local delicacy of mountain goat and bananas cooked in their skins. Golda did not disappoint her hosts; she ate every bit."

At home, however, preferences are decidedly less exotic. Golda likes simple Jewish cooking and her only requirement is that it be homemade. Breakfast is most often a cup of coffee, but when time allows, Golda likes a plain roll or toast and sometimes an egg. Although the former Prime Minister could have eaten at any of the capital city's leading restaurants, she preferred to go home, where more often than not she was joined by members of the Knesset and other government leaders. They would sit down to a meal of chopped liver, grilled fish, eggplant, rice with mushrooms, salad and applesauce or stewed fruit for dessert — real "Jewish soul food." Golda did not tell her cook what she wanted to eat each day, as one might expect. She ate what her cook prepared, and Leah must have done something right, because she told us that Golda never complained. Leah is not a professionally trained cook. "Most of what I learned must have simply rubbed off on me. I never took much notice of what was going on in my mother's kitchen, but I cook old-fashioned Jewish food and that is what Golda likes: food with a touch of nostalgia to remind her of her home and parents."

Israel's Chief Grandmother relies on no one to select goodies for her children and grandchildren, who now live with her on Kibbutz Revivim. Like grandchildren everywhere, her two love their grandmother's cooking and she loves to cook for them. Their special treat comes when the former Prime Minister makes them her famous chicken soup with matzah balls or her Middle Eastern specialty, fried eggplant, which can be found under Vegetables on Page 170.

CHICKEN SOUP WITH MATZAH BALLS

1 three-pound chicken (whole or in pieces, with feet)
6 cups water
2 medium-size onions, peeled and sliced
2 stalks celery, chopped

4 carrots, scraped and chopped into half-inch pieces
Pinch paprika
Salt and pepper to taste
3 sprigs parsley, coarsely chopped

Clean the chicken. Immerse the feet in boiling water for a few seconds, then remove the outer skin. Place the chicken in a large pot, add the water and onions. Bring the water to a boil, reduce the heat, skim, then cover and simmer the chicken gently for one hour. Add the other ingredients. Simmer, covered, for another 45 minutes or until the chicken is tender. Strain it, skim off the fat and season to taste.

Use the chicken for salad or serve it on the side, cut up, with soup. One cup of cooked rice may be added if desired, after straining the soup. Mrs. Meir often serves the soup with Kneidlach (matzah balls). *Serves 6.*

Kneidlach

¾ cup matzah flour
2 eggs, slightly beaten
½ teaspoon salt
Pepper to taste

2 sprigs parsley, finely chopped
1 small onion, chopped and fried until crisp in 2 tablespoons oil
1 tablespoon cold water

Mix the ingredients in the order listed. Form the mixture into small balls and drop into the boiling soup; cook over medium heat, uncovered, about 20 minutes. *Makes 20 matzah balls.*

Russian Orthodox Nuns' Unbeatable Borscht

The portraits of the Russian patriarchs looking sternly down upon us lent an air of disapproval to the somber room, but we more than approved of the authentic caviar and vodka which were offered to us when we visited the Russian Orthodox Mission. In the kitchen behind the huge refectory, where nuns were preparing Borscht, we were reminded of the many thousands of Christian pilgrims who had eaten here during their pilgrimages to the Holy Land. Up until 1917 the government of Russia supplied the poor Christian peasant pilgrim to Jerusalem with beds and food in a fine hostel inside the Russian compound, now located next to the Municipality. This meant a big commitment by the Russian government, since up to fifteen thousand poor peasants came yearly to the Holy Land.

In 1860 the Russian government, wanting to establish a presence in the Holy Land for Russian Orthodox pilgrims, acquired property in Jerusalem from the ruling Turkish authorities and began building several churches (foreign governments could construct only religious buildings in Jerusalem). Today two of these buildings are still fine landmarks on the city's skyline — the five-domed Church of the Holy Trinity, with the Chapel of the Ascension, its roofs pale green with age, in the Russian compound, and the beautiful onion-domed Church of Mary Magdalene on the Mount of Olives. Besides the churches, hostels, convents and even a hospital catered to the Russian pilgrims who flocked to the Holy Land before the Revolution. After 1917, when the Orthodox Church lost its official status, most of the property fell into disrepair and few, if any, pilgrims came to visit the Holy Land, since religion was discouraged under the Communist regime. With the creation of the State of Israel in 1948 — interestingly enough, Israel was first recognized in the United Nations by the USSR — politics became entwined with religion, and the official Russian Orthodox Church within Russia maintained the property in Jewish Jerusalem, while the Russian Ecclesiastic Society, headquartered in New York City and still loyal to Czarist Russia, took over the structures in the Jordanian sector.

Today many of the Russian Orthodox priests and nuns in Jerusalem are able to converse with new Jewish immigrants from the Soviet Union in a unique form of ex-countryman socialization. The nun who gave us her Borscht recipe told us about an immigrant from Russia who had come to the mission with a sack of rubles, requesting an exchange in Israeli pounds. Although he did not obtain his money, he did receive hospitality from his native country — in the form of conversation in his native tongue and a delicious sampling of a native dish as well.

BORSCHT (BEET SOUP)

1 large onion, chopped coarsely
1 clove garlic
Oil for cooking
2 pounds beets
¼ cup wine vinegar
1 cup tomato juice

2 teaspoons salt
1 teaspoon sugar
Juice of 1 lemon
½ cup fresh dill
Sour cream

Sauté the onion and garlic in oil until golden. Meanwhile, peel and slice the beets and then place them in a saucepan with the onion and garlic. Cover them with water and simmer gently, covered, for about forty minutes until the beets are tender. Then place the mixture in a blender and purée. Add the wine vinegar, tomato juice, salt, and sugar and simmer a few minutes more. Flavor to taste with lemon juice.

If serving cold, chill Borscht until icy cold. Add the dill just before serving and place a generous scoop of sour cream on top of each portion. If serving it hot, heat it just to the boiling point and proceed as above with sour cream and dill.

If you are serving Borscht with Pirogen (see Page 67) put a dish of sour cream on the table for both dishes. *Serves 4–6.*

WINTER BORSCHT (MEAT-VEGETABLE SOUP)

6 cups water
2 pieces marrow bone
2 pounds lean bottom round,
   blade or chuck steak
2 pounds beets
½ small white cabbage
2 carrots
1 large onion
3 stalks celery

1 green pepper
1 red pepper
1 potato
2 or 3 garlic cloves, minced
Salt and pepper to taste
1 teaspoon sugar
Juice of 1 lemon
Oregano to taste

In a large kettle bring water to the boil. Add the meat and marrow bones and cook over medium heat until froth forms on the surface; skim off.

While the meat is cooking, clean and peel the vegetables; grate all of them on the large holes of the grater. After the froth has been removed add the grated vegetables to the meat and season with garlic, salt, pepper, sugar, lemon juice and oregano (a sweet and sour taste is desired). Cover and cook over low heat for 2 hours. After cooking, check again for seasoning, and add as needed. *Serves 4–6.*

A Yemenite's Recipe for a Long and Good Life

According to some theories the "real" Jews of the Diaspora lived in Yemen, a country in southwest Arabia bordering on the Red Sea. These Yemenite Jews spoke Arabic with their Moslem neighbors but Hebrew among themselves and always yearned to return to the Holy Land. Since they have rarely married outside their group, their chiseled dark features are considered by some to be the purest Jewish features. Yemenite families began immigrating to the Holy Land as long ago as the sixteenth century. With the birth of the State of Israel in 1948, the Zadok family and thousands of their fellow countrymen finally realized their age-old dream: they were carried to Israel by a "great bird," which landed in the midst of a field near Aden, a large port on the Red Sea, and swept them, as if by magic, to what is now the David Ben-Gurion Airport. This feat was appropriately dubbed "Operation Magic Carpet."

To learn more about the Yemenites, we visited in Jerusalem with members of the Zadok family — a name that has become synonymous with Yemenite leadership and fine jewelry and silverwork. In their immaculately clean home — every Yemenite home is spotless — we met Yosef Zadok, the patriarch of the family and rabbi of the local community. Young craftsmen were deeply engrossed in designing silver in one room and Yosef was guiding them with a steadiness of hand remarkable for a seventy-seven-year-old man. To our question about the secret of his obvious contentment and healthful countenance he responded, *"Baruch Hashem* — Blessed be His Name. Everything is fine. The air is better in Jerusalem than anywhere else. What more do I need?" We later learned that ever since Yosef Zadok arrived in Jerusalem in 1948, he has never once left the city.

As it was only 8:30 in the morning when we arrived, we asked if it was too early to talk to him. "No, I have been up since 4:30, when I went to pray at my synagogue. After that I walked to Mahane Yehuda to buy my wife's groceries. I came home to study the Talmud, drank *zhum* and now I'll work until 12:30, when I'll eat a little bread and a small piece of meat" — Yemenites eat most parts of an animal, including genitals, tail, leg, belly and udder. "Sometimes I take a nap for a quarter or

*"Praise be to God, the air is better in Jerusalem than anywhere else
in the world. What more do I need?" says Yosef Zadok*

half hour — not more — then back to work until 5:30, when I go to
synagogue for two more hours of prayer. The rest of the evening I spend
studying."

When we asked about the delicious aromas coming from the kitchen,
Yosef replied that his wife, Yona, was cooking, not so much for him as
for the craftsmen. "My secret is to work hard, keep clean, and eat just
enough. *Baruch Hashem*, my sons are following me in the same tradition." In fact, we later discovered that not only do his two sons Avram
and Haim make jewelry, but also his grandson is beginning to learn,
and next year, after his bar mitzvah, is looking forward to praying each
morning and evening with his father, uncle and grandfather.

YEMENITE SOUP — A MEAL IN ONE

½ pound beef shoulder or ribs
(remove fat)
3 pieces of marrow bone
6 to 10 garlic buds (according to
taste) unpeeled

1 large onion, peeled, whole
1 carrot whole
1 large tomato, almost quartered
but not cut apart at bottom
4 sprigs parsley

4 sprigs dill
2 chicken legs, including thighs
1 zucchini
2 potatoes, peeled
4 celery stalks
½ teaspoon salt

1 teaspoon curry powder
¼ teaspoon black pepper
¼ teaspoon ground cumin
1 cup cooked noodles or rice
(optional)

In a soup kettle, place the beef and marrow bone pieces with 1½ quarts water. Bring them to a boil and skim the froth from the surface, removing every bit. Lower the heat and add the garlic buds (by being left unpeeled, they do not get soft in cooking). Add the onion, carrot, tomato, parsley and dill. Cover the pot and cook, simmering, for 20 minutes. Remove the marrow bones. Add the chicken legs, cover and simmer another 20 minutes. Add the zucchini, potatoes and celery, cover and simmer another 20 minutes. Add the salt and additional spices and cook for final 10 minutes. Remove the garlic buds.

When serving, place a portion of rice or noodles in a large soup plate. Pour in some soup liquid and add meat and vegetable portions. *Serves 4.*

The Judge Enjoys "Trying" Good Soup

". . . And never the twain shall meet." But East meets West and the two blend beautifully in the Jarrallah home on Nablus Road in east Jerusalem. A child's baseball bat has been casually left on an ornate Damascus-style chair; a four-foot-high brass coffeepot outshines the modern lamp nearby, and there are a television set, an Oriental rug, paintings by the Judge's father, the son's framed diploma from an American university and a copper pot in which meals for fifty people were once prepared. The Jarallah guests are just as varied: an American marine, an Israeli lawyer, and a U.N. official were enjoying the hospitality the day we visited.

Since there is no priesthood in the religion of Islam, nor lawyers — in the sense that Islam recognizes no legislative function other than the law of God — there developed a class of professional men of religion who fulfill the tasks of both lawyer and priest. Judge Nihad Ali Jarallah, descendant of one of the oldest Moslem families, going back to the time of Saladin, has maintained the family tradition of serving justice in the city. His late uncle, the Mufti of Jerusalem, had the authority for judgment in court cases. Consequently, the name Jarallah has become synonymous with jurisprudence and is respected throughout Jerusalem. Judge Jarallah's father studied law in the Ottoman Empire in Constantinople and trained his son in the traditions embodied in this legal system. The judge studied and practiced under the British until 1948, then under the Jordanians until 1967; today, under the government of Israel, he is a judge at the court of appeals in the nearby town of Ramallah.

Tradition is of great importance to the Jarallahs. Members of the family have occupied the same house on the Via Dolorosa near St. Stephen's Gate in the Old City for 800 years. It is still owned by Judge Jarallah's cousin Salah. When the judge's grandfather built the house where they now live, "Everyone thought he was crazy to build so far away from the Old City . . . there were hyenas and thieves here . . . and the house was surrounded by a forest of olive trees," said the judge with a smile.

Born in Bethlehem, the judge's wife, Hilda, belongs to one of the oldest Christian communities in Jerusalem — the Assyrian Orthodox (Nestorian). Their liturgical language is ancient Syriac, the Aramaic spoken by the Jews at the time of Jesus.

The Jarallah household is open to all. Besides knowing practically every family in east Jerusalem, the judge is sought after by Jews, Christians and Arabs alike for professional advice. Hilda offers each visitor, old friend or new acquaintance her unique combination of Assyrian Orthodox and Moslem Arab cookery. When we asked Hilda how she manages with so many guests of so many different backgrounds, she explained that this is exactly what appeals to her. One of the judge's favorites is Lentil Soup, which Hilda insists has enough protein to nourish her vegetarian son.

SHORABAT ADAS (LENTIL SOUP)

¼ cup olive oil	1 tablespoon parsley
1 large onion, chopped	1 teaspoon cumin
2 cloves garlic, minced	¼ teaspoon thyme
1 stalk celery, chopped	¼ teaspoon pepper
1 carrot, chopped	Pinch saffron
1 pound lentils	1 teaspoon salt
2½ quarts chicken broth	Juice of 1 lemon
1 bay leaf	

In a large saucepan, heat the oil and sauté the onion and garlic until just tender. Add the celery and carrot, stir to coat with oil, cover and cook for 5 minutes. Add the lentils, broth, bay leaf, parsley, cumin, thyme, pepper and saffron. Cover and cook over low heat about 1 hour, until the lentils are tender. Add the salt and lemon juice. If a smoother consistency is desired, whirl in blender and then reheat. *Serves 8.*

MASTE KHEYAR (COLD CUCUMBER–YOGHURT SOUP)

4 small cucumbers
1 teaspoon salt
2 garlic buds, minced (to taste)
1 tablespoon chopped fresh dill
   (or to taste)

Juice of ½ lemon
4 cups plain yoghurt
1 tablespoon chopped fresh mint
   leaves
1 tomato, peeled and chopped

Peel the cucumbers if the skin is waxy. Otherwise draw tines of a fork lengthwise all around so that slices will be scalloped. Slice the cucumbers thin and sprinkle them with salt. Mix them together with the other ingredients, reserving the chopped mint and several cucumber slices for garnish. Place the mixture in a blender and whirl for 30 seconds; the mixture should not be too smooth. Chill well and serve with mint, tomatoes and cucumber slice garnish. *Serves 4–6.*

Main Dishes—
Meat, Poultry
and Fish

Jerusalem's Queen of the Fishes

Until only recently, one of Jerusalem's major problems was lack of water. Since the time of King David water had been dragged, or piped or (more recently) trucked to the residents from faraway fresh-water sources. The only nearby water is the Dead Sea, in which no living organism is able to survive, since it is so heavily laden with potash. And so, fresh fish has always been a delicacy. Sarah Rosenzweig is an example of someone who did something about the availability of fresh fish for the population of Jerusalem.

During the first years of her marriage, in the early thirties, Sarah decided to open Jerusalem's first fresh fish shop; she began with a stall in the Jewish open-air market of Mahane Yehuda. Every morning at five A.M. she took a bus to the Mediterranean port city of Jaffa near Tel Aviv, where she bargained with the fishermen in Arabic or Hebrew, stuffed her purchases into her wicker basket lined with grape leaves, and returned to Jerusalem in time for the eight A.M. opening. If the fish in Jaffa were not first-rate she traveled in the evening as far north as Acre (Acco) and returned to Jerusalem in the early morning of the next day. Sarah's business thrived as customers' tastes for fish grew, and soon she decided to buy a share in a fishing boat, thus ensuring herself of a good corner on the market at all times.

Next, this enterprising businesswoman decided to open a fish restaurant, since there was none in Jerusalem. By that time she was the mother of four children and thought it would be a good investment for their future. Then, after the Six-Day War, Sarah's son Shraga told her about an Arab restaurant which needed some capital to continue operating. Thus the first successful Arab-Jewish–owned eating place in the city opened. Meanwhile, Sarah's other son, Beni, opened West Jerusalem's only fish restaurant which caters to kosher-style eating — that is, it

"Fresh trout from Lake Tiberias!" calls Beni Rosenzweig
at the family fish stall in Mahane Yehuda

does not serve any shelled seafood but only fish with scales and fins. Success breeds confidence; Sarah recently told us of visiting Europe to see if there were any fish restaurants there as good as hers.

SOLE WITH CHEESE AND MUSHROOMS IN WINE SAUCE

Sole
2 pounds sole fillets, cut into
    serving-size slices
1 teaspoon salt
1 tablespoon lemon juice

Wine Sauce with Cheese and
  Mushrooms
1 cup sliced mushrooms
2 tablespoons butter

2 tablespoons flour
¼ teaspoon salt
¾ cup milk
½ cup light cream
4 tablespoons grated Cheddar or
    Parmesan cheese
¼ cup white wine
2 tablespoons chopped fresh
    parsley

Sole: In a large skillet with a cover, heat to boiling 2 inches of water with the salt and lemon juice. Place the fillets in the water, overlapping slightly, but do not layer. Cover, reduce heat and simmer for about 5 minutes until the fish flakes with a fork. Drain the slices and keep them warm while preparing the sauce.

Sauce: In a small pan, sauté the sliced mushrooms in 1 tablespoon butter until brown. Drain on a paper towel and set aside. In a medium-size saucepan, melt the remaining 2 tablespoons butter and quickly stir in the flour and salt. Stir until smooth. Immediately add the milk and cream; cook over medium heat, stirring constantly, until the mixture comes to a boil. Stir in the cheese until blended; then lower the heat. Mix in the mushrooms and wine and cook several minutes longer to blend.

Place the fillets on a serving platter and pour the sauce over. Sprinkle with parsley. *Serves 4–6.*

SOLE WITH ORANGE SAUCE

Sole
2 pounds of sole or 6 sole fillets, cut into serving-size slices
2 eggs
1 tablespoon water
¾ cup flour
1 teaspoon salt
⅛ teaspoon white pepper
¼ teaspoon ground ginger
Cooking oil
1 tablespoon butter

Orange Sauce
Grated rind of 1 orange and 1 lemon
1 cup orange juice (strained fresh or reconstituted frozen)
2 tablespoons brown sugar
1 tablespoon butter
4 tablespoons fresh lemon juice
2 tablespoons cornstarch
⅛ teaspoon salt
¼ cup Cointreau (optional)
½ cup chopped dates or ¼ cup light raisins

Sole: In a large bowl, beat the eggs with the water. In another bowl, mix the flour, salt, pepper and ginger well. Dip each fish slice in the egg mixture, then in the flour mixture, coating well. In a large frying pan, heat the oil and butter to about ¼ inch depth. Fry the fish slices until brown, carefully turning them over to brown the other side. Cooking time altogether takes about 8 minutes. Spoon off any remaining oil and keep the fish warm while preparing sauce.

Sauce: In a medium-size saucepan, mix the orange and lemon rinds, orange juice, sugar, and butter. Bring to a boil and reduce to low heat. Blend the cornstarch with the lemon juice until smooth and stir this into the orange mixture. Raise the flame to medium and cook, stirring constantly, until the mixture thickens — about 3 minutes.

Preheat the oven to 450°.

Let the sauce cool slightly and add Cointreau, if desired. (If a skin forms, stir briskly until the sauce is smooth again.) Place the warm fish slices on an oven-proof serving platter. Pour the sauce over and sprinkle with dates or raisins. Bake, uncovered, for 8 minutes. *Serves 4–6.*

TROUT WITH ALMONDS AND APPLES

6 whole cleaned trout
Flour
¼ cup cooking oil
1 tablespoon butter
Salt and pepper to taste
1 cup blanched almonds

½ cup melted butter or margarine
2 peeled and coarsely chopped
   apples
½ cup thinly sliced mushrooms
½ tablespoon lemon juice
¼ cup chopped fresh parsley

Preheat oven to 400°.
Wash the trout and pat dry. Coat them lightly with flour and fry in the oil/butter combination until crisp. Season them with salt and pepper. Set them aside on an oven-proof platter.
Sauté the almonds in butter or margarine until golden. Mix them with the apples, mushrooms, and lemon juice and pour over the fish. Bake for 10 minutes and garnish with chopped parsley to serve. *Serves 6.*

Alexander of the Greek Colony

"I am the cook in the family," announced seventy-one-year-old Alexander Efklides as we arrived for our lesson on Greek cooking.

Alexander, who lives with his two elderly sisters, loves Greek food and learned to cook it himself because Cleo and Helen were always dieting. "A man could starve around here," he asserted. Now he insists he's the only one in the family who is qualified to prepare the meals.

Born in the Old City, the three children moved with their father in 1905 to a house he had purchased outside the Damascus Gate. It seems that Poppa Efklides had a great deal of foresight, judging from where he chose to buy property and build in that year. Although his holdings were to continue through the rule of several regimes, the rental revenue provided a comfortable income for his three children. It's a good thing too, because Alexander does not like to work and Cleo firmly avows how "lazy" they all are. (In spite of their aversion to routine employment, Alexander worked as an interpreter and teacher for twenty years, and Cleo herself stitched dresses by hand for the city's leading couturier for nearly as long.)

In 1924, the Greek community held a lottery for land near the German Colony not far from the center of Jerusalem. The property was won by the sisters and brother Efklides, and they built their lovely home, where they have lived to this day. Alexander sat in the corner reading his book on the life of David Ben-Gurion, while above him, facing each other kitty-corner, hung two paintings: one of an Arab boy and the other of a Jewish boy.

"You see? We want them to be friends," said Cleo.

Although Greek Orthodox, they all became completely nonreligious in 1916 when their father died during the worldwide flu epidemic. "God was not able to help us then," said Cleo. "However, we were very lucky during the Six-Day War. A Jordanian shell landed on our rooftop and exploded in the boiler. If it hadn't hit that blessed boiler, we would have been dead. The next day a friend of ours, a Greek priest, came to visit. 'How God loves you,' he said when he heard the story and saw the damage. 'It's because we never bother Him,' I told him."

"We have many fond memories of our life here in Jerusalem," reflected Alexander. "One of our favorites occurred just after the Six-Day War. A municipal official knocked on the door with a stack of papers in his hand, saying that his records showed there were two small holes in one of our windows; he had come to arrange repairs." Alexander then proceeded to point out the holes to us. He had purposely not had them repaired; he wanted to keep them as a memento.

When we began to talk about cooking, we could feel Alexander was in his element, and we began to drool as he described his special fish with garlic — a dish to be eaten *only* in the evening because no one could tolerate you if you ate it during the day!

FRIED FISH WITH SKORTHALIA (GARLIC AND POTATO PURÉE)

Fish
1 pound small whole fish or fish
   fillets
2 eggs
2 tablespoons water
1 tablespoon flour
Salt and pepper to taste
Olive oil

Skorthalia
10 garlic cloves
Salt to taste

½ cup plus 1 tablespoon ground
   blanched almonds
½ cup water
3 medium potatoes, boiled, peeled,
   quartered and cooled
Juice of 1½ lemons
½ cup olive oil
1 egg yolk
Freshly ground black pepper to
   taste

Fish: Rinse the fish with cold water and pat dry. Beat the eggs, water and flour to make a dripping batter. Coat the fish pieces thoroughly and fry in hot olive oil until golden brown and cooked through. *Fish serves 2–3.*

Skorthalia: Into a wooden bowl, press juice from the garlic cloves with a garlic press. Add the remainder of cloves from inside the press. Pound with a pestle, adding a few sprinkles of salt. When a creamlike consistency is reached, add the almonds and pound. If this mixture gets too thick, add water. Mash the potato quarters, a few at a time, add the garlic and mix until smooth. Add the garlic and almond mixture to the potatoes. Using a mixer or blender, alternate thin streams of olive oil and lemon juice with the potato-garlic mixture until a purée is formed. Beat an egg yolk slightly and blend well into the purée. Add pepper.

Skorthalia is delicious with salads and on slices of eggplant fried in olive oil and drained.

Can be kept up to one month, sealed tightly, in refrigerator. *Skorthalia makes 2½ cups.*

YAKNE (CHILLED FISH)

Yakne tastes best cold, but may also be served hot.

1 pound fish fillets, fresh or frozen, sliced	6 sprigs fresh parsley, cut coarsely
Olive oil	4 medium tomatoes, peeled, cut in large pieces
6 medium onions, sliced thin	1 teaspoon salt
6 celery stalks with leaves, sliced thin	Freshly ground pepper to taste
	2 tablespoons water

If frozen fillets are used, thaw them slightly. Heat the olive oil in a heavy saucepan and sauté the onion slices until browned but not crisp. Add the celery, parsley and tomatoes to the onions, sprinkle with salt and pepper and stir to mix the ingredients. Stir in the water. Cover and simmer over a low heat for 20 to 30 minutes until all ingredients are tender. Place the fish slices on top, sprinkle them lightly with additional salt and cover. Simmer until most of the liquid is absorbed and the fish flakes with a fork, about 15 minutes. Cool slightly, place in the refrigerator and serve cold. *Serves 3–4.*

MOUSSAKA (EGGPLANT AND LAMB CASSEROLE)

2 medium eggplants (about 2
  pounds total)
Cooking oil
1 large onion, chopped
1 pound chopped lamb or beef
¼ cup fresh parsley, minced
½ cup red wine
2 tablespoons tomato paste
1 teaspoon cinnamon

Salt and pepper to taste
3 tablespoons butter
3 tablespoons flour
2 cups milk
2 eggs, lightly beaten
1 cup cottage or ricotta cheese
1 cup Parmesan cheese
1 cup breadcrumbs

Peel and slice the eggplant. In a large frying pan, sauté the slices in oil and set them aside. Then cook the onion in the frying pan until tender. Add the chopped beef and cook until brown. Add the parsley, wine, tomato paste, cinnamon, salt and pepper. Cover and cook over a low heat until the liquid is absorbed (about one half hour).

In a saucepan, melt the butter and then add the flour, stirring until all the flour is absorbed. Remove from the heat and let it cool slightly. Then gradually add the milk, stirring constantly. Return it to low heat and stir until the sauce thickens. Remove it from the heat and stir in the eggs, cottage cheese and ½ cup of the Parmesan cheese.

Preheat oven to 375°.

Place the following in a large casserole: ½ cup of the breadcrumbs, half of the eggplant slices, all the meat, ¼ cup of the Parmesan cheese, ½ cup of the breadcrumbs, the rest of the eggplant slices, all the sauce and then the remaining ¼ cup of Parmesan cheese.

Bake uncovered for 50 to 60 minutes until top is golden. *Serves 4–6.*

PASTITSIO (BAKED MACARONI AND MEAT)

3 tablespoons olive oil
1 cup chopped onion
1 pound ground lamb or beef
  (more meat if desired)
¾ cup chopped peeled tomato
1½ teaspoons salt
Freshly ground black pepper
¼ teaspoon oregano
½ cup grated Gruyère cheese
1 pound macaroni, cooked and

drained

Sauce
2 tablespoons margarine or butter
1 tablespoon flour
½ teaspoon salt
⅛ teaspoon white pepper
1 cup milk
1 egg yolk
¼ cup grated Parmesan cheese

In a skillet heat the oil; cook the onion and meat over high heat, stirring constantly for 5 minutes. Stir in the tomatoes, salt, pepper and oregano. Cook over low heat 5 minutes. Stir in the cheese and check for seasoning. In a buttered 2-quart casserole, spread half the macaroni. Cover with the meat mixture and then add the rest of the macaroni.

Preheat oven to 350°.

Sauce: Melt the margarine or butter in a saucepan; gradually blend in the flour, salt and pepper. Add the milk gradually, stirring constantly, until the mixture comes to a boil. Cook it over low heat 5 minutes. Beat the egg yolk and cheese in a bowl; add the hot mixture slowly, stirring constantly. Pour over the macaroni. Bake it for 30 minutes until light brown on top. *Serves 4–6.*

An Artist "Designs" Dinner

Most of the early Zionists who built the State of Israel were so intellectually and idealistically socialistic that they felt food was used only to keep body and soul together; one ate to live. And for many of them, not only food but also the need to express oneself in art seemed quite unnecessary.

However, Boris Schatz, a twentieth-century Zionist, felt that all the arts should be important in the new land. Schatz ran away from his native Vilna, Russia, as a young man and studied art in Paris before coming to Jerusalem. Rural Jerusalem did not offer much in the way of either art or cookery, nor was there ever any gourmet food later in his Jerusalem home, as his wife, a Russian art historian, was imbued more with the ideas of spiritual Zionism than with haute cuisine.

Besides having tasted the delicious food of France, Boris had also seen the paintings of the French masters, and he dreamed of a revival of Jewish art and of an art center in Jerusalem on one of the many hilltops. Today the Israel Museum atop the Biblical hill Neve Shaanan (serene dwelling place) is that center and in it is a wing which includes a large collection of Judaica, as well as works by the masters and Israeli painters. In memory of Boris Schatz the wing is called "Bezalel," and justly so, as in the Bible Bezalel, the son of Ur, built the Tabernacles for the Temple and was thus embodied with art talents by God. The name Bezalel has again become synonymous with beauty, for the Bezalel School, which Boris Schatz founded in 1906, is the most important art school in Israel.

Boris's son, Bezalel, as he is not surprisingly named, is one of Israel's leading artists. His wife, Louise, originally an American, is considered one of Israel's finest painters. Not only have the young Schatzes realized Boris's dreams about painting and art, they have also added their own about food. Bezalel was recently president of the Jerusalem branch of the International Society of the Chaîne des Rôtisseurs. Louise also has combined her love of both cooking and art, and she gave us recipes for Sukiyaki and Shrimp Curry accompanied by an original drawing.

SUKIYAKI FOR SEVEN

1 pound lean beef
6 onions
4 celery stalks
½ cup fresh green peas
1 cup bean sprouts
10 lettuce leaves
6 spinach leaves
2 green peppers
1 kohlrabi
½ cup soy sauce
½ cup dry white wine or dry sherry
1 cup beef stock

Salt to taste
1 teaspoon cornstarch
1 tablespoon sugar
2 eggs
1 cup blanched almonds, halved
1 cup sliced mushrooms, fresh or dried, or both
1 cup water chestnuts
1 bunch green onions
1 cup peanut oil
3 pieces pork fat (or substitute), for rendering

Three hours before serving: slice the beef in paper-thin slices. Peel and slice the onions into thin wedges. Arrange them attractively on a serving tray and refrigerate. Slice thin or chop all the vegetables except the mushrooms, water chestnuts, and green onions and place each ingredient in a separate mound on another serving dish, then refrigerate them,

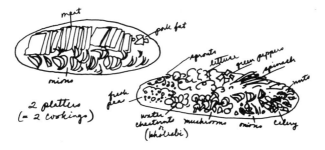

covered with plastic wrap. Mix the soy sauce with the wine, beef stock, salt, cornstarch and sugar. Twenty minutes before serving, break the eggs into a glass and beat slightly. Halve the almonds and slice the mushrooms, water chestnuts and green onions and add to the refrigerated dish. When diners are assembled (it will be about 10 minutes before dish is ready) place the two serving dishes on the table. Pour peanut oil into a wok, heat and cook the pork fat until melted. Discard bits left over and start stir-frying the ingredients as follows: Stir-fry the onions, push them aside, add half the meat, stir-fry, push it aside. Proceed the same way with the peppers, celery, mushrooms, more onions, and peas. Add the bean sprouts, chestnuts and green onions. Pour on half of the soy sauce mixture, add the lettuce and spinach and kohlrabi, stir-fry until limp and add the rest of the soy sauce mixture. Stir in the beaten egg, and serve with steamed rice.

If preparing Sukiyaki at the table, do it in two servings. Do not over-cook. Five minutes is sufficient to keep vegetables crisp. *Serves 7* (a good number for Sukiyaki, according to artist Schatz).

SHRIMP CURRY

2 pounds shrimp, peeled and deveined	1 to 4 teaspoons curry powder
4 onions	Salt and pepper to taste
¼ cup margarine	½ cup dry vermouth or 1 cup dry white wine
⅛ cup flour	½ cup grated Emmenthal or Parmesan cheese
6 tomatoes	
2 cups chicken stock	2 cups rice or buttered toast
4 to 10 drops Tabasco sauce	

Preheat oven to 400°.

Steam the shrimps in a small amount of water in a tightly covered saucepan for 5 minutes until firm. Rinse with cold water, peel and de-vein them. Peel the onions and cut them into quarters. Sauté them in margarine, sprinkling lightly with flour. Peel the tomatoes and chop coarsely. Add them to the onions, cover and simmer for 5 minutes. Add the chicken stock, bring to the boil, lower the heat to moderate, stir and cook to reduce the sauce slightly (the mixture should bubble while cook-ing). Add the Tabasco sauce, curry powder, salt and pepper. Lower the heat and add the shrimps. Pour on the vermouth or wine and sprinkle with grated cheese. Place in the oven to brown. Serve with steamed rice or on buttered toast, with a green salad.

If you wish to prepare the dish ahead, prepare up to where the shrimps have been added. Then, just before serving — because the wine does not improve on standing — add the vermouth or wine and proceed. Can be served with a combination of sour and heavy cream on top. *Serves 4–6.*

British Pilgrims Packed a Kosher Picnic

In 1897 a group of English Jews packed kosher picnic baskets ordered from Lyons' Tea Room in London and journeyed to Paris on the first leg of their Passover pilgrimage to "Eretz Yisrael," the land of Israel. Led by Herbert Bentwich, the "Pilgrim Father," this group of British Zionists was one of the first to arrive in the Holy Land. Thus even before 1917, when on behalf of the British Government Lord Balfour formally recognized the right of the Jews to resettle their national homeland, British Jewry began to strengthen its physical and spiritual bond with Jerusalem.

After independence was declared in 1948, a great wave of British Jews immigrated to the new State of Israel. Among them was Gladys Sabel. Having learned to cook economical and nutritious meals when food was rationed in London during World War II, Gladys was well prepared to overcome austerity in Jerusalem. Her talent for organization and her cooking finesse were soon recognized, and before long she was instructing new immigrants from Yemen and other Arab countries on the many and various uses of dried eggs — a product familiar to her but totally foreign to most of the other new immigrants. In no time her "pupils" were cooking many new dishes with this new staple. Several years later Gladys became the first Israeli representative at an international cooking competition in London. She remembers how the English ladies were shocked to see no gefüllte fish or bagels and lox in her entry. "This can't be Jewish!" they exclaimed.

Today Gladys, whose husband, Harry, announces the seven A.M. English news on the Voice of Israel Radio, is a loving grandmother who keeps her cookie jars filled with goodies for her grandchildren, who are constantly in and out of her home. She enjoys relaxing in her comfortable overstuffed English armchair and reading through her eighty-two cookbooks to provide meals for her family — still using lots of chicken and eggs, a carryover from wartime life in London and her first years in Jerusalem.

CITRUS CHICKEN

1 chicken, about 4 pounds
1 whole orange
½ cup fresh unstrained orange
    juice

1 teaspoon salt
1 teaspoon pepper
1 teaspoon ground ginger
4 to 6 tablespoons liquid honey
½ cup red or white wine

Preheat oven to 350°.

Place the chicken in a roasting pan breast side down. Place a whole orange inside the chicken. Combine the juice, salt, pepper and ginger and pour the mixture over. Roast, uncovered, for half an hour.

Remove the chicken from the oven, turn it over and smear it with honey. Return it to the oven. After five minutes, baste it with wine and juices from the roasting pan. If the breast seems to be browning too quickly, cover it with foil. Baste it once more. Bake it until the drumstick moves easily — about 20 minutes. Remove the orange from the chicken and slice it to garnish when serving.

Good served with green peas and potato balls. *Serves 6.*

COFFEE CHICKEN

1 four-pound chicken, cut into serving portions
¾ cup coffee made by adding 1 tablespoon instant coffee to ¾ cup boiling water
⅓ cup tomato ketchup

3 tablespoons soy sauce
2 tablespoons fresh lemon juice
2 tablespoons wine vinegar
1 tablespoon cooking oil
⅓ cup brown sugar

Preheat oven to 350°.

Place the chicken pieces in a shallow oven-proof dish. Mix the other ingredients in the order listed, in a medium-sized saucepan. Bring them to a boil, reduce the heat and simmer for 5 minutes. Pour the sauce over the chicken pieces. Bake uncovered for about 1 hour until the chicken is tender. Baste occasionally.

NOTE: This sauce is also very good with lamb chops. For 8 lamb chops proceed as above, baking about ¾ hour or until tender.

Nice served with artichoke hearts on top. *Serves 6.*

FRUITED CORNED BEEF

Good served with boiled parsleyed potatoes and a lettuce salad.

1 four-pound piece corned beef brisket (with covering of fat on one side)
Whole cloves
½ cup brown sugar

¼ cup fine breadcrumbs
1 teaspoon dry mustard
Grated rind of 1 lemon
Grated rind of 1 orange
1 cup apple cider or apple juice

Place the meat in a large kettle, cover with cold water. Bring to the boil, boil 5 minutes and skim froth from the surface. Cover tightly and cook over a low heat for three hours.

Preheat oven to 350°.

Remove the meat and place it in a roasting pan. Score the fat with a sharp knife in diagonal lines, making a pattern of diamond shapes. Insert a clove in each diamond. Mix the brown sugar, breadcrumbs, mustard and grated rind with ½ cup of cider. Pat the mixture over the meat and bake for 30 minutes, basting occasionally with the extra cider. *Serves 6–8.*

An Antiquities Dealer's Good Taste

Before we had even been to Jerusalem we had heard of an Arab named Victor Barakat, whose antiquities were some of the finest in the Old City. When we paid him the first of many visits we were surprised at how young he was, in his early thirties.

Wonderful ancient objects filled his shop — a Byzantine incense burner with three chains connected to the pot by a cross, a four-thousand-year-old two-headed cultic figurine, an ossuary (stone coffin) from the Herodian period and necklaces, which Victor designs himself, made of rare old coins and semiprecious stones.

The Barakat shops have become very well known in Jerusalem and its suburbs. Members of the family own antiquity stores in many locations where glass and ceramic pieces dating from as far back as 4000 B.C. can be found. In their other stores, all located on David and Christian Quarter Streets, material handwoven in Gaza, rugs, ancient coins and richly embroidered old Bedouin dresses are for sale.

As a youngster Victor visited his father's store just as his younger brothers do his shop today. Fascinated by the beauty of old stones and ancient pottery, he read everything he could on archaeology and antiquities, and today attends every archaeological lecture in the city. He is so familiar with his pieces that he can discuss the period of each stone, glass or gold object at a glance. Besides his very regular customers including such avid collectors as Moshe Dayan and Mayor Teddy Kollek, Victor's main dealings are with serious private collectors and museums from all over the world. His shop is also busy with people who decide that they are "just looking" — when they hear how high the prices are!

When we were visiting Victor one day, an elderly Arab dressed in a black robe and a kaffiyeh came in clutching a small plastic sack filled

David Street in the Old City, home of Barakat Antiquities
and the original Havilio candy shop

with bronze coins. Victor told us that he was the "middleman"; he goes around to villages, buys old coins and then brings them in to sell. With a professional eye and touch, Victor examined the coins, smiled and said, "They're good but I carry only the very finest — that's why my prices are so high."

Since Victor's special interest is glass from the Middle Egyptian to Islamic periods he carefully showed us some of his favorite pieces. His fingers vibrated when he touched them. "These won't sell. I'll add them to my personal collection, which I hope one day will become a family museum."

When we asked him if he had any other passions besides archaeology, he replied that he was "mad about all good things," including good food, and then he proceeded to describe to us how his mother makes his favorite dish — Mousakhan — broiled chicken with spices and nuts on Pita.

MOUSAKHAN (CHICKEN WITH SPICES, ONIONS AND PINE NUTS)

2 medium-size chickens, quartered
4 large or 8 small loaves Pita bread (see Page 36)
¼ cup margarine
Salt and pepper to taste
6 onions, chopped coarsely
½ cup water
¼ cup olive oil
1 cup pine nuts (pignolias)
1 teaspoon ground cloves
1 teaspoon saffron
1 tablespoon ground sumac (be sure to use commercial variety; some of the wild kinds are poisonous)
½ teaspoon paprika
½ teaspoon pepper

Preheat oven to 350°.

Rub the chicken with margarine or brush with melted margarine. Sprinkle with salt and pepper and place in a baking dish surrounded with coarsely chopped onions and water. Cook 20 minutes, turning occasionally. After 15 minutes are up, sprinkle the chicken with olive oil and cover with a mixture of pine nuts, cloves, saffron, and sumac. Sprinkle with paprika and pepper. Depending on taste you might want to increase amount of cloves, saffron, sumac and pepper. At the end of 20 minutes, transfer the chicken to pieces of Pita which have been sliced lengthwise in half. Broil the chicken and bread with spices and nuts poured over for last 5 minutes.

This dish tastes best when the chicken and bread are eaten with one's fingers. It is also a good recipe for cooking over an outdoor grill. Serve with salad or a green vegetable. *Serves 6–8.*

STEAK WITH APRICOTS

Good served with curry-flavored fried rice.

Steak
2 pounds round steak, cut in cubes
¼ cup cooking oil
2 tablespoons minced onion
½ pound halved dried apricots
½ cup raisins
¼ cup pine nuts (pignolias)
Chopped fresh parsley

Sauce
1 tablespoon margarine
1 tablespoon flour
1 cup cold milk
3–4 tablespoons tomato paste
Salt and pepper to taste

Steak: In a heavy frying pan with a lid sauté the onions and steak cubes in the cooking oil until they are lightly browned on all sides. Then stir in the apricots, add a small amount of water to prevent sticking, cover the pan and cook over low heat 20 to 30 minutes until the meat is tender.

Sauce: While the meat is cooking prepare the sauce. In a heavy-bottomed saucepan melt the margarine, quickly stir in the flour until the mixture is pastelike and immediately add the milk, stirring constantly. Over medium heat, stir the mixture until it thickens, then stir in the tomato paste and cook over a low heat for a few minutes. Season with salt and pepper.

Add the sauce to the meat mixture, stir in the raisins and pine nuts, and garnish with parsley. *Serves 4–6.*

Hungarian Home Cooking

On a shady street in a quiet residential area of Jerusalem a soft-spoken lady with a Mona Lisa smile feeds hundreds of Jerusalemites at lunch and dinner. After only five years, Leah's restaurant has become a Jerusalem institution for good home cooking. Leah Brumer and her husband Ernest have always loved to cook, ever since their honeymoon days in their native Hungary, where together they experimented making chicken paprikas with the six kinds of paprika available to them there. Leah's cooking has a different taste from other restaurants' — no hummus or shish kebab — the more traditional Jerusalem fare. Hers is strictly Hungarian cooking with no Middle Eastern influence. In fact, some of her first customers were enraged by her European menu and left. But professors, students and even government officials return day after day to taste the different specialties. One lady collects chicken bones from all the other customers' leftover stuffed chicken — one of our favorites too — to feed her dog, who also seems to prefer Leah's cooking.

There is something unforgettable about Leah. On her arm and the arms of all the cooks in the kitchen is the all too familiar stamp of the holocaust. Although her past haunts her, Leah is happy with the present and shows the remarkable recuperative powers of so many of her kinsmen who survived the Nazi period. After Leah fled concentration camp, she spent a year in Cyprus before being permitted to enter Israel. The past is the past in everything but her eyes and her arm, and she and her husband, who designed the restaurant himself, are totally engrossed in cooking for and hosting their customers.

When we visited Leah on one of our visits we watched her prepare the Monday specialty, Vadás (or "wild") — a sweet and sour pot roast which we would recommend for Thursday, Friday and Saturday also. . . .

LEAH'S STUFFED CHICKEN

Delicious any time — hot or cold.

¾ cup finely chopped onions	2 eggs, slightly beaten
¾ cup (about 6 ounces) uncooked chicken livers, chopped fine	1 chicken bouillon cube, crumbled
Cooking oil	1 tablespoon chopped fresh parsley
1 slice white bread, dampened slightly in water	1 large roasting chicken
	Salt and hot paprika to taste

Preheat oven to 400°.

Sauté the onions and liver in oil until onions are light brown. Combine the bread, eggs, bouillon, parsley, onions and liver; mix lightly. Sprinkle the inside of the chicken with salt and paprika. With your fingers, push the stuffing mixture under the skin: that is, between the meat and the skin. Do this on the body and legs. Fasten all openings together with skewers and tie the legs together. Brush the skin with oil; sprinkle with salt and pepper. Roast, uncovered, in oven for 1 hour until the drumstick moves easily. *Serves 4–6.*

VADÁS (SWEET AND SOUR POT ROAST)

3 teaspoons sugar	½ cup cooking oil
4 tablespoons Dijon mustard	1½ cups water

| 1 tablespoon wine vinegar | 3 pounds beef chuck |
| 2 carrots | 2 bay leaves |

Mix the sugar and mustard. Add the sugar-mustard combination to the oil, water and vinegar. Peel and slice the carrots, and add them to the first mixture. Place the meat in a casserole, pour the sauce over and place bay leaves in the dish. Cover and simmer over low heat until all liquid is absorbed, about an hour. The longer it is cooked, the better it tastes. Slice the meat very thin.

Good served with noodles and a cucumber salad (see Page 47). *Serves 6.*

Arab Traditions in the Little Town of Bethlehem

Two thousand years after the birth of Jesus, Christians still come from all over the world to Bethlehem on Christmas Eve to celebrate at the traditional place of Jesus' birth. Today Bethlehem is the home of eighteen thousand Christian Arabs who are able to trace their family history back for many centuries in that same town.

The director of Bethlehem's French Hospital, Dr. Michel Dabdoub, and his wife, Julia, are two such residents. Julia has always been interested in maintaining the original Arab traditions native to Bethlehem. Julia and her friends from the Arab Women's Union have renovated an old Bethlehem house and turned it into a display area for cultural and culinary material of the Arab inhabitants. Members of the union go into local villages to seek out examples of handmade embroidery, which is then copied by women at the union headquarters. This is the first opportunity for most of the village women of a world bound by male-governed traditions to do something on their own, not to mention the helpful addition to the family financial situation. They sit together, chatting, sewing and making good use of their skills. The traditional Bethlehem Arab dress is a floor-length, long-sleeved black gown with multicolored handmade embroidery forming a square yoke at the neck and borders around the hem and on the sleeves. The union women turn out these dresses in great numbers, and few tourists who see them can resist buying them. This enterprise of Julia and her friends has given pleasure both to the purchasers and to the women who fashion the lovely gowns.

The Dabdoub daughters attend school in London, Dr. Dabdoub lec-

Above the Little Town of Bethlehem

tures at the hospital in French, and Julia can converse fluently in three languages — yet the Dabdoub home is still a pleasing combination of modern education and respect for the traditions of the past. Julia specifically requested that we use one of her traditional Arab recipes, and she took pains to show us how she grinds her own spices every day in old-fashioned style.

CHICKEN AND CHICK-PEAS

1 three-pound chicken, cut into pieces
Salt to taste
5 tablespoons butter or cooking oil
2 cups chopped onions
1½ cups chick-peas (canned)

1 teaspoon ground cumin
1 tablespoon ground coriander
Freshly ground pepper to taste
1¼ cups chicken broth (made from boiling water and 2 chicken bouillon cubes)

Wash and dry the chicken pieces. Sprinkle with salt. Heat the butter or oil in a heavy saucepan with a lid. Sauté the onions and brown the chicken on all sides. Then add the chick-peas, cumin and coriander and sprinkle with pepper. Cover and cook over low heat about 10 minutes, shaking the pan once in a while so the chicken will not stick. Add the broth, cover and cook ½ hour until the chicken is tender. Remove the cover and cook for an additional 5 minutes. The gravy will be thick and there won't be much of it. Check for seasoning. *Serves 4.*

Horseback Riding to a French Gourmet Dinner

Local people on donkeys laden with baskets, yes; but smartly turned-out men and women in riding dress on properly saddled horses? Horseback riding as a sport is something new in the historic hills of Jerusalem. Trails and destinations of a very different nature from those found in America await the pleasure of visiting riders. One can ride to the grave of the Prophet Samuel, through clusters of lovely Arab cottages, minarets and mosques, or one can pack a picnic and gallop to the hillside where King David built the original city of Jerusalem thousands of years ago.

After such a ride, a magnificent treat awaits. On the outskirts of the city, at a riding stable where horses are available for rent, one can also enjoy a very fine French meal. Michelline Olivesse, one of the best cooks around Jerusalem, is the proprietress of the stable, and she will prepare a meal for the best of equestrians, or even the worst pedestrians for that matter, if she is notified in advance.

Michelline and her husband Claude are the hosts in a beautiful room which might have been plucked out of southern France and set down in Israel. Michelline comes from Baux near Avignon and is from the group of Jews known as the *juifs du pape*. The group got its name in the sixteenth century, when all Jews were expelled from France except those living in Avignon, who were protected by the antipope residing there.

The Olivesses converted a factory without electricity into their home. Claude, whose hobby is carpentry, regretfully put aside his electric saw and cleverly fashioned beautiful wooden furniture with simple hand tools. The pieces are complemented by antique wall cupboards, candles in wall sconces, white lace curtains, flowered china, polished copper pots and gingham tablecloths — all of which create a scene from a cottage in southern France. In addition to building his own furniture, Claude expertly instructs amateur riders, while Michelline prepares wonderful French meals for her by-appointment-only guests, whose favorites are the following dishes.

COQ AU VIN (CHICKEN IN RED WINE SAUCE)

4 slices bacon (or substitute), chopped into small pieces
1 medium chicken, quartered
1 cup fresh sliced mushrooms
1/2 teaspoon salt
1/8 teaspoon pepper
1 dozen small white onions, peeled (optional)
3 potatoes, peeled and cut into

chunks (optional)
1 3/4 cups dry red wine
1 bay leaf
1/2 teaspoon ground thyme
1 teaspoon ground nutmeg
1/2 teaspoon sugar
1 1/2 tablespoons flour
4 pieces rye bread
4 tablespoons butter

Using a heavy saucepan with a tight-fitting lid, fry the bacon pieces until they are limp but not crisp. Remove the bacon from the saucepan and set the pieces aside. Lightly brown the chicken pieces and then the mushrooms in the saucepan. Drain off the remaining bacon fat and season with salt and pepper. Add the onions and potatoes, if desired.

Meanwhile, in a medium-size saucepan place 1 1/2 cups wine, bay leaf, thyme, nutmeg and sugar. Bring to boiling and simmer for 5 to 6 minutes. Stir in a paste made from flour and 1/4 cup wine. Pour the wine mixture over the bacon, chicken, and mushrooms in the casserole. Cover and simmer gently for about 1 hour until tender.

Cut rye bread into 1-inch strips and fry in butter until crisp. When serving, place on top of the chicken. This dish is best prepared in advance, since the taste improves with reheating. *Serves 4.*

POULET À LA CRÈME (CHICKEN IN CREAM SAUCE)

4 tablespoons butter
1 medium-size chicken, cut into
  4 pieces
Salt and pepper to taste
1 teaspoon dried tarragon
¾ cup cognac

2 egg yolks, lightly beaten
¾ cup sour cream
3 tablespoons butter
Fresh parsley, chopped coarsely,
  for garnish

In a large frying pan, melt 4 tablespoons butter until sizzling. Sauté the chicken pieces lightly until the meat stiffens but does not brown. Season with salt, pepper and tarragon while sautéing. Cover and cook over very low heat about one hour, until tender. Remove from pan and keep warm. Add the cognac to the juices in the pan and stir to scrape up the pieces. Boil rapidly to reduce the liquid to half its volume.

In a medium-sized saucepan mix the egg yolks thoroughly with the sour cream and slowly stir in the cognac mixture. Add 3 tablespoons butter, season with salt and pepper if required and cook over low heat, stirring constantly until the sauce thickens. The sauce must be cooked over low heat so that it does not curdle; it will not be very thick.

Arrange the warm chicken pieces on a serving plate, pour the sauce over and sprinkle with parsley. *Serves 4.*

An Ethiopian Monk's Dinner for a Nonfast Day

Each morning at dawn, tall black Ethiopian Orthodox monks leave their cells on the roof of the Church of the Holy Sepulchre and cross over to an adjacent rooftop chapel, where they pray until eight A.M. Soon the sun rises and shines through the tiny chapel window, outlining the slender figures in their black robes and round hats, leaning on T-shaped canes and chanting. In a separate area the priests, dressed

PETER ANDERSON ICP

*An Ethiopian monk in the doorway of his cell on the roof
of the Church of the Holy Sepulchre*

in robes of green, white or yellow, depending on the ecclesiastical season, swing incense burners and conduct the mass.

Ever since the Ethiopian Queen of Sheba came to visit King Solomon in his splendid Temple, Ethiopians have had a close attachment to Jerusalem. Indeed, Ethiopia is cited eleven times in the Old Testament, and an Ethiopian is mentioned in the Acts of the Apostles as one of those who accepted the teaching of Jesus and was then baptized. Unlike other Christian communities in Jerusalem, such as the Armenian and Greek Orthodox, which also date from the earliest days of Christianity but have patriarchates, the Ethiopians maintain monasteries. One is located on the roof of the Church of the Holy Sepulchre and a second is in the Ethiopian Quarter outside the walls of the Old City. For centuries the Church has been sending representatives to administer its sacred sites in the Holy Land, and the presence of Ethiopian monks and pilgrims is recorded in the writings of first-century pilgrims.

On frequent visits to morning services, we were impressed with the apparent simplicity of Ethiopian prayer. Actually, complete concentration and attention to detail pervade the liturgy, and indeed religion governs every aspect of their daily life.

Fasting and eating play a large part in the religion, with over 280 fast days in a year. On these days, the priests pray in church from two A.M. until eight and informally alone in their cells throughout the day until the next organized service, in the evening. Then each returns to his cell and again alone prepares the simplest of meals. Only on feast days do the priests eat together. Then, as a group, they cook all night long, cutting ingredients into tiny pieces characteristic to Ethiopian cooking. This chicken recipe is a typical feast-day dish, tasty and simple to prepare.

WAT (PAPRIKA-LEMON CHICKEN)

1 medium-size chicken, cut into
   8 pieces
¾ cup fresh lemon juice
Cooking oil
6 large onions, chopped coarsely

¾ cup flour
2 tablespoons sweet paprika
1 teaspoon salt
¼ cup warm water
2 tablespoons tomato paste

Place the chicken pieces in a large bowl, pour lemon juice over and rub it well into each piece. Set aside. In a large frying pan with a cover, sauté onions in cooking oil until they are tender and browned, sprinkling them with extra paprika during cooking. Remove and set them aside. In a large brown paper bag, shake the flour, paprika and salt until well mixed. Shake the chicken, 2 pieces at a time, in the mixture, coating well. In the same frying pan, sauté the chicken pieces in cooking oil, with chicken skin side down for 20 minutes and then the other side down for 15 more minutes until tender. Make sure all surfaces of each chicken piece are browned well. Return the onions to the frying pan. Mix the water and tomato paste and sprinkle it over the chicken and onions. Cover and cook over low heat for 10 minutes.

Serve with a lettuce and tomato salad and crusty buttered bread. *Serves 4.*

A Recipe Arrives in Jerusalem Before Columbus Discovers America

Seven years before Columbus discovered America, even before the time of the Spanish Inquisition, when all Jews were expelled from Spain, the first members of the Eliachar family immigrated from Spain to Jerusalem. Although they could have sought refuge in Holland, Turkey, Morocco, France or Italy, they chose instead the place dictated by their hearts, the "Holy City."

As we described in "Sephardic Sabbath Morning Specialties," Sephardim — Jews of Spanish or Oriental origin — formed the majority of Jerusalem's population until the nineteenth century. Their lives were centered around their synagogue, located in the Jewish Quarter of the Old City, and their cultural identity was retained in all aspects of life, including their use of Ladino, a medieval Spanish dialect containing Hebrew, Turkish, and other elements, written with Hebrew script.

Many of Jerusalem's old families can claim one or two community leaders of stature, but the Eliachar family is unique in that every generation, for hundreds of years, has consistently contributed a prominent citizen — a chief rabbi, a mayor, a historian or a leading businessman. Today, within that tradition, Eli Eliachar is president of the Jerusalem Sephardic Community Council.

At home his wife Rachel maintains the traditional Spanish cuisine. She often compares recipes which were handed down to her from her first Jerusalem ancestors with those of the new immigrants from other Sephardic countries — and there is surprisingly little difference! Medias, vegetable halves stuffed with meat, are a family specialty which has been handed down from generation to generation since the first Eliachars arrived in Jerusalem.

MEDIAS (STUFFED VEGETABLE HALVES WITH MEAT)

4 large onions
4 large tomatoes
1 cup chopped beef
1 egg
2 tablespoons chopped fresh
   parsley
2 tablespoons chopped onion

3 tablespoons coarsely chopped
   almonds
2½ or 3½ tablespoons cooking
   oil
Salt and pepper to taste
Flour
Paprika

Peel the onions and slice off the stem ends. Drop the whole onions in boiling water and cook for a few minutes. Remove them and cool slightly. Cut the tomatoes and onions in half crosswise. Mix the chopped meat with the egg, parsley, onion, almonds and ½ teaspoon oil. Season well with salt and pepper. Carefully remove the insides of each vegetable half, leaving about 3 rings of onion and at least ½ inch of tomato shell. Set the pulp aside to use later. Fill each half with the meat mixture, mounding it up on top. Sprinkle the top with a little flour and paprika. In a heavy saucepan with a lid, heat 2 or 3 tablespoons of cooking oil. Place the vegetable halves, meat side down, in the pan to brown for several minutes. Remove with a slotted spoon and set them aside. Chop the reserved onion and place it with the tomato pulp on the bottom of a saucepan. Set the vegetable halves on top, vegetable side down. Sprinkle them generously with salt and pepper. Cover and cook over low heat for ½ hour.

Good served with rice or buttered noodles. *Serves 4.*

TOP OF STOVE STUFFED CHICKEN

1 three-pound chicken
3 tablespoons cooking oil
Paprika
Liver from the chicken
¾ cup cooked rice
1 tablespoon finely chopped fresh
   parsley

¼ teaspoon salt
Pepper to taste
2 tablespoons whole pine nuts
   (pignolias) (optional)
½ cup red or white wine
   (optional)

Rinse the chicken and pat it dry. In a large heavy saucepan with a lid, heat 3 tablespoons of cooking oil. Sprinkle the chicken with paprika and brown it in oil, turning it to brown all sides. Remove the chicken and brown the chicken liver, then chop it fine. Mix the rice, parsley, salt, chopped liver, a generous sprinkle of pepper and the pine nuts. When the chicken has cooled enough to handle easily, stuff it with the rice mixture and sew the openings with a needle and thread or truss it with skewers and string. Sprinkle it with salt and pepper. Drain the remaining oil from the saucepan, leaving just enough to cover the bottom. Place the chicken in the saucepan, breast side up, cover and cook it over very low heat about 1½ hours until tender.

If desired, ½ cup red or white wine may be added to the saucepan with the chicken before cooking it over low heat. But chicken needs no liquid to cook properly. *Serves 4–6.*

Recipes Exchanged through Barbed Wire

For nineteen years barbed wire separated the two sides of Beit Zaffafa, an Arab village inside Jerusalem. Between 1948 and 1967 cousins grew up talking to each other over the rusting coils of wire. The Israeli and the Jordanian sectors of Jerusalem were separated by areas of "no-man's-land" — empty stretches of unoccupied territory. The only part of Jerusalem not bordered in this way was the quaint Arab village of Beit Zaffafa with its narrow streets and ancient olive trees. It was arbitrarily cut through the middle by the existing railroad tracks and the addition of a barbed wire fence. By agreement between the Israeli and Jordanian governments, the Jerusalem–Tel Aviv train continued to run, emphasizing in sound and motion the accidental fate of a small village.

Omar and Suzy Othman, who have always lived on the Israeli side of the village, slowly became accustomed to this division which cut them off from friends and family. As a young boy Omar studied at an Arab elementary school and then earned two B.A. degrees, in Arabic and Education and in Islamic Civilization, from the Hebrew University in Jerusalem. Until recently he was the principal of a school in Abu Ghosh, an Israeli-Arab village between Jerusalem and Tel Aviv. This year, Omar is finishing work for his master's degree and teaching Arabic to finance his studies. He and his wife, Suzy, live in Beit Zaffafa near the house in which Omar was born and grew up.

"Besides talking, we would exchange foods that were scarce, like sugar and coffee," commented Omar. "Fish especially was expensive on the Jordanian side of Beit Zaffafa. Since we could get fish in Jerusalem from the Mediterranean near Jaffa, we used to pass it over to our friends and relatives when the guards were not looking. . . . Every day we would talk over the fence to each other."

"Sometimes we would even exchange recipes taken from the Arabic,

Israeli and Jordanian newspapers," interjected Suzy, the cook of the family.

As we sat in the living room of their lovely home, surrounded by a garden filled with vegetables and flowers, we heard a mixture of perfect Hebrew, Arabic and English. The Othmans' neighbors in Beit Zaffafa are Arabs, and Arabic is their native tongue. Across the street and up the road are Israeli friends, with whom they speak Hebrew. The English Omar and Suzy learned at school is spoken with their American and British friends, many of whom are Omar's pupils.

While Omar was teaching an Arabic lesson to an Israeli woman who wants to learn "because it's essential when living in the Middle East," we talked with Omar's wife and his sister. As we discussed the following Arabic dishes, including one which uses fish from the Sea of Galilee, we tasted the fresh jam which was bubbling on the stove — made from the figs growing outside the house.

MOUSHT (FISH WITH TAHINA)

(Mousht is Arabic for a Sea of Galilee fish similar to trout — appropriately called St. Peter's fish. Trout is easily substituted.)

¼ cup cooking oil
4 small St. Peter's fish or trout
2 medium-size onions, sliced
1 small can tahina

1 tablespoon lemon juice
1 clove garlic, crushed
Salt and pepper to taste

Preheat oven to 325°.

In an oven-proof saucepan heat a small amount of cooking oil and sauté the onion slices for a few minutes. Add the fish and sauté them for a minute or so on each side just to flavor them. In a bowl blend the tahina with the lemon juice and garlic. Sprinkle the fish with salt and pepper and spread each one with the tahina mixture. Bake uncovered for about half an hour or until the fish flakes easily with a fork. *Serves 4.*

Good served with Cucumber Salad (see page 47).

LAHMEH AL WARAK (LAMB ON GRAPE LEAVES)

6 to 8 fresh or canned grape
  leaves (fresh are better)
1 pound lamb, cut in bite-size
  cubes
2 onions, chopped

2 tablespoons oil
Salt and pepper to taste
¾ teaspoon allspice
¼ cup pine nuts (pignolias)
Juice of 1 lemon

If fresh grape leaves are used, soak them in hot water for 5 minutes. Squeeze them dry. If canned or bottled leaves are used, soak them overnight in cold water to get rid of salt. Squeeze them dry.

Preheat oven to 350°.

Sauté the meat and onions in oil until the meat is brown on all sides. Season with salt, pepper and allspice. Place half the leaves in the bottom of a low oven-proof dish. Spread the meat mixture over, sprinkle with the pignolias and place the rest of the grape leaves on top. Sprinkle with the lemon juice. Cover the dish with a larger dish with water in it and bake in the oven for ½ hour.

Tastes good with rice. *Serves 4.*

RUZ TATBILLA (RICE WITH CHICKEN LIVERS)

1 pound chicken livers	Salt and pepper to taste
Oil or butter for cooking	½ cup chopped blanched almonds
1 large onion, chopped	¼ cup pine nuts (pignolias)
2 cups cooked rice	Fresh parsley, chopped

Cut the chicken livers in half, rinse them with cold water and pat them dry. In a large frying pan, sauté the livers and onion in butter or oil until tender, about 8 to 10 minutes.

Meanwhile, sauté the nuts in butter until brown, about 5 minutes.

Add the rice to the meat mixture, stir and cook to heat the rice. Add the nuts, sprinkle with salt and pepper. Garnish with parsley. *Serves 4.*

Creative Cookery— A Scottish Minister's Hobby

From the steps of St. Andrew's Church, which was built in 1927 to commemorate the liberation of Jerusalem from the Turks by the British forces during the first World War, we enjoyed one of the finest views there is of Mount Zion and the walls of the Old City. Nearby is the memorial to the soldiers of the 52nd (Lowland) Division, who died in the war's Palestine campaigns. Jerusalem's first city planner, Sir Patrick Geddes of Edinburgh, who at the request of the British designed several buildings of the Hebrew University complex on Mount Scopus, no doubt contemplated this inspiring view on his many visits to Jerusalem in the twenties and thirties.

It seems that Scots have had an affinity for Jerusalem for centuries. Over six hundred years ago King Robert Bruce, to complete his unfulfilled wish to visit the Holy City, requested that his heart be buried here after his death. Unfortunately, his appeal was never carried out, but today there is an inscription to his memory in St. Andrew's Church.

The Reverend William Gardiner-Scott is the energetic minister at St. Andrew's, which is Jerusalem's only Presbyterian church. This year Queen Elizabeth awarded the Reverend Dr. Gardiner-Scott the Order of the British Empire for services to the church and the British community in Jerusalem. After the Yom Kippur War, the Gardiner-Scotts inspired the raising of funds, among the Jerusalem Christian communities, for wounded veterans still in Hadassah Hospital.

Despite his many commitments, Dr. Gardiner-Scott also tries to find time to enjoy his culinary hobby, to the delight of his family and friends. Interestingly enough, during World War II the Reverend Dr. Gardiner-Scott was in the catering trade in Egypt before becoming a minister. Here are several of his recipes, one of which combines his Scottish love of solid meat like liver with the use of Israeli's fine eggplants and apples.

EGGPLANT BAKED WITH LIVER AND APPLES

1 large eggplant
Salt and pepper to taste
1 pound calves' liver, sliced thin
   (¼ inch thick) into 4 pieces
2 eggs, lightly beaten
1 tablespoon water
½ cup flour

Vegetable oil
3 medium-size onions, chopped
   coarsely
½ cup mushrooms (optional)
3 large apples, unpeeled but cored
   and sliced thin
1 tablespoon butter

Peel the eggplant, slice it thin. Place it in a colander, sprinkle it with salt and let it stand for 1 hour with a heavy saucepan on top so that the bitter juice can drain off.

Preheat oven to 350°.

Dip liver slices in the egg and water mixture, then lightly coat them with flour. Heat the oil in a frying pan and sauté the meat until browned on both sides. Prepare eggplant slices in exactly the same manner. Then sauté the onions until they are tender but not crisp. In a large oven-proof dish, layer ingredients as follows: half the eggplant, onion, mushrooms and liver. (If desired, add sliced, peeled mushrooms to the liver layer.) Sprinkle with salt and pepper and add half the apples. Dot with butter. Repeat once. Bake, uncovered, for 45 minutes.

Good served with mashed potatoes and a green salad. *Serves 4.*

BEEFSTEAK AND KIDNEY PIE

1 half-pound beef kidney
2 pounds round steak or other
    goulash-type lean beef, cut into
    small cubes
4 medium-size onions
Cooking oil

2 cups sifted flour
1 teaspoon salt
1 cup shredded suet (or
    substitute)
1 teaspoon baking powder
Water at room temperature

Remove the membranes from the kidney and chop it into small pieces. In a frying pan lightly brown the beef and kidney in cooking oil. Remove to a plate. Chop the onions coarsely and brown very lightly in the same pan. It is preferable to use a heavy-bottomed frying pan with a lid. Otherwise, place the meat and onions in a heavy saucepan with a small amount of water to prevent sticking, cover them and cook over low heat until the ingredients are not quite tender but definitely not soft.

While the meat is stewing prepare the following crust: mix flour, baking powder, salt and suet in a bowl, adding enough water to make a pliable dough. Roll out fairly thin and fit into the inside of a deep Pyrex dish or other heat-resistant bowl, reserving enough dough to make a layer for the top of the bowl. Place the meat and onions inside and cover with a circle of dough, crimping the edges together. With the tip of a sharp knife, cut out two small circles on the top so that the steam can escape. Cover the bowl with foil or grease-proof paper, tucking the paper tightly under the rim. (Use a circle of paper a bit larger than the circumference of the top of the bowl.) Place about two inches of water in a low cake pan and bring to a boil. Set the pie in the water and steam it gently over medium heat for 2 hours, checking the water level periodically.

Serve with mashed potatoes and glazed sliced carrots. *Serves 6–8.*

TARTAN VEAL

2 pounds veal cutlets
2 eggs
3 tablespoons water
1 cup dry breadcrumbs

1 can mushroom soup, with a
    half-can water and a half-can
    milk

Pound the veal with a meat hammer until it is about ¼ inch thick. Cut it into serving-size pieces. Beat the eggs with water. Dip the veal pieces into the egg mixture and then coat each piece with crumbs. Place them in the refrigerator for 15 minutes to chill so that the coating will not flake off during cooking. Then sauté in hot oil until they are lightly browned on both sides. Place in a shallow casserole (overlapped slightly but not on top of each other) and pour the soup, water and milk over. Cover and bake in 325° oven for about 20 minutes until tender.

Good served with mashed potatoes and candied carrots. *Serves 4–6.*

Cooking Class at an Arab Girls' School

An Arab who was willing to teach right after the Six-Day War was considered either a collaborator or courageous, depending on the point of view of the particular observer. Georgette Maabadi, realizing full well the dangers involved in becoming principal of the Maamouniah Girls' School in September 1967, decided that Arab girls absolutely had to be educated by Arab teachers and took the post. Despite continual threats she stubbornly persisted, and today her school has achieved academic success and has contributed to a decided improvement in the courses offered in East Jerusalem. "At first," said Georgette, "it was 'Take out your Israeli books and then take out your Jordanian books.' Now students have a combined syllabus which will enable them to sit for exams at either the Hebrew University or any Arab university, as they like."

Georgette grew up in Jerusalem. Her mother was Greek Catholic and her father was Roman Catholic and they both liked to cook and to eat. True to her upbringing, Georgette believes that "every Arab meal is a feast" and carries this belief to her teaching. "I like to teach my girls how to present meals in a tempting manner," she explained while instructing a cooking class in how to make an Oriental delicacy — stuffed small zucchinis and rice and meat wrapped in grape leaves. "Since meals are planned around the vegetables in season and no frozen ingredients are used, these girls learn how to make dishes in which the meat, vegetables and starch are cooked together." When we asked Georgette if she ever teaches the girls to make desserts, she answered, "When they are more advanced I teach them to make Arabic sweets like Baklava, which we compare with those in the fine pastry shops in the Old City."

One day Georgette invited us to attend a luncheon for teachers from Gaza who were visiting her school. The whole meal was planned and prepared by her young students, who were quite amazed that we didn't already know how to make stuffed grape leaves; they thought we had been out of school long enough! Here is their recipe, without the giggles.

WARAK ENAB (GRAPE LEAVES STUFFED WITH RICE AND LAMB)

20 grape leaves, fresh, canned or
   bottled
1 cup rice
1 pound chopped lamb
2 tablespoons melted margarine

¼ teaspoon cinnamon
1 teaspoon allspice
1 tablespoon salt
1 teaspoon pepper
⅓ cup fresh lemon juice

If fresh grape leaves are used, soak them in hot water for 5 minutes. Squeeze them dry. If canned or bottle leaves are used, soak them over-night in cold water to get rid of salt. Squeeze them dry. Soak the rice in water for 10 minutes. Drain well, mix with the lamb, margarine and spices. Place a grape leaf back side up and roll around 1 tablespoon of the rice-lamb mixture, turning in the corners. Layer in a heavy saucepan and add water until ¼ inch above the filled grape leaves. Cover and cook over low heat 25 minutes, adding the lemon juice for the last 5 minutes of cooking. *Serves 4.*

FASSOULIA (BEEF AND GREEN BEAN STEW)

1½ cups tomato juice
½ cup water
1 pound stewing beef, cut in small
   chunks
3 tablespoons chopped fresh
   parsley

2 cloves garlic, minced
3 tablespoons butter
1 large onion, chopped coarsely
1 pound fresh green beans
Salt and pepper to taste

In a heavy saucepan bring the water and tomato juice to a boil. Add the beef, parsley and garlic. Cover and simmer for 2 hours. (Do not brown the meat first.) Wash the beans and slice them diagonally into one-inch pieces. In a large frying pan sauté the onion and butter until golden, add the beans, and cook for 10 minutes, stirring occasionally. Add the meat (reserving the sauce), season it with salt and pepper and cook 10 minutes more. Add all the sauce from the meat, cover and cook over low heat for a few minutes to heat through. *Serves 4.*

A Once-Jewish Archbishop

Suppose a person mysteriously found himself across from David's Tower inside Jaffa Gate in the Armenian Quarter, where would he think he was? Certainly not Jerusalem. Most likely he would think of rural England. His guess would be partly correct, as Christ Church, the first English-style building in Jerusalem, was designed after a country church in Anglican England.

In the 1840's the first Anglican bishop *in* Jerusalem (not *of*; that distinction was given to the church dignitaries already here during the Ottoman Empire) was a converted Jew named Michael Solomon Alexander, who came to the Holy Land between 1841 and 1845 with the London Society for Promoting Christianity among Jews, to convert Jews to Anglicanism. On the site of the present church Bishop Alexander set up a free kitchen to provide the poorer Jews of Jerusalem with nourishment. When he found very few takers for his hot soup and bread, he set up a kosher kitchen, which was decidedly more popular — and understandably so.

As a result of the British Mandate in 1920, the British Anglican population in Jerusalem began to increase. Bishop Alexander's successors expanded the activities of the Anglican Church in Jerusalem and founded schools for Arabs and Jews, and today there are several churches, schools and hospitals serving the population. One Anglican hospital, which was used as temporary headquarters for Hadassah Hospital after 1948 when the original was cut off from the city, has become an international school for the children of diplomats, journalists, UN personnel and the many transients living in the city.

When we visited the Anglican School (which no longer has a kosher kitchen!) we glanced through an international cookbook, prepared by the students and reflecting their many backgrounds, and found these special meat dishes, as well as an equally special eggplant soufflé, which we have included on Page 169 under Vegetables and Salads.

CARBONNADE À LA FLAMANDE (BEEF IN BEER)

¼ cup butter or margarine
¼ pound bacon (or substitute), diced
1¾-pound braising steak, cut in medium slices
5 small onions, sliced
2 tablespoons sugar

2 small bottles good-quality beer
2 teaspoons thyme
Salt and pepper to taste
1 bay leaf
6 slices rye bread with crusts cut off
French mustard

In a heavy-bottomed saucepan melt the butter or margarine until it is golden brown, and sauté the bacon, beef and onions until they are brown. Push this mixture to the sides of the pan, leaving the butter (or margarine) in the center, stir the sugar into the butter, and continue stirring the mixture until it is golden and caramelized. Then mix together all the ingredients in the pan and add the beer, thyme, salt, pepper and bay leaf. Cover the pan and cook slowly for about 1½ hours. Add more beer from time to time if necessary.

To serve, spread each slice of bread with mustard, place it on a dinner plate and top with a portion of Carbonnade. Serve with mugs of cold beer and buttered boiled potatoes sprinkled with parsley. *Serves 3–4.*

NOTE: Carbonnade can be made equally well in a covered casserole in an oven or in an electric Dutch oven.

MINT LAMB

3 pounds shoulder lamb with
  bones
2 large onions, quartered
Salt and pepper to taste

4 potatoes, peeled and halved
1½ cups fresh green peas
¾ cup fresh mint leaves

In a large kettle place the lamb bones and meat with the onions. Cover with water and bring to the boil. Skim the froth from the surface and season with salt and pepper. Add the potatoes, cover and simmer until the meat is tender, about 2 hours. Fifteen or 20 minutes before serving, add the peas and mint leaves, cover and simmer until tender. The excess liquid may be used for a gravy. *Serves 4.*

Jerusalem's "Perle Mesta" during the Siege of 1948

During the siege of Jerusalem in 1948, everyone living in the area around the city needed ingenuity and initiative to survive. Marian Lewin-Epstein, a former American now living in Jerusalem, fascinated us with tales of how her mother-in-law coped with the situation.

The elder Mrs. Lewin-Epstein, an American Zionist, was a trained nurse and the wife of a prominent dentist. During the time of the siege her home on Princess Mary Street near the Old City was in a dangerous spot, and so she converted it into a first-aid station. She used her husband's medical supplies and often went out into the street under fire to bring the wounded into her home for treatment. Food was dangerously scarce, and Mrs. Lewin-Epstein, like so many other women, had to use her creativity to find food to feed a starving population. The only real foodstuff to be found was in the available plants growing near the city. One "delicacy" was the buckthorn, which was sucked for its juice. Often dinner consisted of fried orange peels, which tasted like chicken. Marian explained that her mother-in-law opened her house in 1948 not only to the wounded but also to the first groups of American students in 1946 as well as to distinguished people visiting the city. In addition, the Lewin-Epstein home was the traditional gathering place for Americans at Thanksgiving.

During the austerity period in 1951, the singer Lena Horne was a guest at the elder Mrs. Lewin-Epstein's home. In honor of her visit, Mrs. Lewin-Epstein served mock chicken liver consisting of onions, oil, breadcrumbs, and fresh yeast. Surprisingly enough, several years later Lena Horne commented on it to a Jerusalemite in Los Angeles as the best chopped liver she had ever tasted.

In more prosperous times, Marian now cooks with ready-made authentic ingredients, and perhaps cooking in this way is less of a challenge. In any case, it is recipes with these "real" ingredients that we accepted from Marian, who with the death of her mother-in-law has become Jerusalem's Mrs. Lewin-Epstein.

POLENTA WITH MEAT AND TOMATO SAUCE

Polenta
2½ cups water
1 teaspoon salt
1 cup cornmeal
1½ cups cold water

Sauce
1 medium-size onion, chopped
   fine
1 tablespoon olive oil

½ pound ground beef
½ green pepper
¼ pound fresh mushrooms, sliced
⅓ cup sweet red wine
1 small can tomato paste
1 garlic clove, mashed
¼ teaspoon basil
½ teaspoon oregano
Salt and pepper to taste
¼ cup grated cheese (optional)

Polenta: Using the top of a double boiler as a saucepan, bring the water and salt to a rolling boil over direct heat. Mix the cornmeal and cold water to a smooth paste and add it to the boiling water, stirring constantly. Cook and stir over low heat until the mixture bubbles. Set the pan over boiling water in the lower part of the double boiler, and cook, covered, until the mixture is the consistency of thick smooth purée — about 40 minutes.

Preheat oven to 350°.

Grease a 9 inch square pan, pour the mixture in and chill until it is firm. Cut it into squares and place them on a buttered baking sheet.

Bake in the oven 15 minutes or under a broiler until crisp on both sides.

Sauce: Sauté the onion in oil, stir in the ground meat, green pepper and mushrooms and cook for 5 minutes. Add the wine, cook and stir. Mix in the tomato paste, garlic and seasonings. If necessary, thin the sauce with a little warm water. Cook, covered, for 25 minutes.

To serve, arrange Polenta squares on a serving dish and pour the sauce over them. Sprinkle with grated cheese, if desired. *Serves 4–6.*

PRACHES (SWEET AND SOUR STUFFED CABBAGE ROLLS)

1 large green cabbage
2 pounds chopped beef
2 eggs
1 large onion, chopped fine
½ cup warm water
½ cup uncooked rice
Salt and pepper to taste

1 large onion, sliced
¾ cup ketchup
1½ to 2 cups water
¾ cup brown sugar
Juice of 1 large lemon
½ cup raisins

Remove the core from the cabbage. Separate the leaves and place them in a large dish. Pour boiling water over the leaves and set aside to soften for 5 to 10 minutes. Mix together the meat, eggs, chopped onion, water and rice. Season to taste with salt and pepper. Drain the water off the cabbage leaves and place a portion of the meat mixture on each. Roll, folding the ends in first.

Preheat oven to 300°.

In a large oven- and flame-proof casserole, place the unused cabbage leaves. Then add the onion slices in a layer. Place the cabbage rolls on top, seamed sides down. Add water (enough to come up just to the top of the rolls). Mix the ketchup, brown sugar, lemon juice and raisins and add to the casserole. Bring them to a boil on top of the stove and then bake, covered, for 1½ hours. This is a good dish to prepare ahead; reheating in a slow oven improves the flavor. *Serves 4–6.*

ROAST BRISKET WITH SAUERKRAUT

2½ pound piece of double brisket
   or short ribs of beef
4 garlic buds, crushed
Salt and pepper to taste
1 teaspoon cinnamon
Cooking oil

6 large tomatoes, halved, or 1
   small can tomato paste
3 large onions, sliced
1 can sauerkraut
6 tablespoons sugar

Rinse the meat with cold water. Pat it dry. Rub the meat on all sides with crushed garlic and then sprinkle it with salt, pepper and cinnamon. Heat a small amount of oil in a heavy-bottomed kettle and brown the meat slightly on all sides. Add the vegetables; cover and cook over low heat from 3 to 4 hours, until the meat is tender.

One half hour before the meat is done, drain the sauerkraut, place it in a saucepan and cover it with cold water. Bring it to a boil, add the sugar and some of the tomatoes and onion slices from the meat. Cover and cook over low heat for a half hour. Serve the meat with the sauerkraut. *Serves 6.*

From Thanksgiving Dinner to Chinese Food at the Y.M.C.A.

Until the Six-Day War in 1967, the tower of the YMCA building in West Jerusalem was the highest point in the Israeli section of the city. Visitors to Jerusalem could climb the tower to get the best panoramic view of the whole city. On the tower is a figure representing the angel that appeared in the Prophet Isaiah's vision, and on the top of the front wall is inscribed the traditional watchword of the Jewish faith: "Hear O Israel, the Lord our God, the Lord is One."

The YMCA, in addition to being a beautiful building, provides social, cultural and athletic activities for anyone of any religion. An annual treat there is Thanksgiving Dinner — guaranteed to cure homesickness for both resident and visiting Americans. Not only are there American-style turkey, sweet potatoes and cranberry sauce, but also pumpkin pie. It took a while for local cooks to learn how to make pumpkin pie, however, since Jerusalemites do not know what American pie is, nor are they familiar with pumpkins.

The Reverend Herbert Minard, the energetic director of the "Y," has been in Jerusalem since 1950. From 1948 to 1950 he and his wife did missionary work in China, where they learned much about Chinese cooking. Recently, many people in Jerusalem have wanted to learn some of Marcella Minard's Oriental culinary secrets, so she agreed to give a Chinese cooking class at the Y. Although many ingredients are difficult to find in Jerusalem, Marcella has learned to improvise. She grows her own bean sprouts and buys kohlrabi, a chunky vegetable easily substituted for water chestnuts. Marcella's recipes are a culinary combination of her American upbringing, her Chinese experience and the availability of products in the Middle East.

CHINESE BEEF WITH VEGETABLES

4 teaspoons cornstarch
2 tablespoons soy sauce
¼ teaspoon pepper
2 teaspoons Worcestershire sauce
1 teaspoon salt
1 pound very thinly sliced flank steak with membranes removed, sliced at an angle (place meat in freezer for 10 minutes to firm for easier slicing)
1 cup chopped celery (½-inch cubes)
1 cup very thinly sliced string beans or carrots, sliced at an angle
Vegetable oil
1 cup sliced mushrooms (use fresh mushrooms only)

Mix together the cornstarch, soy sauce, pepper, Worcestershire and salt. Add the beef strips and stir to coat well. Set this aside while preparing the vegetables. Cook the celery and beans or carrots in boiling water, uncovered, for 5 minutes. Immediately drain off the water into a bowl for later use. Heat a small amount of oil in a frying pan. Sauté the beef strips, stirring constantly, quickly and until dark in color (about 2 minutes). Remove them from the pan and set them aside. In the same pan sauté the vegetables, including mushrooms, for a few minutes. Add the beef strips, then stir in ½ cup of the reserved vegetable water and stir. Cook for a few seconds. Serve with rice and add more soy sauce to taste. *Serves 4 as a main dish and 8 as one of several in a Chinese meal.*

EGG ROLLS MINARD

Batter for Pancakes
1 cup flour
¼ teaspoon salt
1 egg, unbeaten
1¼ cups water

Filling
2 tablespoons margarine for sautéing
2 stalks celery, sliced thin (¼-inch pieces)
1 cup bean sprouts or 1 cup green cabbage, sliced thin
5 large mushrooms, sliced
1 cup leftover cooked ham, chicken, pork or veal chopped very small
2 tablespoons soy sauce
½ tablespoon red or white wine
Salt to taste

Batter: Sift together the flour and salt. Make a well in the center and drop in the egg. Gradually stir in the water and beat the mixture until it is smooth. Set it aside for one hour while preparing the filling.

Filling: Melt 2 tablespoons margarine in a frying pan. Sauté the celery and bean sprouts for about 2 minutes. Add the mushrooms and meat; sauté for 2 more minutes. If you are using cabbage instead of bean sprouts, add it and stir after the mushrooms and meat. Add the soy sauce and wine; stir to blend and turn off the heat. Season with salt and set the mixture aside to cool.

Pancakes: Very lightly grease a 6-inch or 7-inch frying pan with margarine or vegetable oil and warm it over low heat. (If the pan is too hot, the batter will stick). Pour about 2 tablespoons of batter into the pan and immediately tilt the pan to cover the surface evenly. (The first one or two will be "test" pancakes; they should be wafer-thin, and a little practice is needed). Cook each pancake over low heat on one side only. Shake the pan, and when the pancake is loose, slide it off and place it, cooked side down, on a counter top. Do not pile the pancakes on top of each other. Continue cooking pancakes until about 2 tablespoons of batter are left; keep this to seal pancakes later.

To fill, turn each pancake cooked side up. Place a small amount of cooled filling in the center of the pancake. Fold all sides in (like an envelope) and seal the edges with a small amount of leftover batter. Turn the pancakes sealed side down to set.

In a deep frying pan, heat corn oil to a depth of 6 inches until it is very hot. (To test if the oil is at the correct heat, drop in a thin slice of raw potato. If it sinks to the bottom and rises immediately, the oil is ready.) Fry the egg rolls, 2 or 3 at a time, until they are light brown and crisp. The egg rolls tend to float, so turn each once.

The egg rolls can be prepared ahead to the stage before frying. However, it is best to leave them at room temperature for about a half hour so that they do not chill the hot oil. *Makes 10 egg rolls.*

Olé for Imports from Argentina

"Since we never prayed in our small town in Argentina, where we were the only Jews, the only connection I had with Judaism was through gefüllte fish and matzah ball soup," commented Ilana Perelstein Ben Ami, a new immigrant from South America. Although Argentina has the fourth largest Jewish population in the world, Ilana, like many other Diaspora Jews, was so assimilated into the Argentinian way of life that she knew more about Christianity than Judaism. On a visit to Israel she began to understand who the Israelis really were — a new breed of "un-Jewish" Jews — and she returned to Argentina enchanted with the spirit of the new state. In 1967 she left her luxurious life there, determined to begin anew in the exciting young country.

Ilana arrived in Israel not knowing a word of Hebrew and spent her

CLADPOLE BOOKS

Miles Costello

38 Hampers Green, Petworth, West Sussex GU28 9NW England

Tel: 01798 343227

milescostello@hampersgreen.fsnet.co.uk

C
B

first six months in an *ulpan*. Until recently when she married Oved Ben Ami, the Mayor of Natanya, she held an interesting job at the Ministry of Tourism, where her fluency in Spanish was an asset to her. Immediately after the 1973 Japanese terrorist attack at Lod Airport, Ilana was called upon to assist wounded Puerto Ricans; she was able to comfort them in their native tongue and ease the communication problems in this emergency situation.

Usually Ilana's job involved more cheerful encounters, and she still enjoys entertaining visitors to Israel in her own home. When Clement Freud, grandson of Sigmund Freud and the "Craig Claiborne of England," was in Jerusalem on a visit, Ilana offered him the use of her kitchen. After touring one of the open-air markets, where he discovered many "marvelous ingredients," Mr. Freud was eager to cook a meal — something he could not do in his hotel. At Ilana's home he turned out a tasty fish stew and an elaborate meat and eggplant dish; unfortunately he did not leave the recipes behind and since "Fish à la Freud" is not exactly an Argentinian dish anyway, Ilana shared with us instead three of her favorite native recipes, Carbonada Criolla, Pastel de Papa and Humita, a corn casserole which can be found under Vegetables and Salads on page 170.

CARBONADA CRIOLLA (BEEF STEW WITH VEGETABLES AND FRUIT)

Well worth the effort.

½ cup olive oil
1 large onion, chopped coarsely
4 garlic cloves, mashed
2 pounds stewing or goulash meat, cut in chunks
1 pound tomatoes, peeled and chopped coarsely
1 bay leaf
2 tablespoons chopped fresh parsley
1 teaspoon oregano
1 teaspoon paprika
Salt and pepper to taste
1 carrot

1 beef bouillon cube, dissolved in 3 cups boiling water
2 sweet potatoes, peeled, chopped coarsely
2 white potatoes, peeled, chopped coarsely
6 dried apricots
1 can kernel corn
1 small can or 1 package frozen green peas
1 cup uncooked rice
6 dried prunes
1 small can peach halves, drained
1 large yellow squash

In a large heavy saucepan, sauté the onion and garlic in oil. Add the beef, stir, and cook it until it is brown on all sides. Add the tomatoes, bay leaf, parsley, oregano and paprika. Season with salt and pepper.

Cover and simmer 10 minutes. Add the carrot, bouillon and potatoes, simmering for 15 minutes more. Add the apricots and corn to the peas and rice. Simmer for 15 more minutes. Add the prunes, simmer 5 minutes and just before serving, add the peach halves to heat.

Preheat oven to 400°.

Meanwhile, cut the squash in half, remove the seeds, sprinkle it with salt, dot with butter and sprinkle it with a little water to keep it from drying out. Bake it until it is tender. Place it in a large serving dish and pour the prepared Carbonada over and around it.

Cut the leaves of the squash into flowers with which to decorate the serving plate. *Serves 6–8.*

PASTEL DE PAPA (POTATO MEAT PIE)

8 medium-size potatoes	1½ teaspoons paprika
1 tomato, chopped	Salt and pepper to taste
2 large onions, chopped	4 hard-boiled eggs, chopped
1 green pepper, chopped	1 cup raisins
2 pounds ground beef	1½ cups pitted green olives,
Cooking oil	halved
½ cup warm milk	1 teaspoon butter
4 tablespoons butter	

Preheat oven to 400°.

Peel and boil the potatoes, covered, for about 20 minutes. Meanwhile, sauté the tomatoes, onions, green pepper and beef in hot oil until the meat is brown. Mash the potatoes and add the warm milk, butter and salt. Beat the potatoes until they are creamy. Remove the vegetable and beef mixture from the heat and stir in the paprika, salt and pepper. Stir in the eggs, raisins and olives; blend well. Place the meat mixture in an oven-proof casserole and cover it with mashed potatoes, sprinkle with additional paprika and dot with butter. Bake, uncovered, for about 20 minutes, until the crust is golden. *Serves 8.*

The Angel Baker's Wife Deserves a Halo

Since we come from the United States, we think we are very up-to-date on ways to save time in cooking. Or that is what we thought until we visited Eva Angel in her kitchen. Beside her large refrigerator stands an even larger freezer, and to look inside truly boggles the mind. The shelves are laden with neat packages of just everything: out-of-season fruits and vegetables cooked and wrapped in portions all ready to heat, chopped and measured fresh ingredients ready to be added to a dish for instant entertaining, and cookie and cake dough ready for the oven. Eva has itemized and recorded all the food stored in the treasure chest, and in this way she saves time and has the luxury of being able to eat almost anything at any time. During our visit, while the coffee bubbled on the stove Eva whipped a package out of her freezer, heated some cooking oil and dropped the contents into it. In five minutes we were sitting in the living room eating hot, homemade *beignets* — triangles of dough wrapped around cheese and fried crisp and golden.

Over coffee we commented on the ancient Syrian marriage contract framed on the Angels' wall. Eva told us that it had belonged to her grandparents and showed us that after her grandfather had written blessings for long life and a happy marriage he had signed a statement that he "valued" his wife at £100,500, "so much money that he couldn't possibly afford to divorce her." In the Angel family cooking tradition, the wife certainly earned her keep.

Avraham Angel runs Israel's largest bread bakery, a heritage from his grandfather, who, when he was in the grain business, acquired a flour mill in lieu of money as payment from a debtor. Their son, carrying on the family interests, studied at the only university in the world which gives a degree in baking. He took us on a tour of the factory late one Thursday evening to see how Challah is made for the Sabbath. Six-story-high mixing machines and block-long ovens where thousands of loaves were slowly reaching golden perfection held us in awe. But as competent as the Angel males may be at bread making, they stay clear of cooking at home, where Eva is chief cook, and these recipes show why.

KTSITSOT (SUPERIOR MEATBALLS)

"Ktsitsot" means "chopped" in Hebrew.

2 pounds ground beef	1 tablespoon cooking oil
2 potatoes, peeled, boiled and mashed	3 eggs, slightly beaten
	Breadcrumbs
1 zucchini, finely grated	2 cups warmed beef bouillon
2 stalks celery, finely chopped	Oil or margarine
2 tablespoons flour	

Mix all the above ingredients except the beaten egg, the breadcrumbs and the bouillon. Form medium-sized meatballs and roll each in breadcrumbs. Dip them in the beaten egg and fry them in the heated cooking oil or margarine, turning them to brown on all sides. When they are browned, pour off the remaining oil and pour the bouillon over the meatballs. Cover tightly and simmer over low heat for 10 to 15 minutes.

These juicy, tasty meatballs are good with noodles, rice or crusty bread. *Makes approximately 36, serving 4–6.*

STUFFED ONIONS SUPREME

4 large well-shaped onions	2 beef bouillon cubes
1 cup uncooked rice	Juice of ½ lemon
½ pound ground meat, uncooked	1 cup boiling water
1 teaspoon cooking oil	1 tablespoon grenadine (optional)
1½ teaspoons allspice	

Peel off the papery outer layers of the onion skin. Slice off the ends. With a sharp knife, slice from the top to the bottom through the center of each onion. In kettle of boiling water cook the onions until just soft. Drain them immediately and let them cool. Mix the rice, meat and allspice with oil, adding more oil if needed to hold the mixture together. The onions will now be ready to separate into individual layers. Each layer of the onion is stuffed. Place a large spoonful of the meat mixture in each layer and roll. Place the layers, side by side, rolled side down, in a flat heat-proof dish. Blend the bouillon cubes, lemon juice and boiling water until the cubes are melted. Pour the mixture over the stuffed onions and sprinkle with grenadine if desired. Cook, covered, over a medium heat for one hour.

Needs only a green salad to make a meal. *Serves 4.*

Eleventh-Century Food at a Twentieth-Century Institute

On a hilltop midway between the ancient cities of Jerusalem and Bethlehem, overlooking the most meaningful sites of Christendom, sits the ultramodern Ecumenical Institute for Advanced Theological Studies. It is here that theologians of all Christian faiths are able to gather for study and meditation.

Following his visit to Jerusalem in 1964, Pope Paul VI decided that the time had come to reunite the two Catholic Churches, which had been separated in the tenth century when the Orthodox Church established its head in Constantinople. Just ten years after this historic visit, the institute, under the leadership of the Reverend Theodore M. Hesburgh, C.S.G., President of Notre Dame University, has already become a leading institution in the city of Jerusalem and the world at large.

Each year as many as fifty scholars study at the institute, with its large library, simple chapel and quiet contemplative atmosphere. One of the institute's aims is to further theological study along lines not found in the usual academic setting of one library or another but rather stimulated by a living environment speaking on all sides of the roots of Christianity and presenting the scholar with a gamut of human situations both religious and secular. Once a year Orthodox, Protestant and Roman Catholic members of the Academic Council meet together in Jerusalem, which Father Hesburgh fondly calls the "theological umbilical cord of the world."

According to Father Hesburgh, to whom we talked during his annual visit to the institute, Jerusalem is not only the "holy city of the three major religions and the center of Christian mysteries, it is also a place of affluent and poor, where East meets West, and old and new merge together. In a sense," he says, "I feel that the institute is the first attempt to get Christianity back to where it began. With the roots of unity which we hope to recreate here, we can reach out to a greater unity for peace everywhere.

"Here three times a day we eat together from the land around us, we look out at Bethlehem, and our conversation is so stimulating that I even forget about what I am eating," commented Father Hesburgh laughingly, as we drank our Turkish coffee after a delicious lunch in the cedar dining room with its stone walls covered in Oriental tapestries.

After lunch, when we told Father Hesburgh about our cookbook, he laughed and said, "You have the wrong guy! I am more interested in ideas than in food. I can recognize bad food, but frankly I have already forgotten what I just ate. But I do enjoy our communal meals."

"Arabs really enjoy a good meal," said Dr. Penelope Johnstone, who was sitting at our table. She is a Catholic scholar from Oxford University, doing research for her book on Arabic medicine. Penelope then showed us a copy of a manuscript written around the year 1000 which she is using for her study. Translating classical Arabic into English, she said, "Al-Zahrawi, a famous surgeon in eleventh-century Moslem Spain, said, 'Religion and medicine are closely related' and 'Possession of a healthy body is necessary for the performance of religious duties.' Here's a recipe which Al-Zahrawi says both nourishes and strengthens."

Cooked today, 974 years later, it is still delicious and is now a new "nourishment" at the twentieth-century Ecumenical Institute.

NOURISHING DISH (LAMB AND BARLEY STEW WITH VEGETABLES)

3 tablespoons cooking oil
2 onions coarsely chopped
2½ pounds stewing lamb, cut in small pieces
3 cloves garlic, minced
2 teaspoons cider vinegar
2 stalks celery with leaves, finely chopped
1 small bunch fresh mint, coarsely chopped
2 tomatoes, peeled and chopped

4 cups boiling water
1 pound zucchini, cut in ¼-inch rounds
Pinch of saffron
1 cup barley
5 tablespoons chopped fresh dill
½ teaspoon salt
Pepper to taste
2 eggs
Juice of 1 lemon

In a heavy pot heat the oil and sauté the onions until transparent. Add the meat and garlic and brown. Sprinkle with the vinegar. Then tie up the celery and mint in a square of cheesecloth and add it, with the tomatoes and water, to the meat. Cover and simmer 1½ hours. Remove the celery and mint and add the zucchini, saffron, barley, dill, salt and pepper. Cover and cook one half hour. In a small bowl beat together the eggs and lemon juice. Stir in a small amount of the juice from the pot and add this mixture to the large pot, stirring constantly to make sure the liquid does not boil. Stir until the stew thickens, and then serve.
Serve in large soup bowls. *Serves 6.*

Dreaming of Couscous While in Prison

"He couldn't hurt a flea," we thought as "André Bébert" sat down to talk with us. This mild-mannered man with baby-blue eyes looked as though he could never have been involved in underground activity! Yet he was and still is; he travels abroad under an alias, with a false passport, since he is a member of Israel's Intelligence and poses as a lab technician.

"I was twenty years old during World War II and living with my family in Tunis, our home for many generations. All my life I considered myself a Tunisian and a Frenchman. I attended French schools, as did other Europeans living in Tunis, until I was told that I could not fight in the French army under the Vichy régime nor could I pursue my studies at a French university. It was then that I learned I was a Jew. When I started reading the underground Zionist newspaper, *Gazette d'Israël*, I further understood what it was to be a Jew in the 1940's and became deeply involved in Zionist activities."

Eager to leave for Palestine, André arranged a fictitious marriage with a young girl who had been given an entry visa by the British, and together they entered the country by train from Cairo in 1945.

André knew where he wanted to go — straight to the Jerusalem head-quarters of the Hagana (the major Jewish underground armed forces during the Mandate). He worked to aid the illegal entry of European Jewish refugees. By 1947 André was traveling throughout Europe helping to purchase arms in preparation for the new state in 1948.

It was not long before the British learned of André's activities and he was imprisoned in a jail inside the Old City. André lived in appalling conditions, but he drank British tea instead of water with his bread. All prisoners dream of good meals and André recalls dreaming of the traditional Couscous, a meat and chicken stew with a semolina-like rice base, which he had loved to eat as a child in Tunis.

Meanwhile, another member of the underground, a young lady named Shoshanna, was in prison in Bethlehem for her part in illegal immigration. Shortly after being released from prison at the end of the Mandate in 1948, these two young idealists met as they rode with the food convoys up the treacherous road from Tel Aviv to the besieged city of Jerusalem. As their truck climbed the mountain road, André and Shoshanna each kept one eye out for terrorists and the other on each other. As André told her of his life, he mentioned how he missed only one thing from Tunisia — Couscous. Shoshanna surprised him by replying that she had learned how to make this special dish. The love story continued with marriage. Today the Bébert household has become a center for Israelis from Tunisia who are homesick for this delicious, but difficult to prepare, specialty. Even native-born Tunisians admit that Shoshanna has become an expert in cooking this Tunisian fare, traditionally prepared in a special *couscoussière*. To them, a dinner invitation to André and Shoshanna's means a nostalgic evening and a memorable meal.

TUNISIAN COUSCOUS

Please read the recipe through before starting.

Chicken and Meat Stew
Cooking oil
1 large onion, peeled and cut in
 half
2 pounds stewing or goulash beef
 (not chopped)
1 large tomato, cut in half
1 kohlrabi, cut in half (optional)
1 turnip, cut in half (optional)
3 stalks celery, cut in half
3 zucchini, cut into halves
2 tablespoons tomato paste
3 carrots, cut in half
1/2 teaspoon pepper
1 1/2 teaspoons salt
1/2 medium cabbage cut in
 quarters
3 whole potatoes
1/2 chicken cut in pieces

Couscous
1 two-pound package prepared
 couscous

Meatballs
1 1/2 onions, grated finely
10 stalks parsley, chopped finely
1 tablespoon salt
6 slices dry white or rye bread
1/2 pound chopped beef
2 eggs
Pinch of saffron
Pinch of pepper
3 potatoes
1 can artichoke hearts

1 tomato
1 green pepper
Vegetable oil
Flour for dredging
14 tablespoons tomato paste

Chick-Peas
2 cans chick-peas, drained
1 teaspoon cumin
1/2 teaspoon salt

Marmouna (Spicy Salad)
1 zucchini, sliced thin
2 tablespoons oil
2 garlic cloves, cut in half
1 hot pepper, cut in strips
2 green peppers, sliced thickly
3 tomatoes, quartered
1 teaspoon salt
1/4 teaspoon saffron

Eggplant Salad
1 eggplant
Juice of 1/2 lemon
1 tablespoon hot pepper sauce
1 teaspoon salt
1 teaspoon oil

Additional Salads
1 tomato
1 cucumber
3 carrots
Pepper sauce to taste
5 hard-boiled eggs

Stew: Heat some cooking oil in a large "couscoussière" or deep soup kettle and add all the stew ingredients in the order given, except for the potatoes and chicken, stirring and cooking for a few minutes. Add warm water to cover and cook covered over low heat for 2 hours until the meat is tender. Add the potatoes and chicken and cook covered another half hour.

Couscous: Prepare the couscous according to the directions on the package, preferably steaming it in a sieve placed over the stew or in the top part of the couscoussière during the last half hour of cooking.

Meatballs: Combine the onion and parsley with the salt and set them aside to bring out the juices. Cover the bread with water and set it aside for 15 minutes. Squeeze out water from the bread. Add the water to the onion-parsley mixture and drain in strainer, squeezing out water with your hands. Combine the bread with the meat and add the onion-parsley mixture. Stir in 1 beaten egg, half the tomato paste, the saffron and the pepper. Mix well with your hands and then shape into meatballs each the size of an egg. Peel and slice the potatoes thin, halve the artichoke hearts; quarter the tomatoes, removing the seeds, and remove the seeds from the peppers and then cut the peppers into silver-dollar-size pieces. (The size is important.)

Heat oil in a frying pan about one inch deep. Prepare flour for dredging and mix 1 egg with 1 tablespoon tomato paste. Take each meatball and press into its sides either 2 potato slices, 2 artichoke hearts, 2 green peppers, or a piece of tomato. Dip the meatballs into the flour and then into the egg and tomato mixture. Then sauté them until they are very brown on all sides. After the meatballs are cooked, place them in a deep soup kettle or couscoussière; add ½ cup of the remaining oil from frying, the remaining tomato paste with enough water to cover the meatballs. Cover and let them cook until the mixture boils. Reduce the heat and cook one hour over low heat. Turn off the heat and keep covered until serving time.

Add the chick-peas, cumin and salt to the stew after the vegetables and meat have been taken out for serving.

Salads: The accompanying salads should be prepared the night before.

To prepare the Marmouna, sauté the zucchini in oil until brown. Add the remaining ingredients with a little water and cook, covered, over low heat for one hour. Uncover and cook until the water evaporates.

Boil the eggplant in water until soft. Peel and cut it in half. Mash the eggplant in its own juice. Add lemon juice and the remaining ingredients.

Chop the tomato and cucumber and mix them together. Place them on a dish.

Peel and boil the carrots until soft. Slice them in rounds and mix them with the same quantities and types of seasoning used for the eggplant salad. Use pepper sauce to taste.

Cut the hard-boiled eggs in half and place them on a separate dish to serve as another accompanying salad.

To Serve: Place the Couscous in a large serving dish with the chicken and meat on a separate platter surrounded by the vegetables. Place the soup and the chick-peas in another bowl as a sauce for the meat and Couscous.

This dish is an event and should be enjoyed as such. Together or in its separate parts, Couscous is a real treat. *Serves 10–12.*

And Also . . .

ARMENIAN SHISH KEBAB (LAMB BROILED ON SKEWERS)

Sis means skewer in Turkish. This dish, served at the Armenian Patriarchate, is one of Moshe Dayan's favorites. See Page 69.

Marinade
¼ cup salad oil
¼ cup lemon or lime juice
¼ cup wine vinegar
2 teaspoons salt
¼ teaspoon freshly ground
 pepper
1 clove garlic, mashed
1 medium-size onion, sliced thin

Kebabs
2 pounds lamb cut in 1-inch cubes
½ pound onions, each cut in thick
 chunks
½ pound bacon slices cut in pieces
 large enough to thread on skewers, but not too large, as they
 will not cook as quickly as the
 meat (optional)
½ pound mushrooms — large
 enough to thread on skewers
Melted butter

Mix the marinade ingredients together, place them in a large glass bowl.
Add the meat and let it stand, covered, overnight.

When ready to barbecue or broil, dip the skewers in oil or run them
through a piece of meat fat. Alternate pieces of meat, onion and bacon.
Leave space on the skewers to add a few mushrooms, which have been
brushed with butter, during the last few minutes of cooking. Excellent
when grilled over a charcoal fire. *Serves 4–6.*

MOSCOW BEEF STROGANOFF

2 pounds porterhouse, tenderloin
 tip or fillet steak
4 tablespoons margarine
1 onion, minced
1 clove garlic, minced
½ pound fresh mushrooms, sliced

1 teaspoon salt
¾ cup beef broth
¼ cup sour cream
1 teaspoon mustard
Fresh dill or parsley for garnish

Cut the steak into narrow strips about 2 inches long. Melt 2 tablespoons
of the margarine, add the onion and cook until golden. Add the meat
and cook, stirring occasionally, until the meat is brown on all sides and
tender; about 5 to 7 minutes. Set aside. Melt 2 more tablespoons of the
margarine, add the garlic. Stir and cook a few minutes. Add the mush-

rooms, cook until lightly browned: about 5 minutes. Stir in the salt. Add the beef to the mushroom mixture with beef broth and stir. Gently mix in the sour cream and mustard. Stir just to heat the sour cream. Garnish with dill or parsley.

Serve with broad noodles. *Serves 6.*

Jerusalem Pasta
and Rice

The Bukharans —
Jerusalem's First "City Planners"

In 1891 Jerusalem's first town planners and city engineers arrived to construct an entire quarter for Jewish immigrants from Bokhara in Central Asia, just north of Iran and Afghanistan, now part of the Soviet Union. This was the Bukharan Quarter, adjacent to Mea Shearim outside the Old City, and the first and only area composed of straight, wide streets and lavish stone houses. Until the Bukharans came to Jerusalem, many of the city's immigrants had been observant Jews of very little means who came to Jerusalem to fulfill their lifelong dream — to die and be buried on the Mount of Olives Cemetery in the Holy City. But the Bukharans, most of them wealthy merchants, were different; they came to visit Jerusalem on pilgrimages and then decided to establish a foothold for their families by building homes here. With their ornate jewelry and richly embroidered clothing they bore a certain inborn dignity in the then rather poor city of Jerusalem. Their pink and green robes, round embroidered caps and splendid jewels provided a rich contrast to their much duller surroundings. With the passing of time and fortunes after the Russian Revolution in 1917, the Bukharan Quarter lost much of its wealth, but even though the large houses have now been divided into small apartments and family riches are no longer what they were, the word "Bukharan" still carries an aura of respect, stateliness and largesse.

When we visited Haim Simchayoff, head of the Bukharan community in Jerusalem, he and his wife Sara showed us the beautifully made traditional garments and old family jewelry, which the Simchayoffs still wear for holidays and the Sabbath. Rather a large man himself, Haim was eating an enormous portion of meat when we first came into their home in one of the original buildings. "Milk products are not filling enough for Bukharan men," said he. "We need lots of meat to keep us going. Why do you think streets in the quarter are so wide? If three Bukharans are walking side by side, no one else can get by. Our engineers knew how to build for us!"

Perhaps all Bukharans are not as hearty eaters as Haim, but the rice Pilaf served to us by his wife helped us understand why he enjoys eating so much.

MINTED PILAF

6 tablespoons margarine
1 large onion, chopped coarsely
2 garlic cloves, crushed
½ teaspoon ground ginger
1 teaspoon ground cloves
1 teaspoon ground cardamom
1 teaspoon cinnamon
1½ cups raw rice (rinsed and strained)
⅛ teaspoon saffron
¾ cup fresh mint leaves, chopped fine
¾ cup fresh coriander leaves
(optional)
1 large tomato, peeled and sliced
¾ cup green peas (fresh preferred, but frozen will do)
3 carrots chopped fine
1 cup light-colored raisins
2 tablespoons lemon juice
3 cups water
½ teaspoon salt
1 cup pine or cashew nuts, lightly toasted or deep-fried
Onion strips or rings

In a large saucepan, heat the margarine and sauté the onion until golden. Stir in the garlic, ginger, cloves, cardamom, cinnamon and rice. Sauté for several minutes. Add the saffron, mint, coriander if desired, tomato slices, peas, carrots and raisins. Stir to mix the ingredients. Add the water, lemon juice and salt. Bring to a boil, reduce the heat. Cover tightly and cook over low heat until all liquid is absorbed — about 20 minutes. Turn off the heat, fluff with a fork when done, replace the cover and let it stand for 5 minutes.

Heap it on a large serving platter and garnish with nuts or onion pieces. *Serves 6.*

Pilaf for a Persian Policeman

A Jew living in New York is a Jew. A Jew living in Iran is a Jew. It is only in Israel that a Persian Jew becomes a Persian. Although police officer Joseph Gabai left Persia illegally as a draft evader thirty-eight years ago to work for the Hagana and has been a ranking member of the Israel police force since its inception in 1948, he is still considered "the Persian." When his chief of police was recently invited to visit Iran, the by now Major Gabai, accompanied by his sabra wife, spent two weeks being officially wined and dined throughout Iran with the official delegation of the Israel police force. "The trip was like a dream," exclaimed Esther Gabai with a happy sparkle in her eyes, "but the fruit wasn't as good as it is in Jerusalem."

First, during the British Mandate as a patrolman in the Jewish Quarter of the Old City and then from 1948 to 1967 as a guard at the Mandelbaum Gate — the only entrance between the two parts of the divided city at that time — Joseph was one of the few Israelis to come in constant contact with East Jerusalemites. At his post at the gate he escorted official visitors and clerics to the Jordanian policeman awaiting on the other side — usually a former colleague or an old friend.

Joseph, like more than 80 percent of Jerusalem's eight-hundred-member police force consisting of Jews and Arabs (including women), speaks perfect Hebrew and Arabic. Until 1948 the Gabais lived in a mixed community near the Mandelbaum Gate, in the American Colony, where Esther, the most renowned cook of all the policemen's wives in the city, shared recipes with her Jewish and Arab neighbors. Now living nearby in the Bukharan Quarter, she also exchanges cooking ideas through the constantly open windows with new immigrants from Persia who have come to live near their old friend Joseph Gabai. Until today, however, no one can rival Esther's Pilaf recipe.

PERSIAN PILAF

1 cup rice	1 teaspoon salt
1 large onion	Margarine
2 large or 4 small carrots	Cooking oil
1 large potato	2 teaspoons saffron
2¼ cups water	½ cup raisins

Place the rice in a bowl and cover it with water (not the 2¼ cups) to soak. Chop the onion coarsely, then clean the carrots and chop them into small pieces. Peel and slice the potato into thick crosswise circles. Drain the rice in a colander and rinse it with cold water. Place the rice and 2¼ cups of water in a pot, sprinkle with salt and quickly bring to a boil. (In order not to waste pots, cook the rice in the same pot you will use later — a fairly large straight-sided pot with a lid, about 9 inches in diameter.) Cover it and cook over medium heat (rice should be just boiling) for 10 minutes.

Meanwhile, in a small pan, cook the onions in margarine until just tender. Set them aside. Remove the rice to a colander and rinse it lightly with cool water. Heat enough oil to cover the bottom of the pot to a depth of about ½ inch, stir in the saffron and place the potato slices in a single layer to cover the surface. Put the rice on top; do not stir it. Cover the pot with a dish towel, place the lid on top and cook over low heat 20 minutes until the rice is fluffy and the grains are separated. While the rice is cooking, add the carrots and raisins to the onions and cook, covered, over low heat until tender, about 15 minutes, adding a small amount of water occasionally if the mixture sticks.

When the rice is done, turn it out onto a serving plate. Place the potato slices, which will be a deep yellow color, around the edge, colored sides up, with the carrot mixture on top of the rice. *Serves 4–6.*

Dome of the Rock's Keeper of the Keys

Family traditions die hard in the Middle East. For centuries the keys to city gates and holy sites have been passed from father to son in a tradition of dignity and prestige. Two Moslem families, for example, have maintained possession of the keys to the Church of the Holy Sepulchre since the era of Saladin in the twelfth century. And in the fifteenth century the Sephardic Jewish community took possession of the keys to the six open city gates when several sultans of Constantinople successively died; each time a new sultan was installed, the keys were anointed with a secret preparation of oil and spices in a Sephardic religious service and then returned to the Turkish civil authorities. Today, the seven gates to the Old City are never locked, but religious shrines still have keepers of the keys.

Mustafa Khalil Ansari, Chief Curator of the Dome of the Rock, inherited the keys to this seventh-century shrine from a line of family members dating back to the beginning of Islam. Mustafa, a venerable gentleman who wears a dark red tarbush (fez) with a tassel, always welcomed our visits to his tiny green wooden office on the steps in front of the Dome of the Rock with warm hospitality. One day he told us that one of his ancestors had accompanied Mohammed on his journey to Mecca and was present when the father of Islam ascended to heaven from the rock over which the Dome of the Rock now stands. From then

Midday prayer outside the El Aksa Mosque

on, members of Mustafa's family have guarded the keys. Mustafa's collection of memorabilia always intrigued us. He proudly displayed his photo albums of the kings, presidents and prime ministers who have visited the Dome of the Rock since he has been its guardian. "My good friend King Hussein gave me this watch, which has his name on it," he said between puffs on his water pipe. Interestingly enough, Mustafa's father-in-law is the guardian of the neighboring El Aksa Mosque, the site of the 1968 fire set by the Australian Michael Rohan, and the major mosque for prayer on the Haram es Sharif.

One day after Mustafa had locked the Dome of the Rock at the end of evening prayers, he invited us to his home. We chatted with his son Khalil, who is studying city planning in London and is married to a French girl from Paris. Khalil and his wife were visiting the Ansaris during a semester break, and it was interesting to hear his answer to our question about the family tradition of handing the keys to the mosque from father to son. "It is a source of conflict," Khalil answered, not looking at his father, and that was all he would say. Mrs. Ansari prepared for us Maklouba, an upside-down eggplant-lamb-rice casserole which is a traditional Jerusalem Arab dish.

MAKLOUBA (UPSIDE-DOWN EGGPLANT-LAMB-RICE CASSEROLE)

There are many versions of Maklouba ("upside-down"), and each Jerusalem Arab housewife has her specialty. Best served with a mixed green salad.

1 cup rice	¾ teaspoon nutmeg
1 tablespoon salt	½ teaspoon allspice
1½ pounds lamb or beef (one third of the meat should be slightly fatty), cut into ½-inch to 1-inch pieces	Pinch of paprika
	Pepper to taste
	1½ cups water
	1 large eggplant
2 large onions, chopped small	Pinch of saffron
¼ cup pine nuts, slivered almonds or chopped walnuts	½ to 1 cup beef stock
	Cooking oil

Rinse the rice, place it in a bowl, cover it with hot water and salt and let stand for one half hour. (This ensures non-sticky rice.)

Meanwhile, sauté the meat, onions and nuts in the cooking oil until the meat is browned on all sides. Stir in the nutmeg, allspice, paprika and black pepper. Add the water, cover the mixture and simmer until it is tender. (Reserve the meat liquid.) Peel and slice the eggplant, then sauté the slices in cooking oil until they are tender; drain them on paper towels. Lightly sprinkle the eggplant with salt. Drain the rice and stir in the saffron. In a heavy saucepan with sloping sides arrange the meat, then the eggplant slices and finally the rice. Pour the reserved meat liquid into a 2-cup measuring cup and add enough beef stock to make 1½ cups of liquid. Pour this carefully over the rice. Cover tightly and cook over medium heat for 8 minutes; reduce the heat and simmer for a half hour.

To unmold the Maklouba, wet a dishtowel with cold water, wring it out and place it flat on a counter top. Set the saucepan on top, then scrape around the inside edge with a long knife. Invert a serving plate on top and turn out the contents. The Maklouba will remain in place until you cut into it to serve.

This is best served with a mixed green salad. *Serves 6–8.*

VARIATIONS ON MAKLOUBA

Maklouba with Carrots

6 to 8 carrots   3 chopped onions

Peel and slice the carrots into 1-inch-thick slices. Instead of adding the onions to the meat, brown the carrot slices and onions in the cooking oil until the onions are golden and the carrots just tender. Substituting the carrot layer for the eggplant layer, proceed as above.

Maklouba with Cauliflower

1 medium cauliflower   Pinch of salt
½ teaspoon cumin

Soak the cauliflower, cut off the stem and the leaves and separate the flowerets. Place it in a saucepan, cover it with water, and add the cumin and salt. Bring the water to a boil and cook for 5 minutes. Drain the flowerets, slice and brown them in cooking oil. Substituting the cauliflower for the eggplant layer, proceed as above. *Serves 6–8.*

SAYADIAH (FISH WITH NUTS AND RICE)

1 cup rice   Cooking oil
1 tablespoon salt   Salt and pepper to taste
1 pound fish fillets (frozen or   2 or 3 onions, chopped small
   fresh)   ½ cup pine nuts (pignolias) or

| chopped almonds | 1 teaspoon cumin |
| 6 carrots | 1 cup boiling water |

Rinse the rice, place it in a bowl, cover it with hot water and salt, and let it stand for a half hour. (This ensures non-sticky rice.)

If they are frozen, thaw the fish fillets just enough to break them apart. Brown the fish lightly in oil and season them with the salt and pepper. In another pan sauté the onions and nuts in oil until the onions are soft. Peel the carrots, slicing them lengthwise and then into long slivers. Cook them in a small amount of salted boiling water until barely tender. Drain the rice and stir in the cumin. In a heavy saucepan with sloping sides arrange a layer of onions and nuts, then the fish, and finally the rice. Pour the boiling water carefully over the rice, top with the carrots and sprinkle lightly with salt. Cover the saucepan tightly and cook over medium heat for 5 minutes; reduce the heat and simmer for 25 minutes. To unmold, follow the directions for Maklouba. This is a fish version of Maklouba. Serve with a mixed green salad. *Serves 4–6.*

Indians in Jerusalem – The "Real Thing" in Curry

Jews have lived in India for nearly two thousand years. The two ancient cultures flourished simultaneously and in perfect harmony. Indian Jews have always called themselves "Benai Israel" (the Sons of Israel), and like Jews all over the world, many of them felt drawn to live in the city of Jerusalem.

Dvora and Isaac Joseph came to Israel from Bombay in 1950, two years after the State of Israel was born. They were the only married couple in a group of seventy-five young Indian immigrants, and they needed all the idealism they could summon up to overcome the problems they encountered in the new, undeveloped, desert country.

In Beersheva, where they settled, the only available homes were tents. Jobs were difficult to find, food was scarce, and there was only one place to bathe in the entire settlement. The shy and modest Indian women would all go to the one public bath together while the men "kept guard" outside — safety in numbers! Most painful to Isaac and Dvora, who had come to live in Israel for the sake of their children, was the complete lack of facilities for Jewish education. After two years of struggling without success, they felt forced to return to India.

"But we just couldn't stay away," Isaac remembers. "We felt an irresistible desire to live in the land of Israel, and a few years later, with three more children and my parents, we came back to try again."

Life was also hard the second time around, but, they say, "the love of Israel somehow pulled us through. The education of our children was our single-minded aim and while we often had only bread and tea for dinner, we did in fact accomplish our goal, and I say this with pride."

Today the Josephs live in Jerusalem, the city that symbolizes their lifelong love of Israel. They are a close-knit family of gentle soft-spoken people. When we visited them we were truly impressed with the respect the three generations showed for each other in this household.

Isaac's and Dvora's mothers sat together in the living room discussing recipes to give us. They spoke in their native Indian dialect, Marathi. Both wore saris and golden hoop earrings, and had their hair knotted in silvery gray buns.

The old saying goes that too many cooks spoil the broth. In the Joseph family, however, two cooks (and two mothers-in-law at that!) cook together and spoil their family — but certainly not the broth!

TAHYER (YOGHURT) CURRY WITH RICE

Eat this dish with gusto! It is *very* hot!

Curry
2 tablespoons cooking oil
6 or 7 mustard seeds
2 medium onions, sliced thick
1 teaspoon turmeric powder
½ bunch coriander leaves
3 green chilies (you may want
    more, depending on how hot
    you want the dish, but remem-
    ber to remove the seeds)
2 garlic cloves
1 one-inch piece ginger root
1 one-inch piece cinnamon
1 pound lamb, cut into ¾-inch
    cubes

1½ cups yoghurt
Salt to taste
1 teaspoon powdered aniseed

Rice
2 cups rice
3 whole cloves
1 one-inch piece cinnamon
2 whole cardamoms
3 whole black peppers
Cooking oil
Butter
2 cups water
Pinch of turmeric

Curry: Heat the oil with the mustard seeds. When the mustard seeds pop, the oil is hot enough to cook the onions. Brown the onions, grind together the turmeric, coriander, chilies, garlic, ginger, and cinnamon, and add to the onions. Cook until the aroma tickles your nose, then add the lamb, browning the meat on all sides. Stir in the yoghurt, salt and aniseed. Cover tightly and cook for 1¼ hours over low heat until the meat is tender.

Rice: Rinse the rice and drain it well. Mix together the cloves, cinnamon, cardamoms, and peppers. Crush them lightly, add to the rice and fry the mixture in cooking oil with a little butter until golden brown. Add the water and turmeric. Cover tightly and cook over low heat until the liquid is absorbed, about 20 minutes. If desired, remove any large pieces of spices which remain.

Serve the meat on the rice. *Serves 3–4.*

"The Street of Bad Cookery"— Good Franciscan Spaghetti

"Here we are in the Street of Bad Cookery," our guide, Father Godfrey, informed us, and we followed his brown-robed figure through the *souk*'s small streets in the vicinity of the Church of the Holy Sepulchre. "And, since you are writing a cookbook, you will be interested to know that the two markets leading off to the right are called the Butchers' Market and the Spice Market, and that the building over there is called the Inn of Olive Oil. Because of the combination of odors coming from the many eating houses on the street we entered from, the Crusaders named it Rue de Malcuisinat — 'Street of Bad Cookery.'" With that Father Godfrey left us to take part in the Friday processional along the traditional Via Dolorosa, also known as the Way of the Cross. Each Friday Franciscan priests and groups of the faithful walk along these lanes in the footsteps of Jesus from the First Station, where he was sentenced, to the Fourteenth, inside the Church of the Holy Sepulchre, where, it is believed by many, the Crucifixion took place and the body was placed. As they walk, with the leader carrying a huge wooden cross, they stop to pray at each Station and the priests explain the events of the last day in the life of Jesus.

Ever since St. Francis of Assisi came to visit Jerusalem in the year 1221, his followers have been the official custodians of the holy places belonging to the Roman Catholic Church. Today over eighty Franciscan priests, representing twenty-five nationalities, live in monasteries in and around Jerusalem. In the Church of the Holy Sepulchre, the priests' duties are to conduct daily services, provide tours for pilgrims and carry out small church repairs. In the Garden of Gethsemane they care for the same olive trees which are said to have shaded Jesus and his disciples when they met after the Last Supper. One group of Franciscan priests maintains an archaeological school on the Via Dolorosa and another teaches Arab children in the Terra Sancta, a convent and school in the Christian quarter of the Old City.

The Franciscan procession along the Via Dolorosa
is a Friday afternoon tradition for Catholics

Father Godfrey is American, but his bustling, brown-robed figure is a real Jerusalem sight — often preceded by his hearty laugh. His warm personality and his complete knowledge of the city (he is the author of two books on Jerusalem and the Holy Land) have led to his being the guide for important English-speaking visitors such as Ted and Joan Kennedy and the Sargent Shriver family. Like his friend Mayor Teddy Kollek, he is a keen archaeology fan; he is often to be seen showing off a recently found artifact which he plucks from the folds of his robe. "In summer this habit is very hot, but it certainly is handy for carrying things around," he says. We managed to sidetrack him long enough to be introduced to the cook at his hostel, whose Bethlehem-made pasta, according to Father Godfrey, tastes "just the way St. Francis would have liked it."

ST. FRANCIS SPAGHETTI SAUCE WITH CHICKEN LIVERS

Tomato Sauce
3 slices bacon, cut into small
   pieces (optional)
¼ cup olive oil
1 medium-size onion, chopped fine
1 garlic clove, minced
3 pounds peeled and coarsely
   chopped tomatoes or 2 large
   cans of peeled tomatoes
1 cup tomato juice
¼ cup fresh chopped parsley

1 bay leaf
Salt and pepper to taste
Parsley sprigs for garnish

Chicken Livers
1 pound chicken livers
2 tablespoons cooking oil or
   butter
Salt and pepper to taste
½ cup dry red wine

Sauce: Sauté the bacon in the olive oil, then add the onion, sautéing until it is golden. Stir in the garlic, tomatoes, tomato juice, parsley, bay leaf and salt and pepper. Cover and simmer, stirring occasionally for a half hour. (You may have to add more tomato juice.) If a smoother consistency is required, press the sauce through a sieve. Cook, uncovered, over a low heat for an additional half hour.

Livers: Wash the chicken livers, pat them dry and cut each in half, removing tissue. Sauté in oil or butter until browned. Season them with salt and pepper, add wine, and cook them over a low heat for 10 minutes.

After the tomato sauce is cooked, add the chicken livers and heat well. Serve over freshly prepared spaghetti or noodles. Sprinkle parsley on top. *Serves 4–6.*

The Simcha (Joy) of an Orthodox Woman

"A woman of valor who can find? For her price is far above rubies. The heart of her husband doth safely trust in her. And he has no lack of gain. She doeth him good and not evil all the days of her life." This is part of the Proverb recited at the Friday night service in Jewish households.

Many feminists today question the woman's role in Jewish tradition, as did Barbra Streisand when she first visited the Western Wall, where a partition separates the praying men and women. However, many religious women wear modest, long dresses, and hair-covering wigs

*An Orthodox Jewish woman in the ultrareligious quarter, Mea Shearim,
takes her Shabbat chicken to be ritually slaughtered*

(scheitels), and take pride in the special role they play in maintaining religious homes. While their husbands spend their days praying and studying the Talmud, wives, mothers and daughters — these proverbial "women of valor" — attend to the practical side of Orthodox Judaism. Sometimes this might also mean maintaining shops to support the family financially while the men study, but no matter what else they do, they must always prepare meals and clean the home.

Throughout the week, except on the Sabbath, the day of rest, Rachel Shapira devotes her energies to purchasing, cooking and cleaning foods according to *kashrut*, ancient Jewish dietary laws which treat food and the Sabbath in a very special way. Since food is an integral part of life, there are prayers recited for everything — over the wine, the first fruits of the year and the daily bread, and thanks at the end of the meal.

Because cooking is prohibited on the Sabbath, three meals for that day must be prepared in advance. And so from Thursday night until Friday at midday, Rachel is busy in the kitchen preparing Gefüllte fish, matzah balls, Cholent and the inevitable Kugel or noodle pudding which has become her trademark. From Friday at noon until *havdallah*, the ceremony signaling the end of the Sabbath and ushering in the new week, the house is filled with relatives who come to enjoy the day of rest. Even before Rachel lights the candles to begin the Sabbath, her husband and children sing praise for the good woman who is the center of the family. For Rachel, seeing her children, grandchildren and visitors enjoying her cooking and hospitality is her pride and joy — described by the Yiddish word *naches*. Rachel explained to us that she creates *simcha* (joy) for her family at the table — indeed the center of the home. Here the Shapiras eat and they pray. She feels she has a greater purpose in life than she would as a housewife who simply went to the grocery store and sought ready-made food. For food is not just physical sustenance, as Rachel puts it, it is also God's providence, and so each food is blessed accordingly.

Every Saturday morning after prayer in the "Presidential" synagogue, where Rachel's husband Eliahu works as a *shamas* (caretaker or deacon) and former Israeli President Zalman Shazar prayed, the participants attend a *kiddush*, a blessing said over wine. They also eat portions of Rachel's Jerusalem Kugel, which over the years became such a favorite of President Shazar's that he received a special one each week for his many guests.

JERUSALEM KUGEL (PEPPERY SPAGHETTI PUDDING)

This peppery noodle pudding is a specialty of Jerusalem's Chassidic Jews. This and the following Kugels are usually kept warm on a hot-plate or cooked in a very low-temperature oven from before dusk on Friday until Saturday at lunchtime.

1 package (8 ounces) thin
  spaghetti
½ cup cooking oil
½ cup sugar
Salt to taste

1½ teaspoons freshly ground
  black pepper
3 eggs, slightly beaten

Preheat oven to 350°.

Cook the spaghetti as the package directs, drain well and set aside in saucepan. In a medium-size saucepan, heat the oil and then add the sugar. Cook over a very low heat, stirring constantly, until the sugar is very dark, almost black, about 10 minutes. Immediately add the spaghetti and the salt, pepper and eggs. Stir well and test to see if it is peppery enough. If not, add more pepper. Place in a greased tube pan and bake uncovered until golden brown on top — at least 1½ hours. Remove from the oven, turn upside down on a serving plate, and un-mold. The Kugel will look like a cake with a golden crust. *Serves 4–6.*

LOKSHEN KUGEL (SWEET NOODLE PUDDING)

Lokshen Kugel means "Noodle Pudding" in Yiddish. This can be eaten as a main course in a *milchig* meal or as a dessert.

8 ounces broad noodles
1 cup pot cheese
½ cup raisins
1 egg, slightly beaten
½ teaspoon salt

1 teaspoon cinnamon
2 teaspoons sugar
¾ cup sour cream
¼ cup margarine or butter, melted

Preheat oven to 350°.

Cook the noodles as directed on the package; drain them well. Stir in the remaining ingredients and half the melted margarine. Place in a greased casserole and pour over the remaining melted margarine. Bake uncovered for 1 hour. *Serves 4–6.*

Vegetables and Salads

Kugels Continued

EGGPLANT KUGEL

1 large eggplant
4 tablespoons margarine or butter
1 onion, chopped small
1 green pepper, chopped small
Salt and pepper to taste

2 small eggs, slightly beaten
1/2 to 1 cup cracker crumbs or
    matzah meal
1/3 cup margarine or butter, melted
Paprika

Preheat oven to 350°.

Peel the eggplant and slice it. Cook it in simmering salted water to cover until it is tender — about 20 minutes. Drain and mash it. Meanwhile, sauté the onion and pepper pieces in margarine until they are tender but not crisp. Mix the eggplant with the slightly beaten eggs. Season to taste with salt and pepper. Add the onions and green pepper to the eggplant mixture. Blend in enough crumbs or meal to give the mixture a good consistency, and place in a greased casserole. Pour melted margarine or butter over the Kugel, sprinkle it with paprika and bake it in oven for 45 minutes, until lightly browned on top and crusty on the sides. *Serves 4–6.*

POTATO KUGEL

7 or 8 medium-size potatoes
1 large onion, chopped
1 tablespoon vegetable oil
Salt and pepper to taste

3 eggs, separated
1/4 cup grated Gruyère cheese
    (optional)

Peel and slice the potatoes. Cook them until tender in boiling water. Drain and mash them well.

Preheat the oven to 350°.

Sauté the onions in the vegetable oil until golden. Add the onions and beaten egg yolks to the potatoes; mix them well. Season with salt and pepper. Clean the beaters and beat the egg whites until stiff, then fold them into the mixture. Place it in a greased baking dish, sprinkle it with cheese if desired, and bake it uncovered about 30 minutes, until lightly browned on top. *Serves 4–6.*

SQUASH KUGEL

1 pound zucchini	¼ cup chopped walnuts
2 teaspoons sugar	3 tablespoons cooking oil or
¼ teaspoon salt	melted butter
1 teaspoon cinnamon	4 eggs, lightly beaten
½ cup raisins	1 small onion, chopped fine

Preheat oven to 400°.

Peel the zucchini, chop it fine or grate it on the medium holes of a grater. Drain it in a strainer. Add the sugar, salt, cinnamon, raisins, nuts and oil. Mix lightly. Sauté the onion until golden and add to the mixture with the eggs. Place in baking dish and bake for 25 minutes until lightly browned.

Good as a side dish with meat. *Serves 4–6.*

A Former Bauhaus Student's Artistic Vegetables

As Paul Klee's youngest pupil at the Bauhaus School in Weimar, Germany, Ruth Cidor studied weaving at the age of fourteen. Her exquisite wall hangings reflect her talent and background, and even her well-known cooking has a touch of the special Klee fantasy world. Ruth's weavings share wall space with her husband Hanan's extensive personal library, and, interestingly, his own pop-art collages. The one we liked best was his portrayal of Eve offering Adam a can of applesauce. Recently the two of them displayed their artistry at a local gallery.

The Cidors came to Israel in 1952 and went directly to an *ulpan* to learn Hebrew. Hanan, of Dutch parentage, had worked with the United

Nations Relief Program in Geneva and was thus a well-qualified candidate for the post of Israel's ambassador to the Netherlands, and not long after their arrival in Israel, Hanan was asked to fill this eminent position. They also Hebraicized Hanan's name from Hans Citroën to Hanan Cidor; it is a rule that everyone working for the Israeli Foreign Office abroad carries an Israeli name.

When the Cidors took up residence in The Hague, they were confronted with the complexities of large-scale, formal entertaining. They did not have the budget for expensive cookery, nor was Ruth an experienced cook. And so Ruth drew upon her artistic talents and impressed her guests with imaginative Israeli-Dutch combinations. Her "Légumes à la Carmel" is a multicolor vegetable combination served on a veritable mountain of rice formed in the shape of the historical Mt. Carmel in Haifa! And in an old Dutch cookbook she found a recipe for "Cotelettes Juives" — Jewish cutlets, a dish which pleased her Jewish Dutch guests.

Today Ruth cooks just for her family and friends. "I like to improvise cooking the way I improvise my weaving: I never make a menu. I look at what is in season at the supermarket and create from there. I hope my meal will at least be colorful." The following recipes are her family's favorites.

CAULIFLOWER GRATINÉ

1 whole cauliflower
2 tablespoons margarine
2 tablespoons flour
¾ cup light cream or milk
1 chicken or beef bouillon cube,
crumbled
Salt and pepper to taste
¾ cup cubed Gruyère or other
  yellow cheese

Wash the cauliflower, remove the green leaves but leave enough to use later as a base. Cook it in boiling salted water 20 minutes. Drain it well. Place the whole cauliflower in a shallow oven-proof dish, flatten out the leaves to form an attractive base.

Preheat oven to 350°.

In a small heavy saucepan, melt the margarine. Stir in the flour until it is blended and add milk or cream and a crumbled bouillon cube. Cook, stirring, over low heat until the mixture thickens. Pour over the cauliflower, sprinkle with salt and pepper if needed, and cover with cubed cheese and bits of margarine.

Bake for ½ hour.

Especially good when served with veal dishes or goulash. *Serves 4–6.*

FRENCH CHAMPIGNONS (BROILED MUSHROOMS)

1¼ pounds mushrooms, cleaned
   and halved lengthwise
2 onions, sliced thin
Corn oil
1 beef or chicken bouillon cube,

crumbled
Salt and pepper to taste
1 tablespoon flour (optional)
½ cup light cream (optional)
Water (optional)

Sauté the onion slices in hot corn oil until they are slightly brown. Add the mushrooms and cover. Cook over low heat for 5 to 7 minutes. Stir in the crumbled bouillon cube and add salt and pepper to taste. If a thicker mixture is desired (as for omelette), stir in 1 tablespoon flour mixed to paste with a little water and ½ cup light cream.

Mushrooms can be served as a meat replacement with potato purée and salad; as a steak accompaniment; or as an omelette filling. *Serves 3–4 as meat replacement; 6–8 as meat accompaniment.*

ITALIAN SPINACH

2 pounds fresh spinach
1 small onion, chopped fine
Butter for sautéing
1 tablespoon tomato paste

2 tomatoes, peeled and chopped
   coarsely
1 beef bouillon cube, crumbled
Salt and pepper to taste

Wash the spinach two or three times, discard any imperfect leaves and dry it with a towel. Chop it coarsely. In a medium-sized saucepan, sauté the onion in butter until it is tender and golden, but not crisp. Add the tomato paste and pieces. Stir to mix the ingredients. Place the spinach on top of the tomato mixture and sprinkle with salt and pepper (do not mix ingredients). Sprinkle with the crumbled bouillon cube. Cook, uncovered, over medium heat for about 8 minutes until spinach is just tender. Mix the ingredients just before serving. *Serves 4.*

"This is Your Life, Itzhak Navon"

A recent hit play, *Spanish Garden* by Itzhak Navon, reminded many Jerusalemites of the times when the neighborhood was the center of everything, when community life was warmer and more joyful than it is today. "Ohel Moshe" (the tent of Moses) was a Sephardic mini-community near the bustling outdoor marketplace of Mahane Yehuda on Jaffa Road. Ladino was the common tongue. Houses were built close together around a common courtyard. Unlike today's apartment houses, where each unit shuts itself off from the next, in Ohel Moshe all doors were open, neighbors were glad to help each other and the term "one happy family" was realized in its true sense. The whole community attended Bar Mitzvahs and weddings, which went on for days.

Itzhak Navon was born and grew up in this community, which he immortalized in his musical comedy. As chairman of the Defense and Foreign Affairs Committee of the Knesset (Israel's parliament), Itzhak represents the younger Labor (governing party) politicians and those of the Oriental Community who have succeeded in advancing into the predominantly East European–controlled political elite. To Jerusalemites he is still best known as the late Prime Minister David Ben-Gurion's right-hand man and advisor for eleven years. Despite Ben-Gurion's powerful personality, Itzhak Navon was one of the few people who never hesitated to contradict Israel's first prime minister when necessary. Itzhak is one of the most respected politicians in the country and is greatly admired for his willingness to listen to the problems of *all* the people.

One way of honoring famous personalities in Israel is to feature them on Israel national television's "This Is Your Life." This surprise greeted Itzhak Navon several years ago. Knowing how fond of Old Jerusalem Itzhak was, his older sister, Esther Kamar, prepared dishes that his mother made, all Sephardic delicacies which she spent many days preparing. As she came on stage with the tray full of Burekas, potato pancakes, artichoke sandwiches and special cookies, the tray fell onto the floor, spoiling hours of labor. Fortunately, Itzhak's culinary sense is as strong as his sense of humor and he quickly guessed which of the delicacies were on the platter, despite their disheveled appearance.

Even with his active life, Itzhak Navon would not miss a family gathering in the tradition of the community he was brought up in, like the one which followed his special television appearance. The responsibility of preparing the old-style delicacies that make these get-togethers such a pleasure falls on Esther. She is the clan's undisputed authority on the preparation of the Sephardic dishes for such events. All these recipes have a nostalgic effect on her family. She gave us the recipes for two of Itzhak's favorites.

CHEESE–STUFFED ZUCCHINI

6 small zucchini or
   3 medium-size zucchini
1/3 cup grated Parmesan cheese
1 egg

1/2 to 3/4 cup fine breadcrumbs
Salt and pepper to taste
2 tomatoes, chopped coarsely

Cut off the stem ends of the zucchini and slice each in half lengthwise. Parboil them, then scoop out the pulp and set it aside. Mix the cheese, egg and crumbs together and season with salt and pepper. Fill each zucchini half with the mixture, packed down and mounded on top. In a low heat-proof dish place the reserved pulp and tomato pieces. Set the zucchini halves on top. Cover and cook over low heat for 45 minutes or until the zucchini softens. *Serves 4–6.*

STUFFED ARTICHOKES

Contrary to popular belief there are no Jerusalem artichokes in Jerusalem. But Jerusalem's artichokes are delicious.

4 large artichokes (about 2
  pounds)
Juice of ½ lemon
1 cup ground beef
1 large onion, minced
1 tablespoon finely chopped
  parsley
2 tablespoons dried breadcrumbs

  or wheat germ
Salt and pepper to taste
2 tablespoons flour
1 egg, beaten
1 tablespoon water
¼ cup cooking oil
1 cup tomato sauce

Cut the artichokes in half crosswise, about 2 inches from the base.

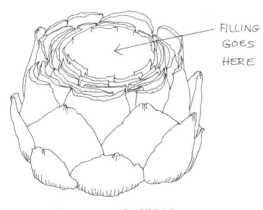

FILLING GOES HERE

SCRAPED-OUT ARTICHOKE

Remove the leaves (and boil them separately to be eaten dipped in butter), and with a sharp knife scrape out and remove the inner hairlike part of the artichoke.

Bring to a boil enough water to cover the artichokes well, add the lemon juice and cook the artichokes, covered, over medium heat for a half hour. Mix the meat, onion, parsley and breadcrumbs; season with salt and pepper. Pack one-fourth of the mixture tightly into the hollowed-out artichoke. Cover the surface with some of the flour and pat it down tightly to seal in the meat filling. Dip the floured surface into the egg mixture. Heat the cooking oil in a frying pan, and sauté the artichokes, floured surface down, until they are browned. Heat the tomato sauce until it simmers, in a saucepan large enough to hold the artichokes, and place them, upright and side by side, in the sauce. Cook gently, covered, for one half hour. *Serves 4.*

Rabbinit Cohen's Vegetarian Kitchen

Names have always been of great significance among Jews. One of the most meaningful is Cohen, that of the family of priests going back before Solomon's Temple. Before the destruction of the First Temple, "Cohenim" served as priests in the Holy Sanctuary. This privilege was originally bestowed upon the descendants of Aaron, Moses' older brother, at the time of the exodus of the Children of Israel from Egypt. The Cohen pedigree carries with it the obligations inherent in the concept "noblesse oblige." Even today members of the Cohen family in any Jewish congregation throughout the world bless the assembled during community worship with the traditional priestly blessing, "May the L——d bless you and watch over you. May He cause His countenance to shine upon you and be gracious unto you. May He turn His face unto you, and grant you peace. Amen."

Once we visited the home of Rabbi David Cohen, a disciple of the famous Rabbi Abraham Isaac Kook, who in his philosophy of Judaism saw the Zionist dream as a stage in the advance toward the Messianic goal. We noticed that in the rabbi's study there was a gathering of men who were praying. Mrs. Cohen explained that Rabbi Cohen always conducts morning and evening communal prayers in his study.

While Mrs. Cohen was bustling about preparing coffee and cake for the congregants following their prayer, she told us that her family has always kept a vegetarian kitchen. Her husband, the august rabbi, wishing to achieve a higher spiritual level, feels that one step in this direction is made by not eating meat or fish, thereby avoiding the necessity of slaughtering living beings. The Cohens' son Sharyashuv, also a rabbi, has followed this dietary tradition as well. His family too enjoys eating the healthy Israeli fruits and vegetables, his wife having learned to cook many vegetarian dishes from her mother-in-law. Today, with health foods so much in fashion, these recipes of the two Mrs. Cohens are apt and appetizing.

LATKES (POTATO PANCAKES)

A favorite eaten at Chanukkah, the Festival of Lights. Each cook has her infallible recipe, but we liked this version, which we found to be especially light.

3 large potatoes	½ teaspoon baking powder
3 tablespoons milk	Salt and pepper to taste
1 egg	Cooking oil

If the skins of the potatoes are thin and unblemished, do not peel the potatoes but scrub them well. Otherwise peel them; then grate 1 potato on the large holes of a grater and the other 2 on the medium holes. Beat in the milk, egg and baking powder. Season with salt and pepper; blend well. If there is a large amount of liquid in the mixture, drain off some of it. Heat a scant ½ inch of oil in a large skillet until it is very hot but not smoking. Drop the batter by large spoonfuls, flatten them slightly. Turn them once. When they are golden brown on the bottom side, cook them several minutes longer and drain them on paper towels. (The Latkes will have crisp edges.)

Serve hot with sour cream or applesauce. *Serves 3–4.*

ZUCCHINI APPETIZER SALAD

Dressing
½ cup fresh lemon juice
½ cup salad oil
1 large garlic clove, pressed
Salt and pepper to taste
2 pinches sugar

Salad
8 zucchini, each about 4 inches
   long
Lettuce leaves

2 medium-size tomatoes, peeled
   and chopped fine
½ small green pepper chopped
   very fine
3 tablespoons very finely chopped
   scallion (use a little of the green
   part)
1 tablespoon capers, chopped fine
1 sprig parsley, chopped fine
1 teaspoon basil
½ teaspoon oregano

Dressing: Combine all the ingredients. Set them aside.

Salad: Simmer unpeeled whole zucchini in salted water for about 5 minutes, uncovered. Pour off the hot water and immediately rinse with cold water to stop the cooking process. Drain. Cut each zucchini in half lengthwise. Carefully scoop out the pulp, leaving a thin shell. (The pulp may be reserved for fritters, as in the next recipe.) Lay zucchini, cut sides up, in a flat nonmetal dish. Cover them with half the dressing. Cover them tightly with foil, place them in the refrigerator and allow them to marinate at least 4 hours.

When you are ready to serve, drain off and discard the marinade. Arrange lettuce leaves on a serving plate; place the zucchinis, cut side up, on top. Combine the other half of the dressing with the salad ingredients and mix well. Pour into and over the zucchini shells, heaping into the hollows and around. *Serves 4.*

SPINACH FRITTERS

Other vegetables may be substituted for spinach.

1 pound fresh spinach	1/2 teaspoon pepper
3 eggs	2 tablespoons minced onion
2 tablespoons milk (fresh or sour milk or buttermilk)	1 tablespoon chopped celery
	1 tablespoon flour
1 teaspoon salt	Cooking oil

Rinse the spinach well, drain and chop it fine. Separate the eggs and beat the whites until they stand in soft peaks. Combine the egg yolks with the milk, salt, pepper, onion, celery and flour. Fold in the beaten egg whites and the spinach, mixing well. Shape into eight 3-inch patties. Fry in cooking oil until the fritters are brown and firm. The surface will be slightly crisp. Drain them on paper towels.

Good served with macaroni and cheese. *Serves 4.*

Maimouna—A Moroccan Community Picnic

Folklore customs often change when ethnic groups leave one country for another, and ever since the Jews became dispersed through the world their holidays have taken on different customs and traditions, all variations on the original significance of each occasion. A unique end-of-Passover tradition, called Maimouna, is celebrated in Israel by a group of the country's most ebullient and colorful immigrants, the Moroccan

Jews. In Morocco, Maimouna was celebrated on the evening of the last day of Passover and was followed by a trip to the countryside or seashore. On that evening Moslem friends visited their Jewish neighbors to wish them happiness and prosperity, bearing trays of fresh yeast (leavened bread is prohibited during the eight days of Passover), fresh bread, honey, flour and butter among flowers, greens and lettuce. Often a fresh fish, symbolizing fertility, was placed in the center of the tray, to be cooked the following day with lots of almonds, a springtime delicacy in Morocco. With the emigration of Jews from Morocco after 1948 the locale changed, but not the festivities.

Jews from Morocco celebrate the end of Passover and the arrival of springtime at the Maimouna festival

Nowadays in Israel, on the day after the end of Passover thousands of Moroccans flock to Jerusalem from all the country to congregate in a large park reserved for the celebration. Moroccans are excused from work on this special day, and in fact the Histadrut (the national labor union) closes the entire port of Ashdod and charters buses so that the employees are free to visit the Holy City. They celebrate the arrival of spring in a spirit of fraternity with their neighbors, friends, and relatives. For many of the participants who live far apart in Haifa, Tel Aviv, Ashdod or Jerusalem it is a rare opportunity to visit each other, since many are religious Jews to whom it is forbidden to travel on the Sabbath, the one day of rest in our one-day-weekend country.

The overall scene is one of bright color and noise. Women wearing headdresses decorated with coins flash their long skirts as they dance to Moroccan music and the hearty singing of their friends. Men in embroidered caps stamp their feet in accompaniment and everyone expresses their feelings of joy by sending forth what can only be described as a "war whoop" — a special cry emitted to show pleasure. (The same cry is also heard at Moroccan Bar Mitzvahs, weddings and other special occasions.) The aromatic smells of frying fish, garlic, Turkish coffee and honeyed sweets are in the air, and delicacies are sold throughout the celebration. All around, many different traditions are being carried out: in one group, the elderly grandfather gives his family a blessing accompanied by a piece of lettuce dipped in honey for a happy and "sweet" year; in another, someone is placing a coin in a sack of flour — "a lucky dip" — to ensure a prosperous year.

One explanation for the exotic-sounding name of the holiday is that "Maimouna" means "bring happiness" in Arabic. Another is that the day is celebrated to commemorate the death of Rabbi Maimon, father of Moses Maimonides, the philosopher, theologian and physician who lived in Morocco for a long period of time in the twelfth century. Whatever the original meaning of the word, these salad recipes are colorfully placed in dishes on blankets during Maimouna.

FANES DE BLETTES (BEET TOPS)

Greens and stems from 1 pound
   of beets
3 tablespoons cooking oil
2 cloves garlic, minced

2 tablespoons lemon juice (or to
   taste)
Salt and pepper to taste

Wash the beet tops, shake them dry, and cut them into one-inch-long pieces. Boil them in water to cover until tender, about 5 minutes. Drain, and squeeze out the excess water. Heat the oil in a frying pan and sauté the beet tops for 15 minutes over low heat. Stir in the garlic and lemon juice and season with salt and pepper. Cook over low heat 5 more minutes. Serve hot or chilled. *Serves 2.*

PIMENTS ROUGES (ROASTED RED PEPPERS)

4 large red peppers
4 tablespoons cooking oil

Salt to taste

Preheat oven to 400°.

Place the whole peppers on a flat baking tray and roast them, turning them often, until the skin is soft, about 20 minutes. Remove and peel them. Cut the peppers in half and remove the seeds. Sauté the peppers in oil until they darken; season them with salt. Serve them hot or chilled, as a side dish or a salad. *Serves 4–6.*

SALADE DE BLETTES (BEET SALAD)

1 pound beets	3 tablespoons minced parsley
⅓ cup vinegar or lemon juice	2 cloves garlic, minced
2 tablespoons vegetable oil	Salt and pepper to taste

Leaving the beets whole and unpeeled, with one inch of stem and the root attached, scrub them thoroughly and boil them gently in water to cover until just tender, from 30 to 60 minutes (depending on size). Drain, peel, and cut the beets into strips. Blend the oil and lemon juice, add the beets, parsley, and garlic; stir gently. Season them with salt and pepper, chill them well to serve. *Serves 3–4.*

SALADE DE CAROTTES CRUES (RAW CARROT SALAD)

1 pound carrots	3 tablespoons minced parsley
⅓ cup vegetable oil	2 garlic cloves, minced
2 tablespoons vinegar or lemon juice	Salt and pepper to taste
	¼ teaspoon sugar (optional)

Peel the carrots and grate them finely. Mix the oil and lemon juice together, add the carrots, parsley and garlic. Season with salt and pepper. If a sweeter taste is desired, add sugar. *Serves 6–8 as a side dish.*

SALADE DE PIMENTS VERTS (GREEN PEPPER SALAD)

4 large green peppers	2 garlic cloves, minced
⅓ cup vegetable oil	Salt and pepper to taste
2 tablespoons lemon juice	

Preheat oven to 400°.

Place the whole peppers on a flat baking tray and roast them, turning them often, until the skin is soft. Remove them from the oven and peel them. Remove the seeds and cut the peppers into strips. In a nonmetal dish, mix the oil, lemon juice and garlic. Stir in the pepper strips, season with salt and pepper, and chill. *Serves 4–6 as a side dish.*

SHAKSHOUKA (EGGS IN TOMATO SAUCE)

Leshakshek means "to shake" in Hebrew. Every cook from North Africa has her own personal version of this egg and tomato dish. Whatever vegetable is used, it must be fresh, not canned.

1 large onion, chopped small	4 eggs
Cooking oil	Salt and pepper to taste
6 medium tomatoes	

In a large frying pan with a cover, sauté the onion pieces in cooking oil until they are light brown. Meanwhile, grate the tomatoes on the largest holes of a grater. Add the liquid pulp to the onions, cover and cook over low heat for 25 minutes. Remove the cover and break the eggs over the surface. Stir gently to break the yolks, cover and cook for about 3 or 4 minutes until the eggs are set. Sprinkle with salt and pepper.

Serve on toast for breakfast or on rice for a luncheon or supper dish.

VARIATIONS: One minced garlic clove can be added to the onion pieces, or 3 or 4 slices of red pimiento may be sautéed with the onions. *Serves 4.*

And Also . . .

ANGLICAN EGGPLANT SOUFFLÉ

1 large eggplant	½ teaspoon freshly ground black pepper
½ teaspoon salt	½ cup grated Parmesan cheese
2 tablespoons flour	4 egg yolks, beaten
2 tablespoons butter	4 egg whites, beaten until stiff
1 cup light cream at room temperature	

Preheat oven to 450°.

Bake the whole eggplant until it is charred and soft, about 30 minutes. Remove it and reduce the oven temperature to 375°. Cool the eggplant, peel and mash it thoroughly with salt. In a medium-sized saucepan, melt the butter and quickly stir in the flour. Add the cream right away, stirring constantly, and cook over low heat until it is thickened. Stir in pepper and cheese. Cool the mixture slightly and add the egg yolks, stirring well. Add the eggplant mixture, stir well, and then fold in the egg whites. Grease a 6-cup soufflé dish, pour in the mixture and bake it for 45 to 50 minutes. (This soufflé will not rise as high as some soufflés made of lighter ingredients.) *Serves 4–6.*

HUMITA (SPICY CORN CASSEROLE)

1 medium-size onion	One 1½ pound package frozen
½ cup butter	corn kernels or 1 can corn
4 tablespoons cooking oil	1½ teaspoons salt
1 red chili pepper	Dash freshly ground pepper
2 large tomatoes, peeled	1 cup milk

Chop the onion coarsely. Heat the butter and oil until they are bubbly, sauté the onion pieces until they are light brown, but not crisp. Chop the pepper into small pieces and add to the onion. Chop the tomatoes coarsely and add them to the onion-pepper mixture with the corn kernels. Lower the heat, cook 10 minutes, stirring constantly. Season with salt and pepper. Stir in the milk, cover and cook over low heat for 20 minutes. *Serves 4.*

PRIME MINISTER EGGPLANT À LA GOLDA

1 large eggplant	Oil for frying
Salt	1 cup tomato purée
3 eggs	¼ teaspoon salt
2 teaspoons water	⅛ teaspoon pepper
¾ cup finely grated Parmesan	1 teaspoon sugar
cheese	2 tablespoons lemon juice

Peel the eggplant and slice it thinly crosswise. Sprinkle each slice with salt and set it aside so that the bitter juice can drain off. Beat the eggs with water, salt and cheese. Dip each eggplant slice in the egg-cheese batter and fry it on both sides in very hot oil. Remove and set it aside on a paper towel. In the same frying pan, with the remaining oil, blend the tomato purée, salt, pepper, sugar and lemon juice; cook it over low heat 5 minutes. If the mixture is too thick, add more oil. Add the eggplant slices, cover and cook over low heat for 25 minutes. Stir occasionally to prevent the eggplant from sticking to the bottom. *Serves 4.*

Desserts

Everybody Loves Friday Night

Most of the world's best-known cities are large in size and densely populated. It is quite a surprise for many a visitor to discover, therefore, that Jerusalem's population is just 305,000, making this world-famous city the same size as Birmingham, Alabama. Situated high in the mountains of the Judean Hills, Jerusalem maintains an aspect of aristocratic isolation. Tel Aviv is much more westernized and typical of a modern city, where social life continues and even gains momentum in the evenings, and it is only forty miles away — a short commuting distance for many Americans. But Jerusalemites do not rush for entertainment to their closest big-city neighbor, and entertainment here is done in a very personal way. Beginning in public school, native-born Jerusalemites form their *chevra* — group of friends — and as friends participate together in the country's youth movement, serve in the army at age eighteen and then often attend the same university together.

Dan and Tammy Horowitz have a *chevra* of forty to fifty old friends, many from the Hebrew University in Jerusalem, where Dindrish (Dan's nickname) is a professor of political science. Tammy does research in sociology at the Szold Institute and is a part-time sociology lecturer in the Department of Criminology. Friday evening is set aside for home entertaining and many, if not all, of these friends gather in one another's homes in what has now become a tradition among them. Guests arrive fairly late after Friday night dinner with their families, around 9:30 or 10:00, the men casually dressed in sandals and open shirts and the women in slacks or, often, long skirts. The ambience is one of comfortable informality. Dips and nuts are the most popular *nosh* and Israeli cognac, beer or a fruit punch — never mixed drinks — is used to toast "l'chaim" (to life). Latecomers wander in, weekly domestic news may be exchanged, and then the conversation zeros in on everyone's (especially

Dan's) favorite subject — the intricacies of Israeli politics. Around mid-night, home-made cakes and coffee are served to fortify the political pundits.

Over the many years and many good times, Tammy has accumulated a good collection of recipes for entertaining a large group of people. Different visitors have contributed their own favorites, like the Coconut-Cointreau Torte which is a specialty of Tammy's friend Sara. The Mulled Wine Pears are something a little different — they can be served warm during the winter and are delicious cold on a hot summer night.

COCONUT–COINTREAU TORTE

6 eggs, separated
1 cup sugar
1 cup walnuts, chopped coarsely
2 cups unsweetened shredded
   coconut (sweetened can be
   used)

¾ cup orange juice
¼ cup Grand Marnier or
   Cointreau
1 cup whipping cream
1 square bittersweet chocolate for
   garnish

Preheat oven to 325°.

In the big bowl of an electric mixer beat the egg whites with ½ cup of the sugar until the mixture holds stiff peaks. Without washing the beaters, beat the egg yolks in the small bowl with the rest of the sugar until they are light and fluffy. Add the yolks to the whites, but do not stir. Add the walnuts and gently fold the ingredients together; then do the same with the coconut, 1 cup at a time. Pour the cake batter into a greased 9-inch spring-form pan and bake it for 45 minutes, until it is lightly brown on top. Remove it from the oven, let it cool a few minutes. Mix together the orange juice and the Cointreau or Grand Marnier and pour them over the cake while it is still in the pan. When the cake is thoroughly cool, place it in the refrigerator until you are ready to serve it. Spread whipped cream over the surface and garnish with bittersweet chocolate shavings. Store it in the refrigerator.

MULLED WINE PEARS

1 quart bottle dry red wine
½ cup sugar
4 cinnamon sticks
8 whole cloves

2 teaspoons lemon juice
8 large pears
1 cup heavy cream
1 teaspoon vanilla

Place the wine, sugar, cinnamon, cloves and lemon juice in a large saucepan. Simmer them uncovered for about 10 minutes until the mixture thickens slightly. Peel the pears but leave the stems on. Place them in the wine mixture, cover and cook them for a half hour — the wine should be simmering gently. Baste the pears occasionally. Beat the cream until it is stiff and fold in the vanilla.

The pears can be served warm or chilled. If possible stand each pear, stem up, in a glass dessert dish and pour the wine around it. If desired, serve with a side dish of the whipped cream for each person to help himself (do not add before serving, as the mixtures curdle). *Serves 8.*

An Old Jerusalem Family — A Blend of Ashkenazi and Sephardi

"As long as I can remember, our house was always a meeting place for Jews from many countries," commented Hemda Zinder, descendant of one of Jerusalem's oldest families. "Both my great-grandfathers, one who came from Russia on the so-called European *Mayflower* and the other a member of a Spanish family which came to Jerusalem in the fifteenth century, were determined to promote the intermingling of Jews who then lived in the Old City of Jerusalem quite separately from each other." Both these men decided to brave the dangers involved and moved outside the walls.

Hemda Zinder's Sephardic great-grandfather, Rahamim Natan Meyouhas, whose family had already lived in the Old City for generations, shared with the Zionists of Europe the deep conviction that in order to deserve their land, the Jews had to work it themselves. He decided to leave the confines of the walled city and to begin farming in Silwan (the Biblical Siloah), a nearby Arab village. He was the only Jew to make such a decision.

Just two years after the family resettled in the village, Rabbi Meyouhas became ill and died, leaving a wife and five children. Hemda's great-grandmother, however, was a proud woman and wanted to continue to pioneer in the same way her husband had. Her Arab neighbors, traditionally hospitable, were very kind to the widow and her children. But keeping the family together was quite a problem. Her eldest son, Yosef, aged ten, helped the family along in many ingenious ways. Being nearsighted, he used his ability to write in minuscule script and decorated grains of wheat with the words "Land of Milk and Honey" and wrote the entire Song of Songs on eggshells, which he then sold to delighted tourists. At the same time he continued his studies in Jewish and general subjects and at the young age of fourteen was asked to become a teacher. With Yosef's imaginative assistance, the family maintained itself and stayed on in the village. Yosef never forgot his neighbors' kindnesses and throughout his life, he lectured, researched and published many works on the Arabic language and Arab customs and culture. To this day, the village where they lived is nicknamed "Minhas" by its inhabitants, a corruption of the Meyouhas name.

Hemda's other great-grandfather, Yachiel Michal Pines, having arrived here from Russia in 1872, was at the same time carving out his own niche in the history of the country. Believing that Jews constituted one family rather than a disjointed group of separate ethnic cultures, Yachiel opened his home to young intellectuals from all groups. Thus it came about that three of his four daughters met, fell in love with and married Sephardim, and Margaelit Pines eventually became Hemda's grandmother. Then the family became a dynamic blend of East and West.

"My family has always been a variety of backgrounds and the food we ate reflects it. Even on Passover we ate eastern European Gefüllte Fish followed by *akutas* (thistles), which is a vegetable similar to an artichoke, filled with meat and is a special Spanish dish. Second only to Mother's European strudel were her Burekas." Hemda loves to cook and generally does not use recipes.

Perfect for Passover is her almond cake with lemon glaze, an old European recipe passed from mother to daughter. And while the chocolate birthday pie is not an old recipe, it is Hemda's "invention," created when her children were tiny, and is still a family celebration dessert. On ordinary days, the Zinders, like most Jerusalem families, eat fresh fruit for dessert.

ALMOND-LEMON TORTE

This recipe is so successful at Passover that it has become a year-round favorite.

Cake	*Glaze*
7 eggs, separated	1 egg yolk
¾ cup sugar	½ cup lemon juice
2 cups coarsely ground	½ cup sugar
blanched or unblanched	Rind of 1 lemon
almonds	1 teaspoon butter
Rind of a large lemon	

Cake: Preheat oven to 325°.

Beat the egg whites until they are stiff, and set them aside. Beat the egg yolks slightly and mix them well with the sugar, then add the ground almonds and lemon rind. Fold in the egg whites. Grease and flour with matzah meal a springform pan and pour in the mixture, which will be very thick. Bake for 1 hour.

Glaze: A few minutes before removing the cake from the oven, beat together the egg yolk, juice, sugar and rind, then place the mixture in a saucepan and boil it, stirring constantly until it thickens. Stir in the butter.

With a toothpick, poke holes in the top of the cake so that the topping can soak in. When the cake has cooled just slightly, still in the springform pan, pour the glaze over it. Let it stand a few minutes so that the glaze melts into the cake, then remove the cake from the pan.

CHOCOLATE BIRTHDAY PIE

Crust
1 cup flour
¼ teaspoon salt
¼ pound butter or margarine
3 tablespoons sour cream

Filling
½ cup butter or margarine
1 cup confectioners' sugar

3 egg yolks, well beaten
1½ ounces unsweetened
  chocolate, melted
½ teaspoon vanilla (optional)
½ teaspoon rum
3 egg whites, beaten stiff
1 cup heavy cream
Sugar to sweeten whipped cream
Grated chocolate for garnish

Crust: Sift the flour with the salt. Cut in the butter or margarine with two knives or pastry blender until the mixture is crumbly. Add the sour cream. Toss with a fork until the mixture forms a ball. Chill 2 hours.

Preheat oven to 425°.

Roll out the crust to fit a 9-inch pie pan. Prick all over the bottom and sides with a fork. Bake it for 15 minutes or until just brown. Cool it on a rack.

Filling: Beat the egg whites first, then, to save washing beaters, beat the egg yolks directly. Cream the butter and sugar well. Add the beaten yolks, chocolate, vanilla (if desired) and rum. Mix well. Fold in the egg whites. Whip the cream and add sugar to taste.

When the pie crust has cooled, pour in the chocolate filling. Spread the filling with whipped cream and garnish it with grated chocolate.

You can freeze this pie up to the whipped cream stage. *Serves 6–8.*

The American Colony —
Teatime in an Enchanting Garden

The great fire of Chicago in 1870 devastated the home of Horatio and Anna Spafford, and in an effort to recover from the shock Anna and her four daughters set off on a cruise to England, only to become the victims of a tragic shipwreck. Anna, a woman of great strength, cabled her husband from London: "Survived alone," and returned to Chicago, where the Spaffords remained for eleven more years. In 1881, still needing spiritual comfort, they decided to come to the Holy Land with their new infant daughter, Bertha. In Jerusalem's Old City they began life anew, forming a small colony with other Presbyterian friends from the United States and Sweden. One day a young local mother came to their home seeking help for her sick child, for whom she was unable to care. This was the beginning of the now famous Spafford Child Care Center, still located in the original building inside the Damascus Gate in the Moslem Quarter and today functioning as a child welfare center providing in-patient care and education in health, education and maternity for the local Arab women.

Soon the Spaffords' quarters, with the already active children's home, were too small for the growing spiritual community. In 1895 they moved to a beautiful house, owned by a pasha, not far from the Damascus Gate — about a half mile away, this time outside the walls; the area soon became known to the local residents as the American Colony.

To support themselves financially the American Colony pooled resources and began the first Jerusalem kibbutz, with some residents working as carpenters, gardeners, cooks and cobblers and others helping with the baby home inside the Old City. One of the daily projects was to deliver homemade cakes and bread by horse-drawn cart to private homes in the neighborhood. The colony rules were so strict that there was a prohibition against "hired labor"; no money was accepted for work and all activities had a purely social and moral motivation.

It was the actor Peter Ustinov's grandfather who later suggested that the next generation of Spaffords convert their beautiful home with its flourishing garden into a hotel, and today it is one of the loveliest in Israel. Full of warmth and charm, it has become a favorite refuge for visiting journalists, including David Brinkley of NBC and James Reston of the New York *Times*, as well as writer Saul Bellow, architect Moshe Safdie and of course Peter Ustinov. Horatio and Valentine Vester (Horatio's maternal grandparents were the original Spaffords) have kept the special charm of the beautiful buildings and gardens and added their own touch as well.

*The enchanting garden of the American Colony Hotel enjoyed by the
proprietor, Horatio Vester, and his sister, Frieda Ward*

It is one of our favorite pastimes to sit in the garden of the American Colony Hotel, perhaps under the very palm tree planted by the elder Mr. Ustinov himself, sipping English tea and enjoying a colony specialty: Chocolate-Almond Cake. The hotel is famous for its Saturday smorgasbord buffet, which offers a wonderful array of delicacies including hot curry, salmon mousse and of course this chocolate cake, which has been handed down through the years since it was first delivered on the colony's horse-drawn cart.

CHOCOLATE-ALMOND CAKE

Cake
8 eggs
1 cup butter, softened (let stand at room temperature ½ hour)
1 cup confectioners' sugar
2 teaspoons baking powder
½ cup sweetened cocoa
1¼ cups finely ground almonds (not blanched) (whirl in blender to obtain right consistency)
½ cup finely ground bread-

crumbs (made from toasted bread)
¼ cup halved, blanched and toasted almonds for decoration (see end of recipe)

Filling and Frosting
½ cup butter, softened
1½ cups confectioners' sugar
¼ cup sweetened cocoa
2 teaspoons rum

Cake: Preheat oven to 375°.

Line a 9-inch cake pan with aluminum foil and grease the bottom and sides. Separate the eggs, placing the yolks in a large mixing bowl and the whites in a deep bowl for beating. Beat the whites until stiff peaks form and set them aside. Combine the yolks and butter well (this can be done by hand or with an electric mixer). In a small bowl, combine the confectioners' sugar, baking powder and cocoa. Add to the yolk mixture and mix well. Add the almonds and breadcrumbs; mix well. Fold the egg whites into the mixture until the two are combined smoothly. Pour the batter into a cake pan and spread it evenly. Bake it for 25 minutes or until a knife inserted in the center of the cake comes out clean. Cool the cake in the baking pan on a cake rack.

Filling and Frosting: Cream the butter with a fork. Mix the sugar and cocoa together and add them to the butter. Cream all the ingredients until they are well blended and add the rum, mixing well.

When the cake has cooled, remove it from the pan, peel off the foil. Divide it crosswise into three equal parts. Put the three layers together with filling-frosting between the layers and on top. Decorate it with the toasted almonds.

Best served slightly chilled. Store the cake in the refrigerator. Slice it thin, as this cake is very rich.

BANANAS CARAMEL

8 bananas, cut in chunks
1 cup whipping cream
1⅓ cups brown sugar
4 tablespoons whipping cream
4 tablespoons butter

1 tablespoon rum
1½ teaspoons vanilla
½ cup blanched slivered and
    toasted almonds

Whip 1 cup of the cream until it is stiff; set it aside in the refrigerator.

In a small saucepan, mix the sugar, remaining cream and butter. Stirring occasionally, cook them about 5 minutes to caramelize them, but do not let the mixture become too dark. Stir in the rum and vanilla. Place the bananas in a low serving dish and pour the sauce over them. Place them in the refrigerator until they are chilled, and when you are ready to serve, top them with the whipped cream and almonds. *Serves 8.*

SPAFFORD FRESH FRUIT MOLD

2 oranges
1 grapefruit
2 apples
1 pear
2 bananas
1 cup diced melon (optional)
6 maraschino cherries, quartered
6 eggs, separated

1¼ cups sugar
1½ tablespoons gelatin soaked in
    ¾ cup cold water
¼ cup Grand Marnier, kirsch, or
    Cointreau
2 cups strained orange juice (fresh,
    frozen or canned)

Grate finely the skins of the oranges and grapefruit, set the gratings aside in a large bowl. Peel all the fruit and cut it into cubes as for fruit salad; drain it. Beat the egg yolks with the sugar and blend them with the grated rind. In a large saucepan, heat the gelatin and water mixture until it is boiling; lower the heat and add the Grand Marnier and orange juice. Add this liquid mixture to the egg yolk and fruit. Beat the egg whites until they are stiff and fold them into the fruit mixture. Chill this in the refrigerator 2 hours.

Serve in deep dessert dishes. *Serves 6–8.*

The Ambassador's Wife Serves Flowers!

"It's always slightly nerve-racking to serve dinner to a prime minister — and you never know if he really enjoys it. Usually he doesn't call the next morning to chat about it or ask for a recipe!" Yael Avner told us. "But once, after we had entertained Lester B. Pearson, the late prime minister of Canada, I heard by chance that he told a friend, 'The wife of the Israeli ambassador serves her dinner guests flowers for dessert.'"

Yael's "flowers" are actually chocolate mousse served individually in small clay flowerpots. A fresh flower is "planted" in each pot, chocolate sprinkles give an earthy look, and the garden scene is completed when the pots are "watered" with brandy from a small watering can.

Born in Germany as Lotte Vogel, Yael met Gershon, also a native German, in London after World War II. Gershon's family had already emigrated to Palestine in 1933 and he was finishing his studies at Oxford University. During their courtship, Gershon's enthusiasm for the new state led him to encourage Lotte to change her name to Yael, as a demonstration of identification with the new homeland.

The young couple settled in Jerusalem, where Gershon joined Israel's diplomatic service. Since then, Gershon has held many posts in the diplomatic corps and has represented Israel in Budapest, Sofia, Oslo, London and Ottawa. Each of their three children was born in a different world capital. Several years ago, the Avners finally resettled in Jerusalem, happy to know that further moves abroad are not imminent.

A man of wide diplomatic experience, Gershon until recently served as the director of Israel's newly created Ombudsman's Office. The office acts as an agent for citizens' complaints against governmental agencies. If the complaint is found to be valid, it is then investigated with the purpose of obtaining justice for the citizen. A large staff of lawyers with a variety of specializations handles each case. It is here that Sam or Sarah Citizen gets his or her chance to cut through bureaucratic procedures and have his or her individual voice heard with professional assistance. Gershon must have been good at handling complaints. Prime Minister Rabin has made him Secretary to the Cabinet.

Although the Avners still entertain a great deal, their dinners are much less formal than they used to be. "To me, a recipe is a chemical formula," Yael says, "and I measure everything carefully. I only make my special cheesecake or chocolate flower mousse for favorite guests, and either dessert is always a smashing success" — no complaints in this department!

CHEESECAKE FAVORITE

1½ cups crumbs (graham
   crackers or crisp cookies)
4 tablespoons margarine or
   butter, melted
1 pound cream cheese
2 eggs

1 cup sugar
1 teaspoon vanilla
1½ cups sour cream
1 teaspoon vanilla
¼ cup sugar

Preheat oven to 300°.

Combine the crumbs and melted margarine and press this crust over the bottom of a deep 9-inch pie plate. Mix the cream cheese, eggs, sugar and vanilla and pour them over the crumb base. Bake for 25 minutes. (Do not turn off the oven afterward.)

Cool the cheesecake for 10 minutes while preparing the topping. Combine the sour cream, vanilla and sugar until they are well blended; pour this over the surface of the cake and bake it for 15 minutes more. Cool it slightly, then set it in the refrigerator to chill.

FLOWER MOUSSE

6 ounces bitter chocolate
6 eggs, separated
1 tablespoon rum, Cointreau or
   Grand Marnier

¾ cup whipping cream
Chocolate sprinkles
8 carnations or other small flowers
Brandy

In the top of a double boiler, over simmering water, melt the chocolate. Remove it from the heat, allow it to cool. Beat the egg whites until peaks form and the mixture is glossy but not dry; set them aside. Beat the egg yolks lightly with the rum and stir them into the chocolate. Without cleaning the blades, whip the cream until it is stiff; add it to the chocolate mixture, then fold this mixture into the egg whites until the mousse is well blended. Divide the mousse among 8 small dessert dishes, custard cups, or crème pots and chill it. Before serving, wrap 8 flower stems (cut to suit the height of the dishes) in foil, sprinkle the surface of mousse with chocolate sprinkles and insert the flowers in the mousse. At the table "water" each dish with brandy in a small watering can or jug. *Serves 8.*

7 ounces bitter chocolate
1 tablespoon water
1 tablespoon sugar
1 tablespoon butter

2 tablespoons Cointreau or Grand Marnier
3 eggs, separated

In the top of a double boiler, over simmering water, melt the chocolate with the water and sugar. Beat the egg whites until peaks form and the mixture is glossy but not dry. Beat the egg yolks lightly and add them to the chocolate mixture with the butter and Cointreau. Fold the chocolate mixture into the egg whites and blend until everything is evenly mixed. Divide the mousse among 8 demitasse cups or small dessert dishes (it is very rich). *Serves 8.*

REFRIGERATOR LEMON CHEESECAKE

NOTE: This cheesecake must be made a day before serving.

Base
1½ cups cookie crumbs
2 tablespoons melted butter
2 tablespoons sugar (less may be required if cookies used for crumbs are sweet)

Filling
4 egg yolks, slightly beaten
1 scant teaspoon salt

¾ cup milk
1 cup sugar
2 tablespoons lemon rind
2 tablespoons gelatin softened in ½ cup cold water
1⅔ pounds cream cheese, softened and mashed
⅓ cup lemon juice
1 cup whipping cream
4 egg whites, beaten stiff

Base: Combine the ingredients and press the crust into the bottom (not the sides) of a 12-inch square pan.

Filling: In a heavy saucepan place the lightly beaten egg yolks, salt, milk and sugar. Cook and stir this over medium heat until the mixture thickens slightly. Add 1 tablespoon of the rind mixed with the gelatin and water; cook and stir the mixture until it is blended. Remove it from the heat and chill it; the mixture will thicken. Beat in (with an electric mixer) the cream cheese, the remaining rind and the juice. Beat the cream until it is stiff, fold it into the cheese mixture; fold in the beaten egg whites, blending well. Pour the filling into the pan containing the base and chill the cheesecake overnight in the refrigerator. *Serves 10–12.*

The Sisters of Zion

In the midst of the Six-Day War, the late Sister Aline of the Catholic Sisters of Zion felt that somehow her convent on the Via Dolorosa would soon link the two sides of the divided city. Then even before the dust of battle had settled, a representative of the Hebrew University knocked at the convent door and presented Sister Aline with the idea of starting a special language center there where Jews could learn Arabic and Arabs could learn Hebrew. Sister Aline responded with enthusiasm, and two weeks later the first class of thirty Christians, Jews and Moslems began studying each others' languages. Today hundreds of Jews and Arabs meet here several times a week to study in the ulpan, and the convent has truly become the cultural and social bridge that Sister Aline envisioned.

The Convent of the Sisters of Zion, one of the most picturesque in the Old City, was built over the ruins of the courtyard of the old Antonia Fortress, which at the time of Jesus towered above the northern side of the Temple area. The fortress was strengthened and armed by King Herod, who called it "Antonia" in honor of his friend Mark Antony. In the cellars of the convent, there is part of a large square paved with stones on which games were inscribed by Roman soldiers who entertained themselves while stationed there. On one wall is embedded part of an arch where it is believed that Pontius Pilate pointed out Jesus with the words "Ecce homo!" (Behold the man!) Thus the Convent of the Sisters of Zion is often referred to as "Ecce Homo" Convent.

The Sisters of Zion are Dominicans from various European backgrounds. The "Ecce Homo" Convent and another beautiful convent of the Sisters of Zion in neighboring Ein Kerem, birthplace of John the Baptist, also serve as hostels for pilgrims and other tourists. The two convents, pacesetters in community relations, also have reputations for fine cooking. The Ein Kerem convent accepts reservations for lunch and has become a popular dining place for both Israelis and tourists. The sisters serve simple but hearty fare, much of it prepared from fruit and vegetables grown on their hilltop gardens, and the visitor, together with the sisters, pilgrims and visiting clerics, dines on plain wooden tables decorated with wild flowers. One of the nuns, Sister Florengina from Roumania, creator of the convent's well-known fruit pies, kindly shared these recipes with us.

APPLESAUCE MERINGUE TART

Dough
1½ cups flour
½ teaspoon salt
Rind of 1 lemon, finely grated
1 tablespoon sugar
9 tablespoons margarine
1½ tablespoons cold water

Filling
1 cup thick sweetened applesauce
¼ teaspoon cinnamon
1 tablespoon very finely chopped
   lemon rind

Meringue
2 egg whites
2 tablespoons sugar
¼ teaspoon cream of tartar

Dough: Mix together the flour, salt, grated lemon rind and sugar. Cut in the margarine with two knives or a pastry blender until the mixture is crumbly. Work in the water with your hands until the dough is well blended. Chill it for a half hour.

Preheat the oven to 475°.

When the dough has chilled, press it evenly into a 9-inch layer cake pan or a 9-inch flan pan (pan with a removable bottom), bringing the dough up the sides almost to the top of the pan and keeping it an even thickness throughout. Make holes all over the bottom and along the sides of the shell with the tines of a fork, and bake the shell for 8 to 10 minutes until it is lightly browned. Remove it from the oven and let it cool. Do not turn the oven off.

Filling: Mix the applesauce with the cinnamon and the chopped lemon rind.

Meringue: Beat the egg whites and cream of tartar until soft peaks form. Beat in the sugar, 1 tablespoon at a time, and continue beating until stiff peaks form.

Procedure: Pour the applesauce into the cooled shell. Pile the meringue in spoonfuls over the surface and blend it together with a spatula, being sure that the meringue touches the edges all around. Bake the tart until the meringue is browned lightly — about 8 to 10 minutes.

Serve at room temperature. Store it in the refrigerator. *Serves 8.*

PLUM TART

1½ cups flour
½ teaspoon salt
Rind of 1 lemon, grated
1 tablespoon sugar
9 tablespoons margarine

1½ tablespoons cold water
2 pounds fresh purple plums
1 tablespoon lemon juice or
   1 tablespoon sugar (see below)

Walking from the New City to the Old, passing David's Tower

Custard Topping
1 cup light cream
2 eggs plus 1 egg yolk, slightly
   beaten

2 tablespoons sugar
4 teaspoons rum
Nutmeg and sugar for garnish

Procedure: Mix the flour, salt, lemon rind and sugar. Cut in the marga-rine with two knives or a pastry blender until the mixture is crumbly. Work in the water with your hands until the dough is well blended. Chill it for a half hour.

Preheat oven to 400°.

Press the dough into a 9-inch layer cake pan or a flan pan (pan with a removable bottom), bringing the dough up the sides almost to the top of the pan, keeping the thickness even all around.

Cut the plums in half and remove the pits. Place the plum halves, skin side down (so that the juice doesn't run out) and slightly overlapping each other, in a circle until the dough is covered or all the plums are used. If the plums are very sweet, sprinkle them with 1 tablespoonful of lemon juice. If they need sweetening, sprinkle 1 tablespoonful of sugar over the surface. Bake the crust and plums for 25 minutes or until the plums are tender when pierced with a fork. Do not turn off the oven.

Custard Topping: In a medium-size saucepan, heat the cream just un-til bubbles form around the edge. Beat together the eggs and egg yolk with the sugar. Add them to the cream and cook over medium heat, stir-ring constantly, until the mixture thickens. Stir in the rum and cook for 2 more minutes. Set the custard aside until the tart is cooked.

Remove the tart from the oven and carefully pour the topping over the surface. Sprinkle it with nutmeg and a little sugar. Place the tart back in the oven for 15 to 20 minutes until the topping is lightly browned and a knife inserted in the deepest part of the custard comes out clean.

Serve slightly chilled. Store the tart in the refrigerator. *Serves 8.*

Yankee Cooking on Mount Zion

Question: What is an old-fashioned American apple pie doing on Mount Zion? *Answer:* Being eaten with great gusto by the students at the American Institute of Holy Land Studies. *Question:* How did it get there in the first place? *Answer:* It was cooked with TLC (tender loving care) by Georgina Young, whose husband, Dr. G. Douglas Young, founded the institute.

The "why" of the institute was explained by Dr. Young. "When people talk about prophecy, they should know Jews and something about them. If students learn about each other, they have added an extra dimension to their lives and therefore can be more useful human beings," he told us. Dr. Young, an evangelical Protestant, is a well-known figure in Jerusalem. While his main interest is archaeology, which is also taught at his school, he discourses enthusiastically and knowledgeably on theology and Biblical studies to young men and women from all over the world who come to learn at the institute. It is rare to hear a student rave about the food served at his school, but we found the exception at the Institute of Holy Land Studies. The students were more than happy with the food at the institute — especially the desserts.

Georgina Young, who is known to her many friends as "Snook," makes sure that the resident students at the institute are eating well and that the day students at the morning Hebrew classes enjoy coffee breaks where home-baked brownies, Chocolate Almond Ice Cream and other Yankee goodies are served. Snook's kitchen is pure Americana. Its décor includes a black pot-bellied stove and beside it a wicker basket containing two curled-up kittens, shiny copper molds twinkling in an antique carved cupboard, an old bentwood rocking chair, flowered chintz curtains on brass rings at the leaded-glass windows, and a bookcase crammed with all types of cookbook. The windows overlook a garden of bright flowers and — as if to remind one of where one is — the Tomb of David is visible from one side of the room and the Church of the Dormition, with the Hall of the Last Supper, from the other.

Snook described her responsibilities as the chief dietitian planning the meals served to the institute's several hundred students as well as her frequent entertaining as wife of the director. She had to adjust her cooking in moving from America to Israel, but the change did not faze her. While teaching the Arab cooks how to prepare fried eggs and pancakes, she was pleased to learn from them how to master shish kebab and Turkish coffee.

CHOCOLATE ALMOND VELVET (ICE CREAM)

1 16-ounce can chocolate syrup	4 cups whipping cream
1 16-ounce can sweetened condensed milk	2 teaspoons vanilla
	½ cup blanched almonds

Before starting, make sure you have a very large plastic container with a tight-fitting lid and enough room in your freezer to store it. (Measure 6 cups of water into the container and see if there is enough space left to use an electric beater without it spattering over.)

Mix together the syrup, milk and cream until blended. Pour the mixture into the plastic container, cover it and place it in the freezer to get icy cold. Meanwhile, chop the almonds coarsely and sauté them in a little butter until they are golden. Remove the mixture from the freezer, stir in the vanilla, and beat the ice cream at high speed with a hand mixer until it is the consistency of softened ice cream. (This takes a fair bit of time.) Fold in the almonds. Store the ice cream in the freezer. (It is better if made one day ahead.) *Makes about 1½ gallons.*

DATE CAKE PUDDING

1 cup dates, pitted and cut up small	½ cup brown sugar
2 tablespoons margarine or butter	1 teaspoon baking soda
1 cup boiling water	½ teaspoon baking powder
1 egg, lightly beaten	½ teaspoon salt
1½ cups flour	½ cup chopped walnuts or pecans
½ cup sugar	1½ cups brown sugar
	1½ cups boiling water

Preheat oven to 375°.

Add the margarine or butter to the boiling water and stir to melt. Place the cut-up dates in a baking pan and pour the water mixture over them. Stir to soften the dates. Cool the mixture. Mix in the egg and sugars. Sift together the dry ingredients and add the nuts; stir until blended. Stir this into the date mixture in the pan and smooth out the batter. Sprinkle it with 1½ cups more brown sugar and slowly pour 1½ cups boiling water over all. Bake the pudding in a lightly greased 9-inch square or round pan about 40 minutes. Serve it warm with ice cream or whipped cream. *Serves 8.*

LEMON MERINGUES

Meringues	*Lemon Filling*
6 egg whites	6 eggs yolks slightly beaten
1 teaspoon cream of tartar	½ cup sugar
2 cups fine sugar, sifted	2 tablespoons flour
2 teaspoons white vinegar	¾ cup water
1 teaspoon vanilla	Juice and grated rind of 1½ lemons

Meringues: At high speed on the mixer, beat the egg whites with cream of tartar just until soft peaks form. Gradually beat in the sugar, ¼ cup at a time, beating well after each addition. Beat in the vanilla and vinegar. Continue beating 12 minutes longer. The meringue batter should be very thick.

Preheat oven to 200°.

Grease two cookie sheets, and with an ice cream scoop or a large spoon, mound the meringue on the cookie sheets, keeping each ball smooth. Make a deep pocket in the center of each by twirling the back of a teaspoon around. Bake for 1 hour. Turn the oven off and leave the meringues for another half hour. Cool and fill them with lemon filling.

Lemon Filling: To the slightly beaten yolks add the flour, water, sugar and lemon. Cook them in the top of a double boiler over hot water, stirring constantly, until thick. Cool. *Complete recipe makes and fills about 18 shells.*

ORANGE RUM CAKE

Cake
1 cup softened butter
1 cup sugar
Grated rind of ½ large orange
(keep fruit for topping)
Grated rind of 1 lemon (keep fruit
for topping)
2 eggs
2½ cups sifted all-purpose flour
2 teaspoons baking powder
1 teaspoon baking soda
½ teaspoon salt

1 cup buttermilk (sour cream may
be used instead)
1 cup finely chopped walnuts

Topping
Juice of 1 lemon
Juice of 2 oranges
1 cup sugar
2 tablespoons light or dark rum
(brandy may be used instead)
1 cup whipped cream (optional)

Cake: Preheat oven to 350°.

Cream the butter and sugar until they are light and fluffy. Add the grated fruit rinds and the eggs, one at a time. Beat well. Sift together the dry ingredients and add them to the butter mixture alternately with the buttermilk; beat the batter until it is smooth. Fold in the nuts. Pour the batter into a greased 9-inch fluted mold or ring mold or a 2-quart tube pan. Bake for 55 to 60 minutes or until a knife blade inserted into the center comes out clean.

Topping: Strain the juices into a saucepan. Then add the sugar and rum. Bring the mixture to a boil, cook for 1 minute, and turn off the heat.

When the cake is done, remove it from the oven, cool it for a few minutes and then poke holes into the surface with a toothpick. While the cake is still in the pan, slowly pour the topping over it; the topping will soak in and become completely absorbed. Let it cool completely and turn it out onto a serving plate. This is a moist dessert cake; eat it with a fork. If you desire to, you can garnish it with whipped cream. Store in refrigerator.

Forbidden Fruit from the Biblical Zoo

"In five days God created day and night; heaven, earth and the seas; sun, moon and stars; plants, fish and birds. On the sixth day he created the beasts and man in his own image; male and female" (Genesis 1).

If you are a child and if your name is Ayel or Dov or Zvi, you can enter Jerusalem's Biblical Zoo without paying even one *agora* (one cent). The gazelle (*ayel*), the bear (*dov*) and the deer (*zvi*) are all animals mentioned in the Bible and as such are among the residents of Jerusalem's Biblical Zoo. Ever since this unique zoo was founded in 1939, animals described in the Bible have been rounded up from all over the world and now live in the land about which the Bible was written. The appropriate verse from the Bible where, for example, the giraffe or elephant or hippopotamus is mentioned is written on a plaque attached to the cage or enclosure. The plaques are written in Hebrew, Arabic and English so that every child who comes to visit can understand.

Sometimes, it is difficult to figure out what exactly was meant by the Biblical name of an animal, since names have changed since then! Today, there is a Names Committee at the Academy of the Hebrew Language which works to solve this interesting problem — one of the simpler examples is the behemoth, the huge animal described in Job 11:15–24, which we now know as the hippopotamus. There is another side to animal naming. The Biblical Zoo's donkey (*hamor* in Hebrew) and zebra recently produced a brand new animal which logically was named the "hamzeb" just as its counterpart in New York's Central Park Zoo is the "zonkey." This donkeyesque animal with striped legs has no identical ancestor in the Bible!

Unlike most other zoos, this one encourages visitors to feed the animals, and at the entrance there is even a box marked "Bread for the Animals." Even in wartime they are not forgotten. During the blackout after the outbreak of the Yom Kippur War, for example, high school students volunteered to fill in for the zookeepers.

Jerusalem's Biblical Zoo is not restricted to animals. In keeping with its concept, the surrounding plants and trees are chosen because they too have Biblical "roots." Among the cypress and olive trees an old apple tree reminded us of what Adam's and Eve's Tree of Life might have looked like. The inevitable recipe for the fruit of this Biblical tree is, of course: "Don't bite." But like our forefathers, Adam and Eve, who

"And Noah sent forth the dove out of the ark."
Two descendants at the Western Wall

could not resist, we too have apple appetites and these recipes make good use of the forbidden fruit.

ADAM'S APPLE CAKE

Cake
5 eggs
1½ cups sugar
1 cup vegetable oil
2 cups flour
2 teaspoons baking powder
1 teaspoon salt
1 teaspoon vanilla
6 or 7 tart cooking apples
¼ cup sugar
1 teaspoon cinnamon

Topping
1 cup heavy cream
1 teaspoon rum
¼ cup sugar
½ teaspoon cinnamon
      OR
¼ cup melted butter
¼ cup walnuts
1 teaspoon cinnamon
½ cup sugar

Cake: Beat the eggs together until they are light and frothy; blend them well with the sugar. Beat in the oil. Sift together the flour, baking powder and salt and add this to the egg mixture. Add the vanilla; beat well. Peel the apples and slice them thin. Mix them with the sugar and cinnamon.

Preheat oven to 350°.

Grease a 9-inch by 13-inch baking pan. Pour in enough batter to cover the bottom well — a little less than half the batter. Arrange the apples evenly over the batter and cover them with the remaining batter. Bake for 1 hour.

Toppings: To serve this as a dessert, spread the cake with whipped cream sweetened with the ¼ cup of sugar and flavored with the cinnamon and rum extract.

To serve it as a coffee cake, brush the top with the melted butter. Sprinkle a mixture of walnuts, cinnamon and sugar on top. Then place the cake under the broiler for about 2 minutes. Serve it warm.

APPLE CAKE EDEN

Eve's Specialty.

1¼ cups flour
¼ teaspoon salt
1 teaspoon baking powder
½ cup butter or margarine
¼ cup sugar
Grated rind of one large lemon

1 egg, slightly beaten
6 or 7 medium-size (or 2 pounds) tart cooking apples
½ cup sugar
½ teaspoon cinnamon

Preheat oven to 350° and grease an 8-inch flan pan or a small round springform pan.

Mix the flour, salt and baking powder. With your hands combine the butter or margarine with the flour until the mixture is crumbly. Add the sugar and lemon rind. Blend the ingredients well and set them aside. Peel the apples and grate them on the large holes of a grater; apples are easily handled if they are left whole after peeling. Mix them with the sugar and let them drain for a quarter hour in a colander. Mix in the egg with the crust and knead them well. (The mixture will still be crumbly.) With a fork, press three-quarters of the dough evenly over the bottom and sides of the pan. Add the cinnamon to the apples in the colander. Spread the apples over the dough in the pan. With the remaining dough design a large apple on top of the fruit. Bake for 30 minutes, until the apples are tender. (The recipe may be doubled for a larger cake.) Best served cold. *Serves 6–8.*

Cookies and Sweets

Much-loved Cookies
for Jerusalem's Much-loved Mayor

Who is the mayor of Paris? Rome? Moscow? Peking? If you did not have to vote for one of them, you probably would never know. And yet there are mayors like Daley, Beame and Brandt who are or were synonymous with their cities. Teddy Kollek *is* Jerusalem.

Why is this so? Perhaps it is his life-style. Do guards at Gracie Mansion call Mayor Beame "Abe" whenever they see him? *"Boker tov,* Teddy," reply the guards at Jerusalem's City Hall every morning when the mayor, at six A.M., is the first member of the staff to check in. We wonder if any other mayor, much less any other executive anywhere else in the world, punches a clock. Mayor Kollek does have one special "privilege" — his card is number one.

"I am an old friend of Teddy Kollek's" is a familiar greeting around the office of Jerusalem's burly mayor. He has more acquaintances than almost any other person in the Israeli government, as well as possessing decidedly more energy than most human beings in Israel or elsewhere, and so it is no wonder that the late Adlai Stevenson dubbed Teddy, who was then the director general of Prime Minister Ben-Gurion's office, "Israel's greatest human resource."

True to Israeli custom, the mayor has yet to be seen in a tie and jacket during working hours. He greets his V.I.P. guests in a kibbutz-style open-necked shirt with more savoir faire than the most elegantly attired of men.

One cannot believe how many people Teddy knows in a personal way; he is on a nickname basis with the world's élite. This, of course, takes its toll in the fulfillment of modern civilization's annual duty. Just the word "September" strikes fear in the hearts of Teddy's secretaries. With summer barely over, the Jewish New Year card lists must be updated, a process which invariably means more additions than deletions.

*Mayor Teddy Kollek has more friends than almost anyone
else in the world*

Then come the Christmas lists and mailings for his many Christian friends. At the same time, Id al-Fitr, the feast concluding the fast of Ramadan, sees the mayor visiting his Moslem friends and colleagues with holiday greetings.

Although Teddy is very modern in his approach to realizing projects such as the development of the government tourist office, the Israel Museum and the new Jerusalem Theatre, he still prefers the old-fashioned touch of the homemade food of his native Vienna.

Because Mayor Kollek's life is so hectic, his wife Tamar is always kept busy hostessing expected and unexpected guests. A friendly and independent woman, Tamar has created foods that have become traditions in her household and have won her acclaim. Senator Stuart Symington of Missouri, for example, so enjoyed the homemade plum jelly he ate at a six o'clock breakfast meeting in the Kollek home that this delicacy has now been introduced into Washington circles. When guests arrive at the Kolleks', whether it be for breakfast or late in the evening for a nightcap, they are drawn to the fine collection of antiquities as well as the marvelous collection of old books and maps on Jerusalem. They sip coffee, cider or something stronger and enjoy Küpferlin, Tamar's Viennese crescent cookies, which by now have become a trademark of this well-known household. Tamar gave us two Viennese cookie recipes, both of which she inherited from her mother.

VIENNESE KÜPFERLIN (CRESCENT COOKIES)

1 cup salted margarine (not butter)
½ cup white sugar

½ cup almonds (not blanched), ground very fine
2 cups all-purpose flour

Preheat oven to 250°.

Cream the margarine and sugar. Add the almonds, and then the flour. Using your fingers to mix the ingredients together is best. Take pieces of the dough the size of a plum, roll them into balls in the palm of your hand and then roll the dough into tube-shaped pieces about 2 inches long. Place each tube on a board and shape it into a crescent. Cut with a sharp knife horizontally across the crescent (see diagram) and press

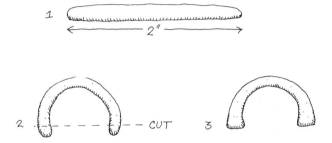

the ends flat. Place the cookies on an ungreased cookie sheet close to each other but not touching. Bake them for 40 minutes, until they are firm to the touch. The cookies should be white in color, not even slightly golden. Remove them from the oven, let them stand a few minutes and, while they are still warm, sprinkle them with sugar. *Makes 5 dozen.*

BAISERS (MERINGUE KISSES)

3 egg whites
1 cup sugar
1 teaspoon cream of tartar

⅝ cup very roughly chopped walnuts

Preheat oven to 275°.

Beat the egg whites until they form peaks. Gradually beat in the sugar and cream of tartar until the whites are very stiff. Stir in the nuts by hand. Drop the batter on a greased cookie sheet in teardrop shapes, using two teaspoons (for shaping); each cookie should be a little larger than a chocolate candy kiss. Bake them about one half hour, checking occasionally, until the cookies are hard but still white. *Makes 50–60 cookies.*

Swedish Christmas
on the Mount of Olives

A winding road up the Mount of Olives leads into the old-world courtyard of the Augusta Victoria Hospital, where the only sounds are the soft whispers of Arabic and the louder whispers of the towering trees moving to and fro in the Jerusalem wind. The elegant stone building, with carved saints piously folding their hands on either side of the main entrance, was completed in 1911 by order of Kaiser William II after his visit to the city in 1898. It was constructed as a hospice for German Protestant pilgrims on a piece of land selected by the Kaiser and named in honor of his wife, Augusta Victoria, as a silver wedding anniversary gift. Soon after its construction, World War I began and the building was never again used for its original purpose. By a strange quirk of fate, it was used as the headquarters of the British High Commissioner after World War I and then during World War II as a British army hospital for the entire Middle East. Today the Augusta Victoria Hospital serves patients from the West Bank and Jerusalem.

Ulla Forshamn, a young Swedish nurse, lives near the hospital on the Mount of Olives in a fairy-tale stone house, one corner of which is a turret with a red tile roof. It is surrounded by tall pine trees and overlooks the eastern part of Jerusalem on one side and the Dead Sea on the other. Ulla was sent here by the Lutheran World Federation, which runs the student nursing program.

She trained in her native Stockholm before joining the Lutheran World Federation, which has taken her to Italy and Nigeria. Now she teaches a class of fifteen Arab nursing students (many of whom are boys from the West Bank and Jerusalem). At the completion of their course they will be qualified nurses, and can work in either Israel or Jordan.

Ulla shares her house with two other Swedish nurses. Although all three have learned Arabic cooking from their students, they still prefer their native Swedish food. In fact, we learned of Ulla's expertise at a local YMCA cooking bazaar, of which her cookies were the highlight. Christmas is Ulla's favorite holiday, celebrated with special cookies such as the Pepparkakor below. According to tradition, friends gather together to help cut out the cookies. When they are baked, everyone does a bit of decorating, followed by the best part — eating them. Ulla, her colleagues and her students continue this Christmas tradition each year in Jerusalem.

PEPPARKAKOR (SPICED MOLASSES COOKIES)

Cookies
½ cup brown sugar
1¾ cups butter
½ cup molasses
¾ tablespoon cinnamon
¾ tablespoon ground ginger
½ tablespoon ground cloves
1¼ cups heavy cream
½ tablespoon baking soda
1 teaspoon water
5½ cups flour

Cookie Paint
1 egg yolk
2 tablespoons milk or water
Food coloring

Cookie Icing
½ cup melted butter
4 cups sifted confectioners' sugar
2–3 tablespoons vanilla
Few drops milk or light cream
Few drops food coloring

Cookies: Cream the sugar and butter until they are very well blended. It is important to blend well. Stir in the molasses and spices. Whip the cream until just stiff and blend it into the butter-molasses mixture, little by little. Dilute the baking soda in the water and blend it well into the batter. Work in the flour until the dough is fairly stiff, cover the dough and let it stand overnight in a refrigerator or cool place.

When you are ready to cut out the cookies, let the dough stand at room temperature about a half hour before starting.

Preheat oven to 350°.

Grease a cookie sheet. Flour a board and rolling pin lightly and roll out a small piece of dough to test if it is of the right consistency. If it is not stiff enough, work in more flour. Roll the dough thin and cut out shapes with cookie cutters.

This recipe makes a huge amount of dough because of the tradition of inviting friends in to help cut and decorate the cookies.

Before baking you can paint some of the cookies (see Cookie Paint) and decorate them with raisins, sprinkles, or candied fruits. Place the decorated and undecorated shapes on cookie sheets and bake them 5 to 7 minutes until they are nicely browned. When cooled, the cookies may be iced (see Icing) and then decorated with nuts, raisins, small candies, candied fruit, sprinkles, etc. Store them in an airtight container. The dough freezes well and also can be kept for a long time, covered, in the refrigerator, before baking and decorating.

Cookie Paint: Beat the egg yolk lightly. Add milk or water. Divide this mixture into as many batches as the different colors you wish to use. Add a few drops of food coloring to each batch. Using a small paintbrush, paint the cookies. This must be done before baking.

Cookie Icing: Mix the sugar with the butter. Stir them until they are well blended. Add the vanilla and a little milk until the mixture is very smooth. The consistency should be quite stiff. Add food coloring. Either use a butter spatula to frost the entire cookie with one color, or use a pastry bag for each color and apply icing to the cookies, creating designs and patterns of your choice. *Makes approximately 200 cookies.*

OATMEAL WAFERS

⅔ cup butter
1 cup sugar
1 cup oatmeal
1 cup flour
½ teaspoon baking powder

¼ teaspoon salt
½ teaspoon vanilla
4 tablespoons heavy cream
4 tablespoons corn syrup

Preheat oven to 350°.

In a large saucepan, melt the butter. Then stir in all the other ingredients in the order listed; blend well. Drop the batter by rounded teaspoonfuls on a heavily greased cookie sheet. (Leave space between teaspoonfuls, as the wafers will spread.) Bake the wafers for 8 to 10 minutes until they are delicately brown and just crisp around the edges. Remove them from the oven, let them cool 1 minute and remove them from the cookie sheet with a metal spatula.

Store the cookies in airtight containers. *Makes approximately 60 wafers.*

A Social Worker, Foster Mother and Good Cook

Traditionally, Arab women do not work outside the home. Times are changing, however, and Salwa Abdo is exemplary of this new life-style. She and several colleagues manage one of the municipal social welfare centers where Arab men and women come for general assistance and counseling on the problems of adjustment that have arisen for them since the Six-Day War.

Like most social service jobs, the work entails many extra hours and much personal commitment — it is never an eight-hour routine. Salwa is a devoted mother, the directress of the welfare center and an enthusiastic social worker. Last year she decided to open her home to several orphaned children and became "mother" to four young Arab boys who are now like brothers to her own young daughter.

It is great fun to visit the home of this lively family, which also includes Salwa's mother, in the northern outskirts of Jerusalem on the road to Ramallah. Friends are always dropping in to the Abdo household, adding to the warmth and gaiety which permeate the atmosphere. On our second visit we were offered the family *narghila* (water pipe). Although the *narghila* may sound very exotic to Westerners, its use is an age-old Middle Eastern custom, one of the many ways in which hospitality is extended and as commonplace here in the Middle East as is pipe smoking in the West. The convivial atmosphere around the family *narghila* lends itself to bright and varied conversations, which range from politics to fashions, food and women's liberation.

Hospitality at Salwa's includes special candies made from figs grown in her garden and preserved for middle-of-the-winter visits such as ours.

MORATUB TEEN (CANDIED FIGS)

Serve in small amounts as a sweet with coffee after dinner or at teatime.

1 pound dried figs	¼ teaspoon cinnamon
1 tablespoon lemon juice	¼ teaspoon nutmeg
1 cup sugar	½ pound walnuts, chopped small
¼ teaspoon ground ginger	

Chop the figs into very small pieces. Place them in a deep bowl, cover them with water and lemon juice and let them soak for one hour. Place the figs and water in a heavy saucepan and cook them over low heat, uncovered, until they are tender. Add the sugar and spices, stir well and cook until the figs are glazed and the mixture is thick and of jamlike consistency. Stir in the walnuts.

Store the confection in the refrigerator. *Makes 2 cups.*

SUM-SUM (SESAME SEED CANDY)

2 cups sesame seeds	2 cups sugar
1 tablespoon water	

Preheat oven to 400°.

Spread the seeds on an ungreased cookie sheet and bake them until they are light brown — about 20 minutes. Place the water in a heavy saucepan and add the sugar. Cook, stirring constantly with a wooden spoon and scraping the sides of the pan often, until the sugar melts. (The sugar will first crumble and lump, then melt and turn dark brown.) Immediately add the roasted seeds, mix them in quickly until blended and remove the saucepan from the heat. Turn the contents into a 9- by 13-inch pan and pat it down to smooth with the back of a large spoon dipped in water. Cut the candy into pieces while it is still warm. Let it set until hard — about 5 minutes.

Variation: A cup of skinned raw peanuts may be substituted for 1 cup sesame seeds. (Roast the peanuts with the seeds.) *Makes 30–40 pieces.*

The City's Sweet Center

In Jerusalem the name Havilio is synonymous with candy: halvah, Turkish delight, Marzipan — whichever most appeals to one's sweet tooth. Originally religious Jews who were expelled from Spain during the Spanish Inquisition, members of the Havilio family have lived in the Old City since the year 1500. Since that time Jewish, Moslem and Christian candy lovers of Jerusalem have been enjoying the products of the Havilio family business.

Before Jerusalem was divided in 1948, the Havilio sweet factory's principal store was on David Street, the Old City's main street. Havilio's was so well known that after the partition of the city, a letter addressed to Nissim Havilio, Confectionery Importers, Jerusalem, was sent from one country to another through the Mandelbaum Gate and reached the Havilios in the Israeli sector.

Jerusalem is definitely a city of varied religious festivals, for each of which special candies are made and then joyfully consumed. Each year three different Christmases and Easters are celebrated, by the Greek Orthodox, the Roman Catholics and the Monophysites, not to mention all the other minor holidays celebrated by all the Christians throughout the year. Then, there is the four-day Moslem feast of Id al-Fitr, celebrating the end of Ramadan, and the Jewish holidays of Rosh Hashanah, Sukkot, Chanukkah, Purim, Passover and Shavuot — all with special sweets. The only times when no sweets are eaten are the Jewish Yom Kippur (Day of Atonement) and during the Christian Lent. Even during Ramadan, after the daylong fast is broken, sweets are permitted. In addition to all these official holidays which each religious group prac-

*Mountains of sweets are ready for Moslems to end their
daily fast during the holy month of Ramadan*

tices with equal spirit, there are also festivities common to everyone
such as births and weddings, the celebrations of which sometimes last
for seven days.

Everyone in the Havilio family is knowledgeable about the customs
pertaining to the different sweets. Marzipan, for example, is traditionally presented to a woman who has just given birth, since this almond
paste delicacy is considered "the richest food on earth." The gift always
includes a piece of *ruda*: a leaf which is believed to ward off the evil
eye. White Jordan almonds, candy-coated nuts, are the traditional sweet
at Christian and Moslem weddings. Often each guest receives a crystal
jar packed with these candies. Blue Jordan almonds are for Christian
baptisms. Sum-sum (sesame seed candy), nougat and the Havilio halvah,
the recipe of which is a secret to this day, are on hand in most homes
for the perpetual unexpected guest who drops in for coffee and expects
a sweet.

Special sweets are eaten during Purim, the Feast of Esther, the Jewish
"Halloween," when children dress up in costumes and the girls vie for
the honor of being dressed as Esther the Queen, who outwitted wicked

Haman in his attempts to do away with the Babylonian Jews in Persia. Candy lollipops in the shapes of scissors, shoes and baby dolls hang from the doorways of houses and *Oznei Haman* (Haman's ears), ear-shaped pastries filled with poppy seeds, figs, or nuts and raisins, adorn the sweet tray in Jerusalem homes.

Interested to see how candy was made at Purim, we paid a visit to the Havilio factory on Jaffa Road in the heart of west Jerusalem. We did not dare interrupt the brothers Havilio or the workmen busily tasting, stirring and dipping. In silence we watched the pieces of Turkish delight being wrapped in squares of cellophane, but we did speak up in time to taste a piece of marzipan, and to request its recipe as well as that of Oznei Haman, which we Americans know in a slightly different version as Hamantashen (Haman's pockets) — both specialties of the matriarch of this family, Sarah Havilio.

MARZIPAN (ALMOND PASTE)

1½ cups sugar
1 cup water
1½ cups finely ground blanched almonds (blender is good for this; ground nuts must be of powderlike consistency)

1 tablespoon strained lemon juice
1 egg white, whisked with fork or egg whisk until soft peaks form
Halved blanched almonds for decoration

Since the lemon juice will be used in two parts, put it in a small glass so it is easily poured. Place the sugar and water in a heavy saucepan over medium heat. Stir it with a wooden spoon, and when the mixture starts to bubble around the edges, add several drops of the lemon juice to keep the mixture from sugaring. Continue cooking and stirring until the mixture is syrupy. Lower the heat, add the ground almonds, continue stirring and scraping around the edges until the mixture forms a ball and is the consistency of a soft dough. Quickly stir in the remaining lemon juice. Remove the mixture from the heat, cool it slightly and beat in the egg white. Let it cool completely, stirring from time to time. Shape the Marzipan into small round balls or flatten out the dough with your fingers and cut it into desired shapes with small cookie cutters. Place an almond half on top of each candy. Store it in a plastic bag or airtight container. *Makes approximately 36 candies.*

OZNEI HAMAN (HAMANTASHEN)

The cookie dough can also be used as crusts for two fruit pies.

Dough
¾ cup light brown sugar
1 cup softened margarine
2 medium eggs
½ cup corn oil
4 cups flour
1 tablespoon baking powder
½ teaspoon salt

Nut and Raisin Filling
1 cup raisins
1 cup chopped walnuts
¼ cup chopped almonds
Rind of 1 orange
Rind of ½ lemon
2 tablespoons butter
½ cup fresh, unstrained orange
   juice
⅓ cup light brown sugar
1 teaspoon cinnamon
½ teaspoon ground cloves

¼ teaspoon ginger
⅛ teaspoon mace

Date Filling
4 cups chopped dates
⅔ cup sweet red wine
4 tablespoons butter
2 teaspoons cinnamon
1 cup chopped walnuts or
   blanched almonds (chopped
   small but not fine)

Poppy Seed Filling
½ cup milk
½ cup sugar
¾ cup poppy seeds
¼ cup breadcrumbs
2–3 tablespoons honey
Juice and rind of 1 lemon
½ cup chopped raisins

Preparation: Preheat oven to 350°.

Cream the sugar and margarine. Add the eggs and oil and beat until completely blended. Stir in the flour, baking powder and salt to form a dough. Since the dough will be too soft to handle easily, roll it into two cylinders approximately 3 inches in diameter and freeze.

Using one cylinder of dough at a time (keeping the unused portion frozen until needed), cut ⅛-inch slices of dough. Roll them out and place 1 teaspoon of filling in the center of each round and draw the three sides together to form a triangle. (The dough will be soft and will require careful handling.) Place the triangles on ungreased cookie sheets and bake them for 20 minutes or until they are golden brown.

Nut and Raisin Filling: Combine all the filling ingredients in a saucepan and cook them over a low heat until a moist cohesive mixture is formed.

Date Filling: Place the dates, wine and butter in a small heavy saucepan. Stir them with a wooden spoon and cook over low heat about 8 to 10 minutes until the mixture is pastelike. Cool the mixture and add the cinnamon and nuts.

Poppy Seed Filling: In a heavy saucepan bring the milk and sugar to a boil. Lower the heat, add the poppy seeds and cook, stirring until the mixture thickens. Remove it from the heat and stir in the remaining ingredients.

Each of the above fillings makes enough for 36 pastries.

Sabbath Dinner in Mea Shearim

Visitors to Jerusalem invariably wander through Mea Shearim, a section of the city where the most Orthodox Jews live. When we were invited to spend a Friday evening with the Zonnenfeld family there, we were delighted to have an opportunity to see what life was like in a community whose religious customs are foreign to our upbringing. In respect for the beliefs of the area's residents, since Shabbat begins at dusk, we walked from our homes and did not carry purses with us, for to the Jews of Mea Shearim (and to other religious groups) the use of automobiles and the carrying of anything from one area to another are forbidden on the Sabbath. We respected the omnipresent "dress modestly" signs. However, even though we both wore dresses below our knees we noticed that the bearded young men with *peot* (sidelocks), *capotes* (long black coats) and *shtreimel* (fur hats) avoided looking directly at us.

Shortly after we arrived at the Zonnenfeld home, the male members of the family returned from the Friday night service. Everyone in the family greeted each other with a "Guten Shabbos" and a Shabbat embrace. Before sitting down to dinner, we all washed our hands and said the traditional blessing for *netilat yadaim* (washing of the hands). Zalman Zonnenfeld chanted the Kiddush over the Sabbath wine and the blessing over the two loaves of homemade Challah. We became members of the Zonnenfeld family for the meal and sat on the female side of the table.

In our honor, the other "members" of the family conversed in Hebrew rather than in their normal Yiddish, which we could not speak well. Although Hebrew is the official language of Israel, it is still considered by many religious Jews to be sacred. To them Hebrew is the language of the Bible and of prayer; Yiddish is the daily secular language. The degree of religious observance in a Mea Shearim family is intensive. However, in the Zonnenfeld family, the older children seemed to be interpreting their own sense of what was religiously acceptable. One son is in the army, two sons are members of the Habad religious movement and two daughters have gone so far as to work as tour guides, escorting groups throughout the country.

During our discussions about life in Mea Shearim, about Israel and tour guiding in Israel, we sat and unhurriedly ate the meal that had been prepared beforehand by Sarah Zonnenfeld and her daughters. We were served a traditional Sabbath eve meat meal which included gefülte fish, soup with matzah balls, chicken and a fruit compote. After the meal, many friends and relatives came to the Zonnenfelds' to visit for the Sabbath and joined the family in singing *Shabbos zmirot* (Sabbath songs), all enjoying the luxury of a leisurely evening as a start to the day of Sabbath rest.

Since no writing is permitted on the Sabbath we came back one day during the week to take down some recipes. In the next room the children were rolling these Knack-Knicks (*knack-knick* means "sausage") in preparation for a neighborhood Purim party.

KNACK-KNICK (CHOCOLATE ICEBOX COOKIES)

1 cup margarine, softened	½ cup sweet red wine
1 cup cocoa	½ teaspoon vanilla or rum
½ cup sugar	4 cups crushed vanilla wafers
1 egg	(about 50)

Cream the margarine and sugar. Blend in the cocoa. Add the remaining ingredients in the order given. Roll the mixture into one or two long sausage shapes and wrap in waxed paper. Freeze for 2 hours, then slice into ¼-inch rounds. No cooking is required!

These fudgy cookies are delicious served topped with ice cream. *Makes 40 cookies.*

COCONUT CRISPS

1 cup butter	2 cups flour
1 cup sugar	1 teaspoon baking powder
2 eggs	1 teaspoon vanilla
1 tablespoon lemon juice	1½ cups shredded coconut
Rind of 1 lemon, grated	½ cup raisins (optional)

Preheat oven to 350°.

Cream the butter and sugar; beat in the eggs. Add the lemon juice and rind. Sift the flour and baking powder; add these to the butter mixture. Add the vanilla. Stir in the coconut — and raisins, if desired. Drop by rounded teaspoonfuls on well-greased cookie sheets; press each very flat with a fork dipped in water. Bake them for 12 to 15 minutes until they are firm on top and light brown around the edges.

ALTERNATE: *Coconut Refrigerator Cookies:* Work the cookie mixture into a roll 2 inches in diameter and wrap it in waxed paper. Refrigerate the roll from 12 to 24 hours. Preheat oven to 400°. Slice the dough thin and place the rounds on an ungreased cookie sheet. Bake for 8 to 10 minutes. *Makes approximately 60 cookies.*

The Ceremony of the Holy Fire: Greek Orthodox Easter

The most populous Christian community in Jerusalem is the Greek Orthodox, whose Patriarch is one of the principal holders with the Armenian Orthodox and the Roman Catholics of the Church of the Holy Sepulchre. Today's Greek Orthodox inhabitants of Jerusalem include native Arabs and six thousand descendants of Alexander the Great, as well as refugees from the Turks in Asia Minor. Many of these people live in a closely knit compound, another city within a city, in the Christian Quarter on Greek Orthodox Patriarchate Street. Others, like Alexander Efklides described earlier, live outside, in such areas as the Greek Colony. They all speak Greek and send their children to Greek-language schools under the jurisdiction of the Patriarch.

The Greek Orthodox Easter, usually celebrated one week after the Western Christian Easter, is the most significant holiday in the Greek Orthodox religious calendar. In fact, the Patriarch greets so many pilgrims who fly over from Greece and Cyprus that the only way he can estimate their number (last year there were seven thousand) is to count the red-painted Easter eggs left over after distribution at the end.of the holiday. The most spectacular ceremony on this holiday is the kindling of the Holy Fire at noon on Easter Saturday, commemorating the light which sprang up at the resurrection of Jesus Christ. By noon thousands of pilgrims have assembled within the Church of the Holy Sepulchre, all clutching white tapered candles in their hands. Then there is great pealing of bells, increased singing and clapping of hands, and the Patriarch, dressed in white satin and wearing a golden crown, blesses the people as he weaves his way through the crowd. He then enters the Holy Tomb and lights a candle, which a parish priest brings to the altar. As the people see the light they chant louder in appreciation and hold thousands of candles in the air. The Patriarch divests himself of his ornate

*Greek Orthodox pilgrims from all over the world celebrate the
Ceremony of the Holy Fire inside the Church of the Holy Sepulchre*

clothes and enters the Holy of Holies while the other Patriarchs wait in
the outer room. They have to wait only briefly; with a cry, the deacon
on guard at the Tomb of Christ holds up several flaming candles, and
immediately the Patriarch emerges, borne aloft on the shoulders of the
crowd, holding a flaming torch, and followed by people struggling for
the honor of lighting their candles from his torch. While the Greeks
receive the fire on one side of the Tomb, the Copts, Syrians and Ethiopians, the minor holders, light their candles on the other side and the
Armenian Patriarch hastens with his light also from the Tomb up to the
ambulatory. The entire church is one great blaze of light and the air
rings with song — a glorious setting for the enraptured faces of these
faithful pilgrims and worshipers. The Jerusalem fire brigade, however,
lives in yearly fear of this ceremony in this ancient and not entirely
fireproof church.

On Easter Sunday the faithful again gather in the church to pray.
Since the Greeks have observed Lent for the past seven weeks, when
they abstained from meat, fish, eggs, butter, milk and cheese, they
eagerly look forward to breaking their fast with the Paschal lamb, often
roasted on a skewer, and ending the meal with these Kourambiedes,
traditional holiday cookies.

KOURAMBIEDES (HOLIDAY BUTTER COOKIES)

1 cup butter
¼ cup confectioners' sugar
1 egg yolk
2 tablespoons brandy or ouzo

2 cups flour
½ teaspoon baking powder
½ cup blanched almonds, finely
  ground

Preheat oven to 350°.

Cream the butter well, add the sugar and egg yolk, and cream these well again. Add the brandy or ouzo. Blend in the flour and baking powder, reserving a small amount of the flour while checking the consistency of the dough — it should not be too soft. Form the dough into balls or oval shapes. Place them on an ungreased cookie sheet and bake them for about 25 minutes. Sprinkle confectioners' sugar over the cookies while they are still warm. *Makes 2 dozen.*

BAKLAVA (HONEY AND NUT CAKES)

Pastry
1 pound fillo pastry sheets
1½ cups (melted) sweet butter
2 cups walnuts, pistachio nuts or
  hazelnuts, roughly chopped
½ cup chopped almonds
5 tablespoons sugar
1 teaspoon cinnamon
Dash of ground clove

Syrup
2 cups water
2 cups sugar
½ cup honey
1 teaspoon lemon juice
3 slices orange and lemon rind
1 cinnamon stick
3 cloves

Pastry: Place sheets of fillo pastry in a 13-by-9-by-2-inch pan, brushing every other sheet evenly with butter. When ten or twelve sheets are in place, combine the walnuts, sugar, cinnamon, and clove, and spread one third of this mixture over the top sheet. Place another five or six buttered sheets of fillo on top of the nut mixture, sprinkle them with another third of the nut mixture, and repeat with buttered fillo sheets on top, carefully buttering every other sheet.

Preheat oven to 350°.

With a sharp knife, cut the Baklava into diamond-shaped pieces. Heat the remaining butter (there should be about ½ cup) until it is very hot and beginning to brown. Pour it evenly over the Baklava. Sprinkle the top with a few drops of cold water and bake the Baklava for 30 minutes. Reduce the temperature to 300° and continue to bake it for 1 hour longer.

Syrup: In a saucepan combine the water, sugar, honey, lemon juice, orange and lemon rind, a cinnamon stick and cloves. Bring it to the soft ball stage (a drop forms a ball when dropped into a cup of cold water) and simmer it for 20 minutes. Strain it. When the Baklava is baked, pour the cooled syrup over it. *Makes 30–36 pieces.*

A Nablus Sweet Adopted by Jerusalemites

Many of Jerusalem's culinary specialties were brought to the city by Arabs from other locales within the Middle East. One of the most famous, called Kinaffah, is from nearby Nablus, the Biblical Shechem; it is now a favorite snack or dessert of Jerusalemites. Originally Kinaffah was eaten to celebrate the birth of a child, and today excited new fathers still travel to Nablus to bring authentic Kinaffah back to their families for the occasion. The perfect Kinaffah from Nablus is eaten in the spring, because it is then that the special sheep's milk cheese is available.

Mohammed Ali Zalatimo, an old man whose tiny pastry shop is located between the eighth and ninth Stations of the Cross on the Via Dolorosa, has become famous for his particular Kinaffah, called *m'batak*. He has been getting up at dawn for thirty-five years to prepare this sweet for his customers, who start buying as early as seven A.M. We managed to arrive in time to watch Mohammed stretching it, twirling it into the air and then stuffing it with goat cheese. Finally he baked it in a huge coal-fed oven and, when it was finished, he poured over it a sugar and water glaze. Since Mohammed refuses to give his special recipe to anyone but his son, who will soon take over for his father, we had to search for someone who would tell us how to make it. At tiny tables in the back of Mohammed's shop, we, together with other customers, savored this delicacy, wiping up the stickiness with our fingers — no forks provided. Sharing our delight over this version of Kinaffah were Fatmeh and Feiz Quttanah, with whom we struck up a conversation.

Several days later we visited Feiz and Fatmeh, who live near Mohammed's shop in an old stucco house which has been in Feiz's family for four hundred years. During our visit they explained to us in great detail about all kinds of Arabic delicacies, and then they let us taste a family sweet which they said was "nothing special." It was special to us, and we suspected it was the most delicious Kinaffah we had tasted. When we asked if this was indeed Kinaffah and if so, how it came to an old Jerusalem household, Fatmeh explained that as a bride she came from a town near Nablus and she wanted to bring her traditional Nablus recipe with her when she married.

Kinaffah delivery in the Old City

While telling us how to make it, Fatmeh apologized for the ready-made pastry — similar to fillo leaves — which she had become accustomed to using since the Six-Day War. "Before we had supermarkets we made our own dough, and consequently my family received this treat less frequently." Having watched Mohammed's extensive preparations to attain the perfect pastry, we could well understand Fatmeh's concession to modern methods.

KINAFFAH (DUNKING DELIGHTS)

The farmers cheese was the best American substitute we could find for the special sheep's milk cheese of Nablus.

Dunkers
1/4 pound fillo leaves
1 cup farmers cheese
1/4 teaspoon nutmeg
1/4 cup ground blanched or
  unblanched almonds

1/3 cup melted butter

Syrup
1 cup sugar
1 cup water
Juice of 1/2 lemon

Dunkers: Remove the fillo leaves from the refrigerator at least 2 hours before beginning.
   Preheat oven to 350°.
   Mash the farmers cheese with a fork until it is crumbly. Add the nutmeg and almonds. Blend well. Taking one leaf of fillo at a time, cut each into a strip about 6 inches by 12. (You may want to vary the size depending on how large a Kinaffah you want.) Butter the leaf, using a pastry brush, and then fold it in half so that it measures 3 inches by 12. Butter it again and place 1 heaping tablespoon of the filling mixture at the bottom of the leaf. Fold the fillo over to make a triangle, continuing until the end of the leaf, buttering after each fold. Place the completed triangle on a greased cookie sheet. When all the Kinaffahs are rolled, brush each again with butter and bake for 20 to 25 minutes until they are golden brown. Keep them warm until you are ready to serve.
   Syrup: Just before serving, bring the sugar and water to the boil and simmer for 5 minutes. Add a good squeeze of lemon juice. Pour the syrup into an attractive serving bowl. Each person dunks his pastry, using a fork or fingers, into the syrup. *Makes 8–10.*

And Also . . .

RUSSIAN CANDIED GRAPEFRUIT PEELS

Shells of 4 thick-skinned
   grapefruit, halved
2 cups water

4½ cups sugar
Juice of 1 lemon

Two days before you plan to prepare the peel, scoop out the grapefruit and soak the peel in cold water in a container which you can cover. Replace the water once during the day.

After soaking for 2 days, the peels will be ready to prepare. Cut each half into 4 lengthwise strips. Place the strips in a large saucepan, cover them with water, bring to the boil and boil them for 15 minutes. Pour out the water. Repeat this process three times. Now add 2 cups of water and the sugar to the strips. Over a low heat, simmer for 2 hours, uncovered (water should be bubbling). When there is no liquid left, add the lemon juice and stir to coat the strips. Drain the strips and immediately cut them into bite-size pieces. Roll each in sugar. Arrange them in a single layer on a plate or on waxed paper and let them set for several hours until they are firm. Store them in an airtight container. *Makes about 4 cups.*

Beverages

"L'Chayim" at Fink's Bar

Fink's Bar is to Jerusalem as Harry's Bar is to Paris or the Algonquin to New York. Since 1933, when David Rothschild and his two partners opened this tiny bar serving drinks and goulash soup, Fink's has been a favorite meeting place of government officials and journalists, first during the British Mandate and later for the State of Israel.

Throughout the past forty years, when other places have closed because of curfews or strained internal relations, Fink's has consistently remained open until the wee hours of the morning. During the War of Independence in 1948 as well as the Yom Kippur War in 1973, when a blackout was imposed throughout the city, Fink's faithful clientèle clinked glasses by candlelight. The familiar *beep, beep, beep* announcing the hourly radio newscasts often catches customers with their swizzle sticks in midair.

A customer's custom at Fink's is to send from home a humorous bar sign, a beer mug or a unique drinking glass. Many are sent, but few are chosen and if Dave Rothschild chooses to display your gift, you've made your mark in the famous spot. After all these years, the walls are covered to the ceiling with tokens of friendship and good memories. The bar boasts a stunning collection of every imaginable type of liquor and even a connoisseur would be baffled by several of the more exotic bottles.

Fink's is the only place in Jerusalem where customers are sure to get a drink the particular way they personally enjoy it. Famous personages such as Mayor Teddy Kollek and former Prime Minister Golda Meir are often seen sipping soup or something stronger after concerts, or they even might just drop in to see who's there. A CBS correspondent relates how surprised he was when Mr. Rothschild politely asked him if he would mind giving up his corner table so that Israel's First Lady would not have to stand at the bar.

During our cocktail interview Mr. Rothschild graciously parted with the recipes for two of his original drinks. We tasted everything from a dry-dry martini to a Sabra Sour. (Needless to say, we checked and re-checked our recipes the next day!)

FINK'S SPECIAL

1/5 vodka
1/5 gin
1/5 white rum
1/5 kirsch
Dash of Triple Sec (white

curaçao)
3 drops Angostura bitters
1 teaspoon lemon squash (syrup)
Cherry brandy

Pour the above ingredients, in order listed, into a chilled sour glass containing one ice cube. Stir well and remove the ice cube. Now carefully pour enough cherry brandy just over the edge of the glass so that it runs down the inside and settles on the bottom of the glass to a depth of ½ inch.

SABRA SOUR

Israel's Sabra liqueur has a chocolaty-orange flavor.

¾ glass Sabra liqueur
2 teaspoons fresh lemon juice

2 teaspoons lemon squash (syrup)

Pour the above ingredients into a chilled sour glass containing one ice cube. Stir well and remove the ice cube. Serve with a hearty "L'chaim" (pronounced "la hi-eem" and meaning "to life").

A Celebrated Bachelor's Punches

"Just be sure to go together. . . . Don't go alone!" we were warned before our interview with one of Jerusalem's best-known bachelors, Gad Granach. Full of fear and trembling (the latter from hunger!), we arrived at Casanova's penthouse apartment with its terrace overlooking the Israeli President's home. Gad's silver MG convertible (the only one in Israel) was parked outside. He and his dachshund, "Brandy," welcomed us to join him and several friends, already comfortably ensconced in an atmosphere of bonhomie and good cooking smells.

Gad's life reflects his personality — neither of which is ordinary. The son of Germany's famous actor, the late Alexander Granach, Gad grew up in Berlin. In 1933 he studied at a training center for young Jews who wanted to emigrate to Palestine. Since his arrival, Gad has worked first on a kibbutz — driving camels to the seashore to transport sand for building projects — spent three years in the Jewish Settlement Police Force, driven a small locomotive around the steaming shores of the Dead Sea, fought in the 1948 War of Independence, and then helped build the railroad running from Hadera (near Haifa) to Tel Aviv. When the Jerusalem Artists' House first opened, Gad supervised the bar, a gathering place for art students and enthusiasts introducing until then unheard-of drinks to this orange-juice-drinking city. It was there that he met the world-famous rabbi-archaeologist Dr. Nelson Glueck, and began yet another career traveling with the late Dr. Glueck on his archaeological expeditions through the Negev Desert. Now Gad is in charge of buildings and grounds at the Hebrew Union College, a part of the Cincinnati-based Reform rabbinical school. This branch was founded by Dr. Glueck ten years ago as a rabbinic seminary and postgraduate school of archaeology.

Gad speaks Yiddish, German, Arabic, Hebrew and English and can make you think he knows any other language in the world. But it's not what he speaks, it's how he uses the language that is so charming. Gad is a raconteur par excellence. His ability to imitate people or sounds is extraordinary. When he was describing to us his days in the German Youth Communist Movement, Gad burst into a one-man, four-part skit — singing songs, "playing" bassoon, providing background talk and simulating the roar of the crowd, leaving us all collapsed in laughter.

Gad cooks like a mad magician. His reputation as a truly creative chef is rivaled only by his reputation as a creative Casanova, and he enjoys both pastimes with equal zest.

BACHELOR PUNCH

2 cups sweetened condensed milk	2 cups crème de cacao
2 cups cognac	Raisins
1 cup vodka	

With an electric or rotary mixer, beat the condensed milk with the cognac and vodka. Beat in the crème de cacao. Serve the punch, well chilled, in small punch cups with a sprinkle of raisins on top. It can be stored, covered, for 2 weeks in the refrigerator. *Makes approximately 20 punch-glassfuls.*

EGG PUNCH

2 sixteen-ounce cans evaporated milk

4 cups water

Sugar to taste

3 or 4 small cinnamon sticks

1½ teaspoons ground nutmeg

4 egg yolks, well beaten

2 cups vodka

In a medium-sized saucepan, cook the first five ingredients together until the mixture comes to the boil. Lower the heat and cook 5 minutes more, stirring constantly. Remove the mixture from the heat, cool it and put it through a sieve. Beat in the egg yolks and put the liquid through a sieve once more if any particles remain. Stir in the vodka (more can be used if desired). Serve well-chilled in punch cups. *Makes approximately 20 servings.*

A Coffee Break with a Bedouin Mukhtar

On a hill looking over the Old City and the Dead Sea, the very hill which the Khalif Omar climbed before he conquered Jerusalem in 637 A.D., lives Hussein Daoud, the thirty-three-year-old *mukhtar* (village chief) of a once-Bedouin village now part of Jerusalem. Actually Es-Sawahira-Gharbi has not been a Bedouin village for over a hundred years, but local Jerusalemites still remember stories about Hussein's ancestors who lived in tents on this hill. Although it is incorporated within the city limits, it is still thought of as a Bedouin village. Within the last century the Daoud clan moved from tents to tin houses until today the village is filled with individual homes faced with Jerusalem stone. "How could anyone wake up without seeing Jerusalem in the morning?" said Hussein wistfully as he looked outside. Others in his village must think this way because of seven thousand, fourteen hundred are related in some way to Hussein — no one leaves! In contrast to the nearby bustling activity of downtown Jerusalem, the serenity of the village and superb view of the surrounding hills reminded us somewhat of the Bedouins in the Sinai Desert, who know how to appreciate quietness and the passage of time in a uniquely relaxed way.

When his father died last year, Hussein became the youngest mukhtar in the city, representing his village in the city government of Jerusalem. His late father chose as his successor the second-born instead of Hussein's elder brother, who had received less schooling. Already the father

Bedouins in the Judean Desert stop for the pause that refreshes
— a cup of Turkish coffee

of eight children (a new one each year), Hussein travels to Jerusalem every day to work in the city's Department of Education and to request new roads, electricity and telephones for his village. In the afternoon he brings back food for his family, including thirty pounds of fresh fruit every few days! The Daouds eat a big midday meal at about three P.M. "My children always wait for me on the road. They know that my arrival means time for lunch."

Sitting in this simple village setting, we could not help noticing Hussein's wife Maissar's bright green eyes, highlighted by a slight bit of eyeliner, which seemed incongruous with her traditional long black dress. When we asked about it, Hussein stoutly insisted that his Maissar never made herself up and was always natural: "I like her as she is!" But we exchanged a knowing wink with Maissar.

In cooking, however, the Daoud family really does stick to tradition, and of course this means the wonderful Bedouin coffee served with such elegant ritual. "In the city they don't know how to make coffee. They serve it in big cups and they make it too sweet. In our village my brother grinds and roasts the fresh green beans, then boils water and adds the coffee with *hel* [cardamom], lets it boil again and then lets it stand the required amount of time." Then Hussein explained the health factor involved in serving small quantities of the bitter Bedouin coffee in tiny cups. "It gives your stomach a chance to rest after you have eaten a big meal!" Just as he finished explaining this, his older brother brought out some Bedouin coffee for us to try — freshly ground by him that very morning. Whether it was this bitter coffee "sedative," the restful atmosphere or the peaceful family, we left Hussein's village with renewed respect for the way of the Bedouin ancestors, which has stayed with them to the twentieth century.

TURKISH COFFEE

Turkish Coffee seems to taste best when prepared in the traditional *feenjan*, but a deep saucepan will do, sized according to how many cups you wish to make. *Feenjans* can be bought in Eastern specialty shops — the pot is wide at the bottom, narrowing toward the top, and has a long handle. Turkish Coffee should be served in small cylindrical cups; espresso cups are suitable.

1 tablespoon finely ground coffee (available at stores specializing in Middle Eastern foodstuffs and certain spice shops)

1 teaspoon sugar (more or less depending on taste)
Cardamom pods according to taste
Boiling water

Place the coffee and sugar in a *feenjan* or a saucepan and mix them together well. Add boiling water (the measure of a serving cup plus a little more), stir well. Add the cardamom pods (you will have to experiment to see how many you like to achieve the desired taste) and bring the coffee to the boil. When the foam on top begins to rise high, remove the coffee from the heat until it settles and repeat the process once. Pour it into a coffee cup, spooning in some of the foam. The coffee dregs will sink to the bottom of the cup; do not stir them up. Serve immediately.

Multiply this recipe by whatever number is required for more than one cup and proceed as above. *Serves 1.*

FRESH LEMONADE

1 cup fresh lemon juice

1½ cups sugar

Stir the juice and sugar together until the sugar dissolves. Store the concentrate in covered glass jars or bottles. For one glass of lemonade, mix ¼ cup concentrate with ¾ cup iced water, or to taste. Serve it with ice and fresh mint leaves.

MINT TEA

Brew your favorite tea and let it stand in a teapot for a few minutes. Serve individual cups with a heaping spoonful of sugar and a sprig of fresh mint.

A perfect ending to a long midday feast.

SAHLAB (MIDDLE EASTERN GROG)

4 cups milk
4 teaspoons sugar
½ teaspoon *sahlab* powder
6 Arabic gums, mashed fine
2 tablespoons cornstarch

4 tablespoons shredded coconut
3 tablespoons crushed almonds,
    pecans or pistachio nuts
2 teaspoons cinnamon

Place the milk, *sahlab* powder, gums and sugar in saucepan. Cook them over medium heat until the gums are melted. Lower the heat. Blend the cornstarch with enough cool water to make it a paste, then stir it into the milk mixture. Stir and cook until the mixture thickens, 10 to 15 minutes. Pour it into cups or mugs. Sprinkle each with a part of the coconut, nuts and cinnamon. Serve it immediately. More sugar may be served with Sahlab if a sweeter drink is desired. Sahlab is perfect on a cold winter's evening or it may be eaten with a spoon as a light dessert. *Makes 4 cups.*

A Guide to
Middle Eastern and
Mediterranean
Food Supplies

The following ingredients can be bought at any food store specializing in Middle Eastern or Mediterranean (Greek, Lebanese, Syrian, Israeli and Armenian) foods. Many supermarkets and most health food stores throughout the United States carry the majority of these products as well.

Arabic gums
Arrack (alcohol distilled from raisins); Pernod or ouzo is a good substitute.
Burghul (cracked wheat), sometimes written "bulghur"
Cardamom
Chick-peas (dried or canned)
Cumin powder
Fillo leaves (strudel-like pastry, fresh or frozen)

Grape leaves (dried, bottled, or canned)
Pine nuts (pignolias)
Pita (open flat bread), called *kimaje* in Arabic and "Syrian bread" here
Sahlab powder
Semolina (prepared couscous can substitute for this grain)
Ground sumac (commercially prepared)
Tahina (sesame seed paste)

Mr. Michael Anasa of Near East Importing and Mr. Harry Gordon of the Government of Israel Trade Center helped us to compile this list of shops that carry Middle Eastern and Mediterranean foods. Also included are local distributors of these foods, who may supply the names of additional shops.

California

CULVER CITY

Amermart Corporation (distributor)
Herbert Block
2921 South La Cienega Boulevard
Culver City, California 90230
213-838-3304

ENCINO

C. Dieber Company (distributor)
Mr. C. Dieber
16200 Ventura Boulevard
Encino, California 91316
213-981-3434

LOS ANGELES

Bezjian Grocery
4725 Santa Monica Boulevard

Codman Trading Company (distributor)
Murray Codman
12036 Washington Boulevard
Los Angeles, California 90066
213-391-6363

Harry Gelman Company (distributor)
Harry Gelman
8344 Melrose Avenue
Los Angeles, California 90069
213-651-2480

Greek Import Company
2801 West Pico Boulevard

Alfred Hart Company (distributor)
Harry Fisher
1650 East Nadeau Avenue
Los Angeles, California 90001
213-581-6161

International Grocery
4820 Santa Monica Boulevard

Park Avenue Imports (distributor)
Joseph Siegel
340 North Madison Avenue
Los Angeles, California 90004
213-666-7420

S. Rimon & Company (distributor)
Mr. S. Rimon
612 North Sepulveda Boulevard
Los Angeles, California 90049
213-270-4513

Service Foods (distributor)
Joe Murez
1933 W. Sixtieth Street
Los Angeles, California 90047
213-750-2910

A-1 Food Distributors (distributor)
2136 South Garfield Avenue
Los Angeles, California 90022
213-685-4898

I. Rudin & Company (distributor)
1522 North Knowles Avenue
Los Angeles, California 90063
213-269-8216

SAN FRANCISCO

Mediterranean and Middle East
223 Valencia Street

SHERMAN OAKS

Les Stiener (distributor)
Mr. Les Stiener
4915 Tyrone Avenue
Sherman Oaks, California 91403
213-986-9823

SOUTH SAN FRANCISCO

J. Sosnick & Sons (distributor)
258 Littlefield Avenue
South San Francisco, California 94080
415-871-5212

TORRANCE

Acron Beverage Company (distributor)
Fred Nielsen
936 Engracia Street
Torrance, California 90501
213-775-4131

Colorado

DENVER

Davis Distributing Company (distributor)
Mrs. Davis
1551 Speer Street
Denver, Colorado 80204

Economy Grocery
1864 Curtis Street

Connecticut

BRIDGEPORT

Bonus Market
500 Iranistan Avenue

HARTFORD

Victoria Importing Company
891 Park Street

NEW HAVEN

China Trading Company
271 Crown Street

STRATFORD

J. Schine Rosenbaum & Company (distributor)
Joel Kaufman
1915 Stratford Avenue
Stratford, Connecticut 06497
203-375-4418

Delaware

WILMINGTON

Calavrita Importing Company
12 East Fourth Street

District of Columbia

WASHINGTON

Acropolis Food Market
1206 Underwood, N.W.

Hellas Greek Importing
1245 Twentieth Street, N.W.

Skenderis Greek Imports
1612A Twentieth Street, N.W.

Florida

JACKSONVILLE

Farahs Imported Food
705 South McDuff Avenue

HIALEAH

Southern Distributing Company (distributor)
Harold Levinson
4570 East Tenth Lane
Hialeah, Florida 33011
305-681-3578

MIAMI

Israel Kosher Sausage Company
230 N.W. Fifth Street

Laurenzo Brothers
1393 N.W. Twenty-first Terrace

T.N.G. Near East Bakery
878 S.W. Eighth Street

Eastern Star Bakery
444 S.W. Eighth Street

Georgia

ATLANTA

Atlanta Wholesale Grocery Company
150 Ottley Drive, N.E.

Roxy's Delicatessen
1011 Peachtree Street, N.E.

Illinois

CHICAGO

Columbus Food Market
5534 West Harrison Street

M. Manischewitz Sales Company (distributor)
Bernie Cohen
4040 West Belmont Avenue
Chicago, Illinois 60641
312-283-3336

Hellenic Enterprises
6058 West Diversey Avenue

International Foods
4724 North Kedzie Avenue

New Deal Grocery
2601 West Lawrence Avenue

Sparta Grocery
6050 West Diversey Avenue

CICERO

S. & H. Food Market
5733 West Twenty-second Street

DES PLAINES
Columbus Food and Bakery
1651 Rand Road

OAK LAWN
Olympia Foods
4909 West Ninety-fifth Street

Indiana

INDIANAPOLIS
Athens Imported Food
103 North Alabama Street

Kentucky

LOUISVILLE
A. Thomas Meat Market
315 East Jefferson

Maryland

BALTIMORE
Imported Foods
409 West Lexington Street

Joffe Brothers (distributor)
Stuart Joffe
Howard and West Streets
Baltimore, Maryland 21230
301-354-2300

BETHESDA
A & L Foods, Inc. (distributor)
Jack Alper
5225 Pooks Hill Road
Bethesda, Maryland 20014
301-530-4466

ROCKVILLE
Skenderis Greek Imports
5558 Randolph Road
Montrose Center

WEST WHEATON
Thomas Market
265 University Boulevard

Massachusetts

BOSTON
Bostonian Foods, Inc. (distributor)
Nat Rotberg
80 Commercial Street
Boston, Massachusetts 02109
617-227-9292

Syrian Grocery Import Company
270 Shawmut Avenue

BROOKLINE
Tripolis Market
133 Harvard Avenue

CANTON
S.W.B. Company, Inc. (distributor)
Harry Leeds
28 Cedar Street
Canton, Massachusetts 02021
617-828-6710

DEDHAM
Homsy Middle East
918 Providence Highway
Route 1

LOWELL
Giavis Market
351 Market Street

Independent Cash Market
374 Market Street

Smyrna Pastry Shop
503 Market Street

LYNN
E. Demakis and Company
37 Waterhill Street

WATERTOWN
California Fruit Market and Produce Center
Company
637 Mount Auburn Street

Michigan

ANN ARBOR
Capitol Market
209–211 South Fourth Avenue

DETROIT
Greenfield Noodle and Specialties (distributor)
Mr. Ernest Greenfield
600 Custer Street
Detroit, Michigan 48202
313-873-2212

Ambrosia Grocery
587 Monroe Avenue

Athens Grocery and Bakery
527 Monroe Avenue

Gabriel Importing
2461 Russell Street

Mourad Grocery Company
2410 Market Street

Oriental Pastry Shop and Grocery
411 Monroe Avenue

GARDEN CITY
Mid Ford Fruit
5636 Middle Belt

GRAND RAPIDS
Russo's Imported Foods
1935 Eastern Avenue, S.E.

RIVER ROUGE
Mediterranean Grocery
11431 West Jefferson

Kitchen Maid Foods, Inc. (distributor)
Stanley Raderman
24660 DeQuindre
Warren, Michigan 40091
313-759-3113

Missouri

KANSAS CITY

Keller Food Company (distributor)
Joe Friedman
2917 Brooklyn Avenue
Kansas City, Missouri 64109
816-921-3500

Minnesota

ST. PAUL

Gourmet Food Company (distributor)
1020 Raymond Avenue
St. Paul, Minnesota 55114
612-646-7817

New Jersey

KENILWORTH

Selected Specialties Sales (distributor)
Jerry Title
20 Lafayette Place
Kenilworth, New Jersey 08033
201-276-6900

LEONIA

International Food
347 Broad Avenue

NORTH BERGEN

Tufayan
9255 Kennedy Boulevard

RIVER EDGE

Olympia Foods of all Nations
908 Kinderkamack Road

ROSELLE

D & E Food Distributors (distributor)
Ronnie Baron and Art Tarshis
280 Cox Street
Roselle, New Jersey 07203
201-241-5200

New York

HEMPSTEAD

Carmel Cheese Company
79 Main Street

NEW YORK CITY

Brooklyn

Alwan Brothers
183 Atlantic Avenue

Beirut Grocery
199 Atlantic Avenue

Beit Hanina Trading
174 Atlantic Avenue

Damascus Bakery
195 Atlantic Avenue

Oriental Pastry and Grocery
170 Atlantic Avenue

Sahadi Importing Company
189 Atlantic Avenue

Manhattan

Near East Importing (distributor)
Mr. Michael Anasa
495 Broome Street
New York, New York 10013
212-226-2071

Government of Israel Trade Center
(distributor)
Mr. Harry Gordon
111 West Fortieth Street
New York, New York 10018
212-594-5215

Bell Bates Company
107 West Broadway

Empire Coffee and Tea Company
486 Ninth Avenue

Friendly Grocery Company
1420 St. Nicholas Avenue

Kalustyan Orient Export Trading Corporation
397 Third Avenue

Kassos Brothers
570 Ninth Avenue

New International Importing
517 Ninth Avenue

Poseidon Bakery
629 Ninth Avenue

Tashjian Grocery
380 Third Avenue

Zabar's Gourmet Foods
2245 Broadway

Triancria Importing Company
415 Third Avenue

Queens

Armen Food
42-20 Forty-third Avenue
Sunnyside

Astoria Superette
29-01 Twenty-third Avenue
Astoria

Plaza Meat and Grocery
30-07 Broadway
Astoria

Friends Food
3502 Ditmars Boulevard
Astoria

Glasser Brothers
2533 Broadway
Astoria

Tonis Lattacini's
41-17 National Street
Corona

K. & S. Meat Market
79119 Thirty-seventh Avenue
Jackson Heights

B. Nesserian
40-07 Queens Boulevard
Jackson Heights

Mediterranean Superette
85-02 Parrons Boulevard
Jamaica

Ohio

CLEVELAND

Marine Midland Foods (distributor)
Max Block and Irving Ginnes
4540 Commerce Street
Cleveland, Ohio 44103
216-391-1005

Athens Pastries and Imported Foods
2545 Lorain Avenue

Imported Products
2217 Ontario Street

Middle East Bakery
1307 Carnegie Avenue

West Side Market
975 Twenty-fifth Street

PARMA

Olympia Import
5435 Pearl Road

TOLEDO

Mazurco
4144 Secor Road

Antonio Sofo & Son
3253 Monroe Street

YOUNGSTOWN

Humble Near East
2933 Market Street

Palestine Market
2100 Market Street

Pennsylvania

CORNWELLS HEIGHTS

Samuel Zuckerman & Company (distributor)
Sam and Sol Zuckerman and Bob Krum
3600 Meadow Lane
I-95 Industrial Park
Cornwells Heights, Pennsylvania 19020
215-OR7-9200

PHILADELPHIA

S. Doucas & Son
929 South Ninth Street

Gary's Delicatessen
790 Garrett Road

Michael's Food Market
230 South Tenth Street

Sun-ni Cheese
371 Averell Road

UPPER DARBY

Parthenon Grocery
7015 Marshall Road

Rhode Island

CRANSTON

Athenian Market
999 Oaklawn Avenue

PROVIDENCE

Near East Market
253 Cranston Street

Texas

DALLAS

Purity Importing Company
4507 Swiss Avenue

Vermont

BRATTLEBORO

Putney Road Market
Putney Road

Index

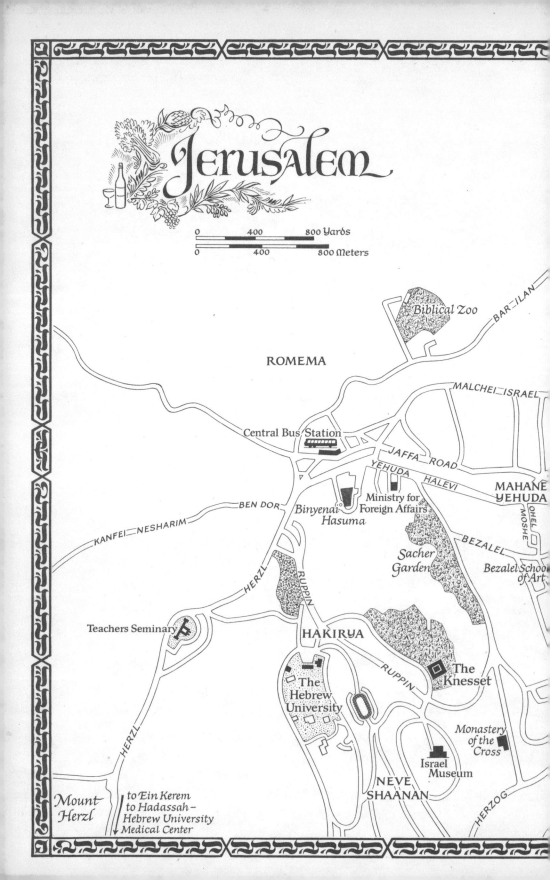